BALLADS

AND

OTHER POEMS

BY

GEORGE LANSING RAYMOND

FOURTH EDITION, REVISED

G. P. PUTNAM'S SONS

NEW YORK AND LONDON

The Knickerbocker Press

The Knickerbocker Press
New York

Made in the United States of America

CONTENTS.

BALLADS OF THE REVOLUTION.

MISCELLANEOUS.

DRAMATIC.

SKETCHES IN SONG.

DRAMATIC.

PATRIOTIC.

BALLADS OF THE REVOLUTION.

REPRESENTING THE SPIRIT AND REASONS
LEADING TO THE
AMERICAN WAR FOR INDEPENDENCE.

———

Third Edition, Revised

BALLADS OF THE REVOLUTION.[1]

OUR FIRST BREAK WITH THE BRITISH.

1765.

GREAT BRITAIN'S lords[2] were planning—
So ran the world's report—
To tax the colonies more and more,[4]
And treat our sires as if they wore
The liveries at the court.

[1] " In writing a ballad the secrets of success are definiteness of aim, directness of execution, and singleness of idea. The language must be simple, but so vigorous that every word tells ; the metre must also be simple, but the versification demands a musical swing, a rush of rhyme, the talent for which is rare. To smell of the lamp is fatal to the ballad ; it should have all the spontaneity of an impromptu. The author must forget himself, for ballad poetry is essentially objective, and a touch of subjectivity spoils it. Each incident must be related as though the writer had taken part in it, and seeing with his mind's eye, he must paint as vividly as though that described were before him in very truth. It is not an easy thing to write a ballad in these days, when the drift of poetic thought is quite in the opposite direction."—*Philadelphia Inquirer*, 1876.

[2] In 1761, " America knew that the Board of Trade had proposed to annul colonial charters, to reduce all the colonies to royal governments."—*Bancroft's Hist. U. S.*, vol. iv., ch. 18, p. 414. " The king, the ministry, the crown officers all conspiring against her liberties. . . . there was no help unless from Parliament."—*Idem.*, vol. v., ch. 11, p. 236.

"The colonies' hope is union,"
    Said Franklin,[3] by and by ;
"Not one of them that stands alone
Can hold its own against the throne.
    We [3] join," he wrote, "or die."

And "Freedom [4] is a birthright
    Our fathers handed down ;
Blood-bought," James Otis [4] boldly said :
"One king of theirs it cost his head ;
    And one his throne and crown.[5]

"Were we to lose it, England
    Would share in our mishap [6] ;
For not a net can harm us here,
But threatens every English peer,
    Whom yet it may entrap.

---

[3] "Franklin looked for greater liberties than . . . Parliament might
inaugurate. Having for his motto ' Join or die.' . . . sketching
the outline of a confederacy."—*Idem.*, vol. iv., ch. 5, p. 116. "William
Penn in 1697 had proposed an annual Congress . . . to regulate commerce. Franklin" in 1752 "revived the great idea, and breathed into it
enduring life."—*Idem.*, vol. iv., ch. 5, p. 125.

[4] "The Board of Trade had proposed . . . collecting the duties
. . . the justice of the restrictions on trade was denied and their
authority questioned ; and when the officers of the customs asked for
' writs of assistance' to enforce them, the colony regarded its liberties in
peril. This is the opening scene of American resistance. It began " in
1761 . . . "in a court-room . . . James Otis . . . stood up . . . the
champion of the colonies."—*Idem.*, vol. iv., ch. 18, p. 414.

[5] "' I am determined,' such were his words, ' to sacrifice estate . . .
life in opposition to a kind of power, the exercise of which cost one king
of England his head and another his throne.' . . . Tracing the lineage
of freedom to its origin, he opposed the claims of the British officers by the
authority of ' reason,' and that they were at war with the ' Constitution '
he proved by appeals to the Charter of Massachusetts, and its English
liberties. . . . 'An Act of Parliament against the Constitution is void,'

" Our laws are in our charters
    For scores of years enjoy'd ;
Nor has the King, or Parliament,
Or both without our own consent
    The power to make them void.[5]

" By them, the Magna Charta,
    And all our Saxon rights ;
By claims of nature, mind, descent,
We ought to send to Parliament[7]
    And show it what it slights."

A protest then we sent it.[7]
    But back came sail on sail ;[8]
And less had leaves of law-books grave
Torn out and flung to wind and wave
    Shown law could not prevail.

he said. . . . ' The crowded audience seemed ready to take up arms.' "—
Idem., vol, iv., ch. 18, pp. 415–6.

[6] " The true interests of Great Britain and her plantations are mutual.
Otis in 1763.—*Idem.,* vol. v., ch. 5, p. 90.

[7] See the Representations of the General Assembly at New York to the
King, concerning the administration of justice in that province, 1762, mentioned in *Idem.,* vol. v., ch. 5, p. 84. " By the laws of nature and of nations, the voice of universal reason and of God, by the statute law and the
common law, this memorial claimed for the colonists the absolute rights of
Englishmen, . . . such were the views of Otis sent by Massachusetts" in
1764 " to its agent in London."—*Idem.,* vol. v., ch. 10, pp. 198–9.

[8] " Less than forty were willing to receive the petition of Virginia. A
third from South Carolina, a fourth from Connecticut, . . . a fifth from
Massachusetts, . . . shared the same refusal. That from New York, no
one could be prevailed upon to offer. . . . The House of Commons would
neither receive petitions nor hear council."—*Idem.,* vol. v., ch. 11, p. 246.
This was in Feb., 1765.

[9] In 1763 Brown, the Governor of South Carolina, " assumed the power
of rejecting members whom the House declared duly elected and returned."—*Idem.,* vol. v., ch. 8, p. 150. In May, 1765, " The Lieutenant-

They broke up our assembly ;[*]
  Supreme their army [10] made ;
Removed the judge [11] who check'd their greed ;
And on the church our fathers freed
  The hands of bishops laid.[12]

"Shall we, whose fathers won us
  Our rights, abide their loss ?
Nay," Mayhew said ; [13] "though these to take
Our Pharoah's hosts of red-coats make
  Blood-red the sea they cross.

Governor " of Virginia " dissolved the Assembly."—*Idem.*, ch. 13, p. 277.
" Fearing a general expression of the sentiments of the people, through
their representatives . . . Tyron issued a proclamation in October
proroguing the Assembly which was to meet on the thirtieth of November,
until the following March. This act incurred the indignation of the people."—*Lossing's Field Book of the Revolution,* vol. ii., p. 568.   Later,
" Townshend's revenue, so far as it provided an independent support for
the crown officers, did away with the necessity of colonial legislatures.
. . . Governors would have little inducement to call assemblies, and an
angry minister might dissolve them without inconvenience to his administration."—*Bancroft's U. S.*, vol. vi., ch. 29, p. 85.   "An act of Parliament "
in 1767 " suspended the functions of its (N. Y.) legislature till they should
render obedience to the Imperial Legislature."—*Idem.*, p. 84.   " Bernard
. . . prorogued them, and then dissolved the Assembly.   Massachusetts
was left without a legislature."—*Idem.*, vol. vi., ch. 34, p. 165,
  10 " This commission . . . established a military power throughout
the continent independent of the colonial governors and superior to them
. . . in 1756 the rule was established . . . that troops might be kept
up in the colonies and quartered on them at pleasure without the consent of the American Parliaments."—*Idem.*, vol. iv., ch. 9, pp. 229-30.
In Feb., 1765, " Welbore Ellis, Secretary of War . . . made known
his intention ' that the orders of his commander-in-chief and . . . the
brigadier generals . . . should be supreme, and be obeyed by the troops
as such in all the civil governments of America ' . . . These instructions
rested, as was pretended, on . . . the commission " (mentioned above)
" . . . prepared for . . . troops in time of war"—*Idem.*, vol. v., ch. 11,
p. 235.
  11 In 1762 " was consummated the system of subjecting the halls of justice to the prerogative. The king . . . instituted courts, named the
judges, removed them at pleasure, fixed the amount of their salaries, and
paid them out of funds that were independent of legislative grants."—
Idem., vol. iv., ch. 19, p. 440.

" The Lord o'errules the waters,
    And He will guard our cause :
And Parliament—let Plymouth Rock
To whelm them all throw back the shock—
    Will bid the tyrant pause."

" God guide the House of Commons,"
    We cried with lifted eyes.
God guided it and us, alas,
But how He scorch'd our heaven to pass
    His finger through the skies !

[12] About 1762 " a fund of two thousand pounds was subscribed to a society which the legislature of Massachusetts had authorized for promoting knowledge among the Indians ; but the king interposed his negative, and reserved the red man for the Anglican form of worship."—*Idem.*, vol. iv., ch. 18, p. 430.　In 1765 " In North Carolina . . . the legislature were even persuaded . . . to make provision for the support of the Church of England."—*Idem.*, vol. v., ch. 13, p. 271.　" For New York, the Lords of Trade refused to the Presbyterians any immunities but such as might be derived from the British Law of Toleration."—*Idem.*, vol. vi., ch. 29, p. 84.　" O poor New England, there is a deep plot laid against both your civil and religious liberties, and they will be lost."—Whitfield in 1764, *Idem.*, vol. v., ch. 10, p. 193.

[13] In Jan., 1750 . . . " Mayhew . . . summoned . . . defensive war against ' tyranny and priestcraft ' . . . He preached resistance."—*Idem.*, vol. iv., ch. 3, p. 60.　In Aug., 1765, " Choosing as his text . . . Ye have been called to liberty . . . he preached fervently in behalf of civil and religious freedom.—*Idem.*, vol. v., ch. 16, p. 312.

[14] " The act seemed sure to enforce itself.　Unless stamps were used, marriages would be null, notes of hand valueless, ships at sea prizes to the first captors, suits at law impossible, transfers of real estate invalid, inheritances unclaimable."—*Idem.*, vol. v., ch. 11, pp. 251-2.

[15] " The publishers of newspapers . . . were . . . called upon to stand the brunt in braving the penalties of the act . . . Timothy Green . . . publisher of the *New London Gazette* . . . fearlessly defended his country's rights . . . On Friday the first day of November, his journal came forth without stamps."—*Idem.*, vol. v., ch. 19, pp. 352-3.

[16] Speaking of Samuel Adams in 1764, " On his motion and in his words, Boston . . . asserted . . . ' If taxes are laid upon us . . . without our having a legal representation . . . are we not reduced . . . to the miserable state of tributary slaves ? ' "—*Idem.*, vol. v., ch. 10, p. 197.

[17] " The strength of the people in America " in 1748 " consisted also in the exclusive right of its assemblies to levy and to appropriate colonial taxes

The Commons framed the Stamp-Act.[14]
    It legal writs refused,
And made our bargains go for naught,
Unless, in all we sold or bought,
    Their stamps were bought and used.

" The stamps are only vouchers,"
    Wrote Green,[15] " to license knaves ! "
" To tax, against their own consent,
Where none," said Adams,[16] " represent
    Our people, brands them slaves."

" Our charter'd free assemblies,
    To which our laws entrust[17]
The right to tax us, and to pay
Each crown-official,—only they
    Can ever keep him just."

Quoth Thomas Chase : [18]   " They only !
    But British agents curse
To find that our assemblies true
Have something nobler here to do
    Than fill a noble's purse."

. . . in America, the rapacity of the governors made it expedient to preserve their dependence for their salaries on annual grants."—*Idem.*, vol.
iv., ch. i, p. 19.
    [18] See note 27.
    [19] March, 1763, " it became lawful . . . for each . . . armed vessel
to stop and examine and, in case of suspicion, to seize each merchant ship
approaching the colonies, while avarice was stimulated by hope of large
emoluments to make as many seizures . . . as possible."—*Idem.*, vol. v.,
ch. 5, p. 92.

"The admiralty," said Hancock,[21]
  "To swell the navy's pelf,
Have pass'd a law that it empowers[19]
To seek in every ship of ours
  A bounty for itself.

"Would we dispute the seizure,
  Our loss can be discuss'd
And righted but in England's courts,[20]
And by a judge whom it supports ;—
  And that, they say, is just.

"No fleet of mine[21] shall carry
  A stamp, though all I lose.
I choose, ere it, to save my soul ! "
The whole land heard, and soon the whole
  Had sworn no stamps to use.

New York had lived by commerce.
  Her merchants vow'd, they all,[22]
Ere stamps they bought, would sail no boats,
And sell no goods, and pass no notes—
  They would not live in thrall.

[20] "The penalties and forfeitures for breach of the revenue laws were to be decided in courts of Vice-Admiralty, without the interposition of a jury, by a single judge, who had no support whatever but in his share of the profits of his own condemnations."—*Idem.*, vol. v., ch. 12, p. 268.
[21] "The first American ship that ventured to sea with a rich cargo and without stamped papers was owned by the Boston merchant, John Hancock."—*Idem.*, vol. v., ch. 20, p. 374.
[22] "The merchants of New York, . . . unanimously bound themselves to send no new orders for goods or merchandise ; to countermand all

Said Isaac Sears : [23] " No wonder
  These human lords combine
The masses' rivalling wealth to steal !
Let them be stript, my lord may feel
  His decency divine.

" For years, to gild the peerage
  Have England's ports been made [24]
The marts by law for all we bought.—
Alas ! in what that we have wrought
  Have they not check'd our trade ?

" The nobles, while their winnings
  Like nuggets clog the sieve
That ours drop through, would not eschew
Their royal rule : ' To others do
  What makes them humbly live.'

former orders ; and not even to receive goods on commission unless the
Stamp Act be repealed."—*Idem.*, vol. v., ch. 19, pp. 351–2.
  [23] " Isaac Sears, the self-constituted, and for ten years the recognized,
head of the people of New York."—*Idem.*, vol. v., ch. 19, p. 355.
  [24] ' The colonists could not export the chief products of their industry
. . . to any place but Great Britain . . . nor might any foreign
ship enter any colonial harbor . . . In all other respects Great
Britain was not only the sole market for the products of America, but the
only storehouse for its supplies. . . . That the country which was the
home of the beaver might not manufacture its own hats, no man . . .
could be a hatter or a journeyman at the trade unless he had served an
apprenticeship of seven years. No hatter might employ . . . more than
two apprentices. America abounded in iron ores. . . . slitting mills, steel
furnaces, and plating forges . . . were prohibited."—*Idem.*, vol. v., ch.
12, pp. 265–7.
  [25] ' We will none of us import British goods,' said the traders in the
towns. . . . North Carolina set up looms . . . and South Carolina was
ready to follow. . . . ' We will have homespun markets of linen and wool-
lens,' passed from mouth to mouth."—*Idem.*, vol. v., ch. 14, p. 288.
  [26] " New England and Pennsylvania had imported nearly one half as

"And shall we not live humbly
   Who but our pride restrain?
And buy at home more homely goods?"—
"Buy homespun!"[25] rang from bay to woods.
   Then rang the looms [25] amain.

But keen and crafty tories,
   They prowl'd around at night,
And plotted long, and bought and sold,
And hoax'd and coax'd the young and old
   Their homespun league to slight.[26]

"We must not wait till England
   Shall send the stamps," wrote Edes.[27]
"Once let our tories own a few,
They soon were sown the whole land through
   To grow like seeds of weeds."

---

much as usual. New York alone had been perfectly true to its engagements,"—the state of things in 1770.—*Idem.*, vol. vi., ch. 44, p. 365.

[27] "The fourteenth of August," 1765, "saw the effigy of Oliver," Boston's stamp agent, "tricked out with emblems of Bute and Grenville, . . . prepared by Boston mechanics, true-born Sons of Liberty, Benjamin Edes, the printer, . . . Thomas Chase, a fiery hater of kings."—*Idem.*, vol. v., ch. 16, p. 310. "Just after dark an 'amazing' multitude . . . made a funeral pyre for his effigy. . . . So the considerate self-seeker . . . gave it under his own hand that he would not serve as stamp officer."—*Idem.*, vol. v., ch. 16. pp. 310–12.

[28] "Everywhere, . . . of themselves, or at the instance of the people, amidst shouts and the ringing of bells and the firing of cannon, or . . . with rage changing into courtesy on the . . . submission of the stamp-master, . . . the officers resigned. There remained not one person duly commissioned to distribute stamps."—*Idem.*, vol. v., ch. 19, p. 351.

[29] "'I am resolved to have the stamps distributed,' wrote Colden. . . . On the thirty-first of October, Colden and all the royal governors took the oath to carry the stamp-act punctually into effect. . . . The governor of Rhode Island stood alone in his patriotic refusal."—*Idem.*, vol. v., ch. 19, p. 350.

The Boston Stamp-man's image
    Men burn'd before his face.
Their roars, like thunder, threaten'd storm ;
And torches flash'd ; the air was warm ;
    The man resign'd his place.

" Resign ! " erelong the echo
    Had roll'd to every town.[28]
None dared resist the people's plea,
And none dared hold a stamp, or be
    The stamp-man of the crown.

" Our governors," growl'd the tories,
    " Will sell the stamps to us."
The governors vow'd this course to take ;[29]
But we, we vow'd, our lives the stake,
    They should not thwart us thus.

The night before the Stamp-Act
    Should rule the colony,
We slept not much ; we melted lead ;
We whetted steel ; we plann'd ahead,
    We " Sons of Liberty." [30]

---

[30] " The SONS OF LIBERTY . . . organized at this time throughout
the colonies."—*Lossing's Pic. Field Bk. of the Rev.*, vol. ii., p. 787.
" The association in New York had a correspondent . . . in London, . . .
from whom they . . . regularly received intelligence of the movements of
the ministry."—*Idem.*, note.

[31] " Friday, the first morning of November," 1765, " broke upon a
people unanimously resolved to nullify the Stamp Act. From New

Then, when the morn was breaking,[31]
   On every hill and plain,
In all the towns, we toll'd the bells,[31]
That all began with doleful knells,
   As though for Freedom slain.

Anon, they rang out madly [31]
   What might have peal'd to be
The land's alarm-bell—only now
They peal'd to hail the new-born **vow**
   Of men that would be free.

New York went wild to hear them.[32]
   Men flooded every way:
They left their shops; they stopt their mills;
And farmers flock'd from all the hills,
   And sailors from the bay.

Now who would buy **a stamp here?**
   Was ask'd in all the ways.
But not a shop was not shut to;
For all had wiser work to do
   On this, our day of days.

Hampshire to the far south the day was introduced by the tolling of muffled bells, . . . a eulogy was pronounced on liberty and its knell sounded,
and then again the note changed as if she were restored to life."—*Bancroft's U. S.*, vol. v., ch. 19, p. 352.
  [32] " In New York the whole city rose up as one man. . . . The sailors
came from their shipping; the people flocked in . . . by thousands."—
Idem., p. 355.

" We would not, and we will not
    Submit," said Isaac Sears.[33]
The governor said: " You fill the street,
But here a fort and there a fleet
    May yet awake your fears."

" Our stamps," cried James,[34] his major,
    " Our stamps, if loaded down
Our cannon here, and scatter'd thence
Among the crowd, would soon commence
    To circulate in town."

" Aha," said Sears in answer,
    " For this you soldiers came ?
For this our wily governor here
Pretended border wars to fear—[35]
    Aha, were we his game ?

" To tax us indirectly,—
    Was it for this, the crown
Bade your imported troopers make
Our town[35] support you ?—for the sake
    Of being thus kept down ?

---

[33] " The leader of the popular tumult was Isaac Sears."—*Idem.*

[34] " ' I will cram the stamps down their throats with the end of my sword,' cried the braggart James, Major of Artillery, . . . 'will drive them all out of town.' "—*Idem.*, vol. v., ch. 17, p. 332.

[35] " The arbitrary invasion of private rights . . . by the illegal and usurped authority of a military chief was the great result of the campaign. The frontier had been left open to the French ; but the . . . example had been given . . . of quartering troops in the principal towns at the expense of the inhabitants."—*Idem.*, vol. iv., ch. 10, p. 241.

" To kill our leaders, was it,
    The crown made them be rank'd
By Braddock's braggarts, who could run
And leave a man like Washington [36]
    By their commands outflank'd ?

" Yes, yes, in genuine danger
    We know who [37] win the day ;
And whose the coin and blood we miss,
That, from our fathers' time to this,
    Have held our foes at bay.

" And need we now your army ?
    You know—your sovereign too,
Our wars are his—He [37] France attacks
And here her colony—when he lacks
    Excuse for sending you.

" How strong, think you, our patience ?
    How long ere it shall tire ?—
Ah, Britain's lion's whelp may get
So tough by cuffs like this, as yet
    To turn and rend her sire ! "

[36] " Washington had left the service on account of a regulation by
which the colonial officers were made to rank under those of the regular
army. . . . Urged by General Braddock to accompany him, he consented
to do so . . . as a volunteer. . . . Through the stubbornness of that general, his contempt of the Indians, and the cowardice of many of his regular
troops, an army of thirteen hundred men was half destroyed. Braddock
fell, and the whole duty of distributing orders devolved upon the youthful
colonel."—*Lossing's Pic. Field Book of the Rev.*, vol. ii., pp. 477–9.

[37] " The King in council . . . having thus invited a conflict with
France by instructions necessarily involving war, . . . neither troops,

" Sheer treason ! " cried the major ;
    And " Treason ! " cried his chief.
Our spokesman's eye their fury brook'd,
Then calmly toward his friends he look'd,
    And gave his thoughts relief.

" Nay, theirs are loyal spirits,
    But when the wrong is great,
And forms of law do not deserve
Their soul's allegiance, then they serve
    The spirit of the state."

With this, he told those courtiers
    Their words would he report.
They heard the people's groans that rose
To greet the words he bore, and chose
    To seek, near by, the fort.[38]

Then from the fort the cannon
    Were turn'd upon the town.
But " If you fire," the people cried,
" We hang the governor here outside,
    Or burn your quarters down."

nor money, nor ships of war were sent over."—*Bancroft's U. S.*, vol. iv.,
ch. 4, p. 102. " *They protected by* YOUR *arms ?* They have nobly taken up
arms in your defence . . . for the defence of a country whose frontier
was drenched in blood, while its interior parts yielded all its little savings
to your emolument."—Barré debating on the Stamp Act in the House of
Commons.—*Idem.*, vol. v., ch. 11, p. 240.
    [38] " Colden himself retired within the fort . . . He would have
fired on the people, but was menaced with being hanged."—*Bancroft's
U. S.*, vol. v., ch. 19, p. 355.

The governor urged his honor ;
   " Had pledged," he said, " his oath,"
And ought to further Britain's aims."—
We thought New York had equal claims
   On oath and honor both.[39]

" And let him pledge his honor
   To let the stamps alone,"
Said Isaac Sears ; and all the crowd
Who heard him say it, shouted loud
   To make his words their own.

The people waited long then,
   And hoped the strife would end ;
But, when this course had nothing won,
No man [40] could check a course begun
   The governor's will to bend.

At night, the boys with torches
   Came trooping out for sport.
They sought the house of James,[41] and took
The army flags his fear forsook,
   And march'd them round the fort.

[39] " Colden pleaded his oath . . . that . . . the Act should be observed, . . . the contempt into which the government would fall by concession."—*Idem.*, p. 357. " In Connecticut, Dyer . . . entreated Fitch (the governor) not to take an oath . . . contrary to that of the governor to maintain the rights of the colonies."—*Idem.*, p. 351.

[40] " Isaac Sears and others, leaders of the Sons of Liberty, who had issued strict orders forbidding injury to private property, endeavored to restrain the mob."—*Lossing's Pic. Field Book of the Rev.*, vol. ii., p. 788.

[41] " A party of volunteers sacked the house occupied by James, and

The governor own'd his coaches,
    And one a coach of state.
They burst his barn-door in with cries [42]
And dragg'd them off before his eyes,
    As trophies of their hate.

An image of the devil,
    And of the governor too [42]
They made, and made them both careen,
While, side by side, through Bowling Green,
    They wheel'd them into view.

At last, of all the coaches
    They form'd a funeral pyre ;
And, full in face of all the town,
Who only roar'd its roar to drown,
    They set the whole on fire.

Then came a wake and wailing,
    As ashes cover'd all ;
And not a clause in laws unjust
The man had thought on us to thrust
    But some one would recall.

bore off the colors of the royal regiments."—*Bancroft's U. S.*, vol. v., ch.
19, p. 356.
   [42] "In the evening a vast torchlight procession carrying, . . . two
images, one of the governor ; the other of the devil, . . . broke open
the governor's coach-house, took out his chariot, carried the images upon
it, . . . to burn them with his own carriages and sleighs before his
own eyes on the Bowling Green."—*Idem.*
   [43] "He has bound himself," they cried, " to be the chief murderer of our
rights." "He was a rebel in Scotland, a Jacobite." "He is an enemy to

" A foe " is he of England ! "
  " A foe to all of us ! "
" In Scotland went with Jacobites ! "
" Has vow'd to murder here our rights !—
  Ere that we toast him thus!"

The colony's council " pass'd then
  A vote opposed by none,—
That England had the stamps assign'd
To agents who had all resign'd,
  Nor was the governor one.

At this the governor waver'd,
  And wrote a message thus :
" I wait the dawn of further light."
Cried Sears then : " Keep the fox in sight !
  He waits till free from us.

" Now send we back this answer :
  'Awhile the town will wait,
But four and twenty hours from now "
Will hold the stamps or else will vow
  To hold no more debate.' "

his king, to his country, and mankind."—*Idem.* " In the opinion of . . .
Colden . . . the democratic or popular part of the American Constitution was too strong. . . . His remedies were a perpetual revenue,
fixed salaries, and an hereditary council of priviledged landholders."—
Idem., vol. iv., ch. 16, p. 371.
  " " The council questioned " (*i.e.*, the colony's council) " his authority
to distribute the stamps, and unanimously advised him to declare that he
would do nothing in relation to them, but await the arrival of the new governor, and his declaration to that effect . . . was immediately published.

The governor begg'd the army,[44]
  The army begg'd the fleet,
To take the stamps and save the fort ;
But neither cared to brave the sport
  Of those who fill'd the street.

The courage of the courtiers
  Had bow'd to wisdom higher :
The power of right that ruled the street
Had overawed the fort and fleet—
  They did not dare to fire.

They did not dare to kindle [46]
  A spark that, should it flame,
Would shed no glory round a throne
Where prince and peer would flush alone
  To blush for their own shame.

So nothing now was left them
  Except to yield us all.[47]
Our mayor took the stamps, at last,
And bore them off, and lock'd them fast
  Within the City Hall.

But the confidence of the people was shaken."—*Idem.*, vol. v., ch. 19,
p. 356.

[45] "'We will have the stamp papers,' cried Sears to the multitude,
'within four and twenty hours.'"—*Idem.*

[46] "Colden invited Kenedy to receive them on board of the Coventry.
. . . Gage being appealed to, avowed his belief that a fire from the
fort would be the . . . commencement of civil war."—*Idem.*, 356-7.

[47] "Colden, perceiving further resistance . . . unavailing, ordered
the stamps to be delivered to the Mayor (Cruger) and Common Council,
the former giving a receipt for the same, and the corporation agreeing to

And loud the people shouted ; [48]
   They felt that right was done ;
Cried " Liberty and Property !
No stamps to curse the Colony ! "
   And parted, one by one.

The next day all the papers [49]
   Without the stamps appear'd.
Men took no notes, but trusted men.
Our ships were off to sea again ;
   And none the navy fear'd.

And none had bought a stamp there,
   Or seal'd himself a slave ;
And half of England, trust my word,
Were thrill'd with joy, when they had heard
   How we ourselves could save. [50]

At last there came a daybreak
   When all the thankful kneel'd ;
And bells were rung, and banners hung ;
And England's weal was drunk and sung— [51]
   The Stamp Act was repeal'd.

pay for all the stamps that should be destroyed or lost. This was satisfactory to the people."—*Lossing's Pic. Field Book*, vol. ii., p. 789.

[48] " In all the streets were heard the shouts of Liberty, Property, and no Stamps."—*Bancroft's U. S.*, vol. v., ch. 19, p. 357.

[49] " The press continued its activity."—*Idem.*

[50] " I rejoice that America has resisted."—William Pitt in the House of Commons.—*Idem.*, vol. v., ch. 21, p. 391.

[51] " On . . . the joyful intelligence of the repeal of the Stamp Act . . . the city was filled with delight. Bells rang . . . cannon roared . . . the Sons of Liberty drank twenty-eight ' loyal and constitutional toasts.' "—*Lossing's Pic. Field Book of the Rev.*, vol. ii., p. 789.

Great Britain's lords in council
    Had talked of fire and ball ;
But, when they touch'd our liberties,
Met manhood in the colonies
    They could not thus inthrall.

THE LAST CRUISE OF THE GASPEE.

1772.

ONE windy day in March,[1]
    Ghost-white against the gray,
A cruiser fleet, through snow and sleet,
    Made Narraganset Bay.

There were smugglers in the bay,
    And smugglers on the shore ;
But loyal still to the royal will
    Ten times as many more,—

Ten times as many more,
    Though every smuggler there
But thrived because of England's laws[2]
    And taxes none could bear.

---

[1] She first appeared in . . . Narraganset Bay in March, 1772, . . . to prevent infraction of the revenue laws, and to put a stop to . . . illicit trade.—*Lossing's Pic. Field Book of the Rev.*, vol. ii., ch. 3, p. 60.
[2] See "Our First Break with the British," notes 5, 19, 20, 24.

Yet the cruiser's captain drawl'd,
The while he quaft his ale,
" These islands low are full you know,
Of fellows fled from jail,

" Of Puritans fled from law
And kings they curse and fear.
Aha !" he laugh'd, " our loyal craft
Has brought the Cavalier !

" Our guns will speak in tones
To make the whole bay ring ;
And teach to each within their reach
The reverence due the king.

" Their ships upon the bay
Shall heed our cannon's call,
And dip their flags,[3] or sail in rags,
And yield us bounties all.[4]

" Their sheep upon the shore,
A royal tax will be.[4]
No lack of food or kindling wood
Is here," quoth he, " for me !"

[3] " Often fired . . . to compel their masters to take down their colors
in its presence—a haughty marine Gesler."—*Idem.*, p. 61.
[4] " Plundered the islands of sheep and hogs, cut down trees, fired
at market boats, detained vessels without any colorable pretext, and made
illegal seizures of goods of which the recovery cost more than they were
worth."—*Bancroft's Hist. U. S.*, vol. vi., ch. 47, p. 417.

There were smugglers in the bay,
And smugglers on the shore;
This craft, I ken, a band of men
Ten times as lawless bore.

Our sheriff went and warn'd
Their captain, o'er and o'er,
To keep in sight the bounds of right,
And not to plunder more.

The captain waved his hand,
Said he: " The fleet has made
A vow devout to carry out
The English ' Acts of Trade.' " [5]

Judge Hopkins [7] wrote him then :
" Our men demand their due."
" I write because you break our laws,"
Wrote Governor Wanton [7] too.

The captain bade them go
To Boston with their plea ;
" Not his affair ; the admiral [7] there
Had sent the ship to sea."

[5] " The Governor, . . . sent a sheriff on board the Gaspee."—*Idem.*
[6] " See *Idem.*, vol. iv., ch. 8.   Also " Our First Break with the British,"
Note 19.
[7] " Hopkins, the Chief Justice, . . . gave the opinion that any person
who should . . . exercise any authority by force of arms without showing his commission to the governor . . . was guilty of a trespass if not
piracy.—*Idem.*, vol. vi., ch. 47, p. 416. The governor, therefore, sent

And then he turn'd away.
One heard him mutter near :
" I think I see the one they fee [8]
    Ship back his bounties here."

The judge and governor wrote
The admiral, who but swore
His fleet would hang [9] the island gang,
    If they should vex him more.

" The navy [10] know their trade,"
His clerk to Wanton wrote ;
" In mere pretence and insolence [11]
    You board the sovereign's [12] boat."

Wrote Wanton : " We shall ask
The throne [13] to judge your note ;
And every time you hint of crime,[13]
    Shall board the sovereign's boat.

" The English crown should serve
The English people's cause,
And honor those, nor make them foes,
    Who stand by English laws."

. . . to ascertain by what orders the lieutenant acted ; and Duddington
referred the subject to the admiral."—*Idem.*

    [8] See " Our First Break with the British," Note 20.

    [9] " As sure as the people of Newport attempt to rescue any vessel,
. . . I will hang them as pirates."—*Idem.*, p. 417.

    [10] " The Admiral answered from Boston : ' The lieutenant, sir, has
done his duty.' "—*Idem.*, p. 416.

But months and months went on.
The cruiser fired away.
None plied an oar, lived near the shore,
But feared to be her prey.[4]

Cried Captain Lindsey [14] then:
"This outrage none should bide !
Rhode Island grit must yet outwit,
And trip the scoundrel's pride.

"He knows my packet here,
And where I sail, and why ;
And if he will may sink me, still
His guns will I defy.

"If down we go, the law,
Will float to stand upon ;
If that go too, this case is through ;
But, Britain, more anon ! "

So high his flag [15] he flew ;
And wide his jib he spread.
The cruiser fired ; her crew grew tired,
Her captain wroth and red.

---

[11] " Your two insolent letters."—*Lossing's Pic. Field Book*, vol. ii., ch. 3.
[12] " I would advise you not to send your sheriff on board the king's ship again on such ridiculous errands."—*Idem*.
[13] " I shall transmit your letter to the Secretary of State. . . . I will send the sheriff of this colony at any time, and to any place within the body of it, as I shall think fit."—*Idem*.
[14] " On the 9th of June, 1772, Captain Lindsey left Newport for Providence in his packet."—*Idem*. " Called the Hannah and sailed between New York and Providence."—*Idem*., note.

"All hands aloft!" he cried;
  "All sail!" and at the words,
The masts were fill'd with sailors drill'd
  To climb and cling like birds.

Wide flew each flapping sheet,
  And sagg'd and bagg'd the gale,
And cloud-like lash'd the waves that dash'd
  As if they felt a flail.

When off of Nauquit [16] Point,
  Shrewd Lindsey knew his ground;
He steer'd afar, and clear'd the bar;
  And then the ship swung round. [16]

Up toss'd her canvas high;
  And dipp'd, as round she ran,
The saucy way that seems to say
  Now catch me if you can.

The cruiser's captain look'd,
  And mouth'd an awful oath:
" Now catch I not, let fire and shot
  Or bottom catch us both.

[15] " As Captain Lindsey, on this occasion, kept his colors flying, the Gaspee gave chase, and continued it as far as Namquit (now Gaspee) Point. The tide was ebbing, but the bar was covered. As soon as Lindsey doubled the Point, he stood to the westward. Duddington, commander of the Gaspee, eager to overtake the pursued, and ignorant of the extent of the submerged point from the shore, kept on a straight course, and in a few minutes struck the sand. The fast-ebbing tide soon left his vessel hopelessly grounded."—*Idem.*

[16] Namquit, according to Lossing; Nauquit, according to Bancroft.

" Mind not the bar," he cried,
  " Straight on !   With depth to spare,[16]
The tide is high, and, sailing by,
  We head them off up there."

  Deep plow'd the cruiser's prow
  The broken waves below,
So bows a bull whose pride is full
  To toss a stubborn foe.

  She plung'd and reel'd and roll'd.
  Ah, better had she tack'd !
The water flew the bulwark through.
  The mainmast **bent and crack'd.**

  The wind, it whistled there ;
  The boatswain whistled here.
The captain swore ; the mainsail tore ;
  The jib had ript its gear.

  A flood was on the deck.
  The crew were floundering round.
Then, clean and chill, **and safe and still,**
  The cruiser lay aground.[16]

---

[17] " Lindsey arrived at Providence at sunset, and . . . communicated
the fact to Mr. John Brown, one of the leading merchants of that city."—
Lossing's Pic. Field Book, v. ii., ch. 3.

When Lindsey saw her fate,
  So loudly cheer'd his men,
The hostile crew, that heard them, flew
  To man their guns again.

But Lindsey kept his course—
  He now could do no more—
And told ere night the cruiser's plight
  To those he met on shore.[17]

" There stays the ship," said he,
  " Till lifted by the tide."
" Till Providence shall lift her thence,"
  John Brown,[17] his friend, replied.

And Providence, at dusk,
  Was routed out to greet
The drumming fierce of Daniel Pierce[18]
  Who cried in every street :

" The cruiser lies aground !
  High tide at three [18] o'clock !
Who care to go and meet her so,
  Come all to Fenner's [19] dock ! "

[18] " At dusk . . . Daniel Pearce passed along the Main Street beating a drum, and informing the inhabitants that the Gaspee lay aground, . . . that she could not get off until three o'clock, and inviting," etc.— *Idem.*

They came to Fenner's dock ;
And found, awaiting there,
Eight [19] yawls, that Brown [19] had lent the town,
In Captain Whipple's [19] care.

The crews that mann'd the yawls
Had muffled [19] every oar ;
And they, and men who join'd them then,[20]
All told, were sixty-four.[21]

Their arms were pick'd with care
From all their friends could loan ;
And all the yawls, for cannon balls,
Were stock'd with paving-stone.[22]

They battled wind and tide,
Three hours [23] amid the gloom.
The midnight pass'd.[23]   They saw, at last,
The cruiser's bulwarks loom.

"Who comes ?" her watch call'd out.
"Who comes !" her captain cried.
Then swift alarm'd, in tones that arm'd,
Her crew that toward him hied.

---

[19] Brown " ordered the preparation of eight of the largest long-boats in the harbor, to be placed under the general command of Captain Whipple, one of his most trusty ship-masters," . . . " the row-locks to be muffled, and the whole put in readiness at half-past eight at Fenner's wharf."—*Idem.*

[20] " The principal actors in this affair were John Brown, Capt. Abraham Whipple, John B. Hopkins, Benjamin Dunn, Dr. John Mawney, Benja-

"Move off!" her captain roar'd,
  His pistol aiming well;
Then fired [23]—alack! fire answer'd back;
  He started, stagger'd, fell.

And then, as dark and fierce
  As tidal waves, where fleets
Are whelm'd and whirl'd and downward hurl'd
  Till death their deed completes,

Our men, at Whipple's[19] cry,
  "Up, up!" clear'd every check;
And dash'd and leapt and slash'd and swept
  Across the cruiser's deck.

But hold!—her men were gone.
  Ours held the deck alone;
Their work had done, nor fired a gun;
  The cruiser's crew had flown.[24]

"Surrender here!" rang out;
  And out the cabin glanced
At first a few, then all the crew;
  Then one and all advanced.

min Page, Joseph Bucklin, Turpin Smith, Ephraim Bowen, and Capt.
Joseph Tillinghast."—*Idem.* "Led by John Brown and Joseph Brown of
Providence, and Simeon Potter of Bristol."—*Bancroft's U. S.*, vol. vi.,
ch. 47.
  [21] "Filled with sixty-four well-armed men, a sea-captain in each boat
acting as a steersman."—*Lossing's Pict. Field Book of the Rev.*, vol.
ii., ch. 3.
  [22] "They took with them a quantity of wood paving-stone."—*Idem.*
  [23] "The boats left Providence between ten and elevan. . . . Between

" First know," said Whipple then,
" That here you sail no more ;
And next prepare your yawls to bear
    Yourselves and yours ashore." [25]

The sailors went and came,
    They came with bags and coats.
They call'd their roll, and said the whole
    They own'd was in their boats.

Meantime our men themselves [26]
    The captain's wound had dress'd ;
And row'd him, sore but safe, ashore
    With all that he possess'd. [27]

" All hands embark ! " rang out ;
    And all the yawls were full ;
Save one whose crew had more to do
    While off the rest should pull.

This crew the cruiser fired, [28]
    Till smoke, well under way,
Flew up the mast as white and fast
    As e'er, of old, the spray.

---

one and two . . . they reached the Gaspee, when a sentinel hailed them
. . . Duddington appeared, . . . and waving the boats off fired a pistol
at them. This . . . we returned . . . Duddington was wounded."—
Idem.

[24] " The crew retreating below."—*Idem.*

[25] " The schooner's company were ordered to collect their clothing and
leave the vessel."—*Idem.*

Then swiftly they embark'd,
And swiftly they withdrew ;
As flash'd the fire, and, streaming higher,
The red flag redder flew.

The cruiser burn'd in state,
Until she burst at last [28]
With every ball she bore and all
Her powder in the blast.

It fill'd the heaven above,
But not to heaven was given :
A wounded cloud roar'd long and loud ;
Then back the whole was driven.

When all was o'er, there seem'd
Faint sparks to fill the place—
" There comes," said one, " the morning sun ;
A new day dawns apace ! "

It dawn'd for these, at least ;
When soon they hove in sight
Of pier on pier pack'd full to cheer
Those heroes of the night.

[26] " Thomas Bucklin . . . fired the musket." . . . He afterwards assisted in dressing the wound, supervised by Dr. John Mawney, an American.—*Idem.*, note.

[27] " All the effects of . . . Duddington being carefully placed in one of the American boats."—*Idem.*

[28] " The *Gaspee* was set on fire, and at dawn blew up."—*Idem.*

But hist ! the cheers were check'd.
  " Keep mum ! " the murmur spread ;
The crown, to get these men, had set
  A price on every head.

" Five hundred dollars down,[29]
  For him who tells of one,"
Was first proclaim'd : but no one named
  A man who aught had done.

" Five thousand," [30] then were pledged,
  " To know who took the lead ;
And half as much to know of such
  As join'd him in the deed."

The King's commission,[31] last,
  Sat half a year or more ;
But not a word it ever heard
  About the sixty-four.

Forgotten were they then ?
  They might have pass'd by day,
Without a wink to make you think,
  Or hint that it was they.

---

[29] " A reward of five hundred dollars for the discovery of the perpe-
trator of said villainy."—*Idem*.
[30] " Afterwards, . . . a reward of five thousand dollars for the leader
and two thousand five hundred . . . the other parties."—*Idem*.

But, when the night had come ;
  And door and blind were lock'd,
And window fast, and blew the blast
  Till all the chimney rock'd ;

When, safe from eyes and ears,
  In homes where all were true,
The way those men were feasted then
  A king, full well, might rue.

And when the board was bare ;
  And round the roaring fire,
The nuts were crack'd and cider smack'd
  Till tooth and tongue would tire ;

When each his tale would tell
  About that ship and night,
And still the way he dodg'd, **each day,**
  The British spy and spite ;

The boys who husk'd the corn
  Would forward bend, and spring,
And draw the ears, like swords, with cheers,
  To make the rafters ring !

---

[31] "A commission of inquiry under the great seal of England . . . sat from the 4th until the 22d of January . . . adjourned until . . . May . . . and sat until the 23d of June. But not a solitary clue to the identity of the perpetrators could be obtained."—*Idem.*

The host who stirr'd the fire
Would stab it through and through :
You might have thought the flames he brought
Had burn'd a cruiser too.

The girls would fancy then
It was the cruiser flared ;
And round the walls would aim like balls
The apples red they pared.

" To arms ! " would cry the men ;
And each a maid purloin ;
While mother's yarn would snap, and darn
The dance that all would join.

Ah, so we hush'd the tale !
Yet spies that nigh would roam
Could not decoy the smallest boy
To tell what pass'd at home.

We hush'd it, till the hush
Became our countersign
To save from those we knew were foes,
And make our men combine.

We hush'd it, till we learn'd
That thousands would be free,
And long'd to know which way to go
And when the call would be.

We hush'd it, till we heard
What Concord had to bear ;
Then shouted loud, a mighty crowd,
" Our heroes lead us there !"

THE LEBANON BOYS IN BOSTON.[1]

The Tea-Party, December 16, 1773.

" NEW trouble brews in Boston,"
    Was told us half the year ;
Yet every week the postman came
    With something new to fear.

" Our freedom," so they wrote soon,
    " Such progress here begets
That England seeks to check it[2]
    With swords and bayonets.

[1] In order to indicate the relations existing, at the time of the " Tea-Party," between Boston and the surrounding towns, as well as to give unity of form to this ballad, the story has been told as given, some years ago, by David Kinnison, one of the survivors of the party, who boarded the tea-ships. He stated that certain young men of Lebanon, Me., united in a secret society—one of many existing at that time—and formed alliances with clubs in Boston and in other places. These young men determined to destroy the tea, and went to Boston for that purpose. Having resolved to stand by each other, to throw overboard those who faltered, and not to reveal each other's names, twenty-four went on board as Indians, half armed with muskets and bayonets, half with tomahawks and clubs, and all expecting a fight.—See *Lossing's Pict. Field Bk. of the Rev.*, vol. 1, p. 499.
[2] In 1770, " September, Hutchinson received the order . . . which marks the beginning of a system of . . . prevention of American in-

" Their foreign ' Board of Customs,'[3]
   Past our laws' reach, they say,
Here pluck from us their living,
   As vultures from their prey.
Ah ! would we keep our freedom,
   We must not basely yield,
But claim our rights,[4] as when of old
   The Stamp Act was repeal'd."

We read, and thought together
   That something must be done ;
And we were those to do it,
   We boys of Lebanon.

The words of Samuel Adams[4]
   We heard a neighbor quote :
" They silence our Assembly ;[5]
   A sword is at its throat ;
Our charter is their target,
   Our judgment-seat their fort,[6]

dependence. . . . Boston was made the rendezvous of all ships . . . and the fortress . . . garrisoned by regular troops. . . . But the charter of Massachusetts purposely and emphatically reserved to its governor the command of the militia of the colony, and of its forts ; the castle had been built and repaired and garrisoned by the colony itself at its own expense ; to . . . bestow it on the commander-in-chief was a plain violation of the charter, as well as of immemorial usage."—*Bancroft's Hist. U. S.*, vol. vi., ch. 45, pp. 368, 369.

[3] " Never was a community more distressed or divided by fear and hope than . . . Boston. There the . . . Board of the Commissioners of the Customs was to be established . . . as the lawyers of England . . . decided," in 1767, " that American taxation by Parliament was legal and constitutional, the press of Boston sought support in something more firm than human opinion. . . . ' The law of nation,' said they, ' is the law of God.' "—*Idem*, ch. 30, pp. 101, 102.

[4] " ' Hancock and most of the party,' said the governor, ' are quiet,

Our men they rob for rations,
　Our boys they shoot for sport ;
Our faith that their horizon burst
　And zenith held not down,
Their Toleration Law [7] would force
　To cringe beneath the crown.
I care not what to others
　A loyal feeling brings ;
To me it still will loyal be
　To serve the King of kings." [8]

We heard, and swore together
　That work must be begun ;
And we were those to do it,
　We boys of Lebanon.

We signed a pledge of " Union."
　To all the land we wrote.
We went to meet the postman.
　We read the Boston note " :

and all of them, exept Adams, abate their virulence.' "—*Idem*, ch. 47, p. 407.

[5] " Bernard . . . dissolved the Assembly. Massachusetts was left without a legislature."—*Idem*, ch. 34, pp. 165. See also " Our First Break with the British," note 9.

[6] " The officers screened their men from legal punishment, and sometimes even rescued them from the constables."—*Idem*, ch. 43, p. 334. See also the whole account, in this chapter, of the Boston massacre.

[7] " For New York, the Lords of Trade . . . refused to Presbyterians any immunities but such as might be derived from the British Law of Toleration."—*Idem*, vol. vi., ch. 7, p. 84. See also " Our First Break with the British," note 12.

[8] " ' It was not reverence for kings,' he (Adams) would say, ' that brought the ancestors of New England to America. They fled from kings and bishops, and looked up to the King of kings. We are free, therefore,' he concluded, ' and want no kings.' "—*Idem*, ch. 36, pp. 194.

"In Union only is there strength ;
    And strength is all our stay.
Alas that some divide us !
    Alas that some give way !
Once none would touch a thing they tax ;
    To-day the weak agree,
And say : ' Enough if none will taste,
    If none will trade in tea.' [9]
The lords have found our weakness out ;
    And now are talking thus :
That India 's losing traders
    May bring tea free to us. [10]
Ay, ay, as if these would not heap
    Her lap with tribute gold,
' Let them,' says England, ' take the tax ;
    Let them the duties hold.'

"Already bound for Boston,
    May tea be on the waves,
A bait flung out to tempt us
    To touch, and then be slaves.

[9] " New York alone had been perfectly true to its engagements . . .
impatient of a system of voluntary renunciation . . . so unequally kept.
. . . Merchants of New York . . . consulted those of Philadelphia on
agreeing to a general importation of all articles except of tea . . . and
now trade between America and England was open in every thing but
tea."—*Idem*, ch. 44, pp. 365, 366. " The students at Princeton burnt the
New York merchants' letter. . . . Boston tore it into pieces " at a full
meeting of the trade.—*Idem*.

[10] " The continued refusal . . . to receive tea . . . had brought
distress upon the East India Company. . . . Praying . . . to export
teas, free of all duties, to America . . . Lord North proposed to give to

And if our strong men falter,
    Nor thrust this bait away,
How can the weak be kept from all
    That makes us England's prey?

" And yet, if we in Boston
    To thwart the throne conspire,
Our town may prove an altar,
    Our fortunes melt in fire.
The sacrifice is ready ;
    Yet first we wait reply,[11]
To know we own a country
    To save, before we die." [12]

We met, and swore together,
    If fighting must be done,
In Boston we would do it,
    We boys of Lebanon.

We started out at midnight,
    And took the Indian suits,
Our fathers' trophies from the wars
    Where all had been recruits.

the company itself the right of exporting its teas . . . the ministry would not listen to the thought of relieving America from taxation."—*Idem*, ch. 49, pp. 457, 458.

[11] " Massachusetts . . . elected its Committee of Correspondence, fifteen in number. New Hampshire and Connecticut did the same, so that all New England and Virginia . . . on the first emergency, . . . could convene a congress."—*Idem*, p. 460.

[12] " ' Brethren,' they wrote, ' we are reduced to this dilemma—either to sit down quiet . . . or to rise up and resist. . . . we earnestly request your advice.' "—*Idem*, p. 476.

We pack'd them up in knapsacks,
    And then with each a gun
And tomahawk away we walk'd
    In pairs or one by one.
By day we kept the forests ;
    But when the sun was down,
We hurried on to Boston,
    And scatter'd through the town.

We hunted out our cousins.
    We told them why we came.
"Aha," said they, "we plot the same.
    We join you in the game."

They show'd us then, at morning,
    The "Tree of Liberty,"
Where those who plann'd the Stamp Act [13]
    Had hung in effigy.
A pole was now beside it ;
    A flag it bore flew high ; [14]
The church bells all were ringing ;
    A crowd had gather'd nigh.
"To see this tree, the agent
    Of stamps," we heard, "resign'd.

[13] See "Our First Break with the British," note 27.   Also *Idem*, vol. v., ch. 16, p. 310.
[14] "A large flag was hung out on the pole at Liberty Tree ; the bells in the meeting-houses were rung from eleven till noon."—*Idem*, vol. vi., ch. 50, p. 473.
[15] "Molineux read a paper requiring the consignee to promise not to

Here too East India's agent
    Should learn the people's mind :
The tea sent here to tax us
    Untouch'd away shall go ;
Or all will brand its consignee,
    Our own, our country's foe." [15]
The people cheer'd the purpose ;
    From lip to lip it pass'd ;
The crowd about went homeward ;
    The sky was overcast.

Each agent heard the message ;
    No promise would he sign. [16]
Again the town demanded one ;
    Again did each decline. [17]
Then Boston's grand " Committee [18]
    Of Correspondence," wrote
To ask the farmers, " Would they stand
    By what the town would vote ? "

From every hill and valley
    Came back, as though one word,
What Samuel Adams read with pride
    Where all the people heard :

sell the teas, but to return them. . . . Then read . . . a Resolve
passed at Liberty Tree that the consignees who should refuse . .
were enemies to their country."—*Idem*, pp. 473, 474.
    [16] " Each and all answered : ' I cannot comply.' "—*Idem.*
    [17] " There was once more a legal Town Meeting to entreat the con-
signees to resign. Upon their repeated refusal, the town passed no vote
. . . but . . . broke up."—*Idem*, p. 475.

" Without a voice dissenting,
    We swear by you to stand.
Our wealth or life preventing,
    The tea shall never land." [18]

Then dawn'd the stirring Sunday [19]
    When swift the news was pass'd,
That one tea-ship they waited for,
    Was in the port at last.
Not many went to church then ;
    But all began to pray,
With eyes to duty open wide—
    The Puritanic way.

In haste we met together,
    Our work must be begun ;
We plann'd, then, how to do it,
    We boys of Lebanon.
With Proctor [20] for our captain,
    We vow'd on hand to be,
And cling like air and water there
    About the ship with tea.

[18] " The Committee of Correspondence . . . authorized Samuel Adams
to invite . . . Dorchester, Rozbury, etc., . . . to hold a mass meeting
. . . the assembly resolved unanimously that ' the tea should be sent
back . . . at all events.' "—*Idem*, pp. 477, 478. See also the reply of
the towns, p. 483.
[19] " Sunday, the 28th of November," 1773.—*Idem*, p. 477.
[20] " A party . . . under . . . Edward Proctor as its captain, was ap-
pointed to guard the tea-ship."—*Idem*, p. 478.
[21] " The select men . . . sought in vain for the consignees, who had
taken sanctuary in the castle."—*Idem*, 477.

The Town-Select-Men waited on
   The vessel's consignees ;
But these were waiting on the fort,[21]
   Well lock'd with English keys.
True courtiers, they would tender
   The governor there their tea.
The governor tried his council ;
   The council[22] said : " Not we ;
Our homes are with the people ;
   And we are not the ones
To hold the cup of serfdom
   To them, ourselves, or sons."

The consignees were waiting
   Until, in forms of law,
Their tea was enter'd at the port,
   When none could it withdraw.[23]
So quick the Town-Committee
   Had made and seal'd a writ,
And pledg'd the vessel's owner's word
   Not yet to enter it.[24]

---

[22] " On the same day, the council, who had been solicited by the Governor and the consignees to assume the guardianship of the tea, coupled their refusal with a reference . . . that the tax upon it . . . was unconstitutional."—*Idem*, p. 478.

[23] " Let the tea be entered, and it would be beyond the power of the consignees to send it back."—*Idem*, p. 477.

[24] " The Committee of Correspondence . . . obtained from the Quaker Rotch, who owned the Dartmouth, a promise not to enter the ship."—*Idem*, p. 477.

At Fanueil Hall,[25] next morning,
    While all the bells were rung,
Men swarm'd, like bees, to buzz before,
    Prepar'd to die, they stung.
The sheriff [26] came and cried aloud :
    " You meet unlawfully ! "
His cry but made them busier buzz,
    With Saxon loyalty.
The consignees were summon'd ;
    " The tea," they wrote, " we stack." [27]
" The tea shall sail for England,"
    The people answer'd back.

And then to ports in England,
    And those at home they wrote :
" Tea-taxers here, or traders,
    Our country's foes we vote.[28]
Think not our men will waver,
    Our wives their vows abate ;
The herbs they steep for tea will keep
    Less bitter than their hate."

---

[25] " Faneuil Hall could not contain the people . . . on Monday."—
Idem, 478.
[26] " The Sheriff . . . entered with a Proclamation from the Governor,
warning, exhorting, and requiring . . each . . . unlawfully assembled
forthwith to disperse. . . . The words were received with hisses, . . .
and a unanimous vote not to disperse."—*Idem,* p. 479.
[27] " We now declare to you our readiness to store them."—*Idem.*
[28] " Every ship owner was forbidden, on pain of being deemed an enemy
to his country, to import or bring as freight any tea from Great Britain
till the unrighteous act taxing it should be repealed, and this vote was

Two tea-ships more were sighted.[29]
   Our guards, like nerves, were strung[30]
From bay to every belfry's bell,
   The slightest move had rung.

Then spoke the vessels' owners :
   " Our tea is legal prey
For fort and fleet, if enter'd not
   Before the twentieth[31] day."
" Then send it off to sea again,"
   The Town-Committee said.
" Too much you ask," was answer'd,
   " For then would blood be shed.
The port's collector warns us
   We must not clear the port.
Without his ' Writ of Clearance,'
   We dare not brook the fort."
They pointed down the harbor :
   There lay the fleet,[32] alas,
Like prongs along the channel,
   To rake whate'er should pass.

---

printed and sent to every seaport in the province, and to England."—
Idem, p. 480.

[29] " Two more tea-ships . . . arrived."—*Idem.*

[30] " A military watch was regularly kept up . . . by night. The toll-ing of the bells would have been the signal for a general uprising."—*Idem.*

[31] " The ships, . . . on the twentieth day from their arrival, would be liable to seizure."—*Idem.*

[32] " The Active and the Kingfisher . . . were sent to guard the pas-sages out of the harbor. . . . Orders were given . . . to load guns at the castle so that no vessel . . . might go to sea without a permit."—*Idem,* p. 482.

They pointed toward the castle,
    And all the guns within
Bespoke how they would treat a prey
    That sought the sea to win.

At this our Town-Committee
    The port's collector sought ; [32]
The governor,[33] too, exulting [34]
    To think his trap had caught.
" You mark the fleet and castle ;
    Should trouble brew," said he ;
" Your Hancocks, Rowes, and Phillips [34]
    Might risk as much as we."
But Molineux [35] said only :
    " They more would risk if slaves ;
For all they then could wish, would be
    Enough to give them graves."
" ' If slaves ' ! " the governor answer'd,
    And rail'd against their cause ;
" Aha !—you talk of ' slaves,' forsooth,
    Because your land has laws !
And you would dare to break them ?—
    And reason, what of it ?—

[32] " A meeting of the people . . . directed . . . the owner of the
Dartmouth to apply for a clearance. He did so. . . . accompanied by . . .
eight others as witnesses. . . . The collector and comptroller unequivo-
cally and finally refused. . . . Then said they (*i. e.*, the people) . . . protest immediately against the custom-house, and apply to the Governor for
his pass."—*Idem*, pp. 483-5.

[34] " ' They find themselves,' . . . said Hutchinson, ' involved in invin-
cible difficulties. . . . The wealth of Hancock, Phillips, Rowe, Dennie,

I trust in human nature,
   When reason should submit."

" We trust in human nature,"
   Said Young,[36] who near him stood ;
" And peace that brooks oppression,
   It does not deem a good.
We trust in human nature ;
   The conscience, ruling there,
May guard the right, full well as kings
   With crowns their dearest care.
Love rules in human nature,
   For, all of history through,
The slaves have been the many,
   The tyrants been the few."

The governor turn'd in anger :
   " Well, well, we then shall see.
Your hint of flint can wring no ' Writ
   Of Clearance ' here from me."

Then met the town together,
   Their final vote to take.
Not one, of seven thousand [38] there,
   Desired the peace to break.

and so many other men of property, seemed to him a security against vio-
lence."—*Idem*, pp. 480-2. " Hutchinson began to clutch at victory."—
Idem, p. 484.

   [35] See note 15 under this Ballad.

   [36] " ' The only way to get rid of it,' said Young (speaking of the tea in
one of the Boston public meetings), ' is to throw it overboard.' "—*Idem*,
p. 478.

Said Quincy :[37] " Crowds and shoutings
   Can never end our strife.
But sadder scenes and sounds await
   Our loss of wealth and life.
The structures fair of freedom
   Men rear beneath the sky,
Press down on deep foundations,
   Where thousands buried lie.
Our course we well may ponder :
   Hope's rainbow in the cloud
May lure a march beneath its arch
   To flash and bolt and shroud."
The people paused and ponder'd ;
   But not a single hand,[38]
When call'd to vote, but voted,
   " The tea shall never land."

And then we met together ;
   If fighting must be done,
We knew we now should do it,
   We boys of Lebanon.
In one day more—one only—[39]
   The fleet and fort would hold
The tea that none could longer keep
   From being bought and sold.

[37] " ' Shouts and hozannas will not terminate the trials of this day. . . .
insatiable revenge which actuates our enemies. . . . must bring on
the most . . . terrible struggle this country ever saw.'   Thus spoke the
younger Quincy."—*Idem*, p. 486.

Close by we sought our quarters ;
   And from our knapsacks quick
We took our Indian guises ;
   And stain'd our cheeks with brick.
Anon, we half were ready,
   With tomahawks in hand [40] ;
And half, with muskets only,[40]
   And heard our last command.
A moment then we waited ;
   We knew the danger there ;
We looked above for courage ;
   We bent below in prayer.
We swore by God in heaven,
   To keep our names from all ;
We swore to stand together,
   Till all in death should fall ;
We swore, by truth and honor,
   Should half essay to flee,
To cast that half the harbor in
   To perish with the tea.[40]

The twilight long had tarried ;
   The darkness deeper grew ;
In old South Church, the people
   Still ponder'd what to do.

[38] " The whole assembly of seven thousand voted unanimously that the tea should not be landed."—*Idem.*
[39] " A few hours would have placed the tea under the protection of the admiral at the castle."—*Idem*, 487.
[40] See note 1 under this Ballad.

The dimness veil'd our coming.
   We listen'd near the door,
Till Samuel Adams rose and said,"
   "We here can do no more."
And then we pass'd the word on :
   "To Griffin's wharf now !—run !"
For we knew where to do the rest,
   We boys of Lebanon.

Then off flew some as pickets
   To stand and sound alarms,
Should coming spies or soldiers
   Compel resort to arms.
The twilight long had tarried ;
   The darkness deeper grew ;
"Full time," said we, "to take our tea !"
   The people thought so too.

To Griffin's wharf we led them ;
   We row'd, and reach'd the ships ;
No captain there, nor sailor,
   Dared open once his lips.
We crowded every gangway ;
   We brought out every chest ;

----

41 " A quarter before six Rotch appeared . . . relating that the governor had refused him a pass. . . . Samuel Adams rose and gave the word : ' This meeting can do nothing more to save the country.' On the instant, a shout was heard at the porch. . . . A body of men . . . disguised as Indians, . . . encouraged by . . . others, repaired to Griffin's wharf, posted guards to prevent the intrusion of spies, . . . and

We smash'd and dash'd it overboard.
   The bay did all the rest.
No time was there for shouting,
   No wish was there for strife ;
Three hours we wrought in silence,
   And thank'd the Lord for life.
Anon, the work was ended ;
   Anon, we back could row ;
The heaven was black above us ;
   The harbor black below.

None thought on shore to cheer us,[42]
   Though all had waited there ;
Their silence match'd the silence.
   Where souls have flown to prayer.
Their silence match'd the silence
   Of war's reserves, whose breath
Is hush'd to hear the order,
   That orders all to death.
Their silence match'd the silence
   Of heavens, close and warm,
Ere, like a shell incasing hell,
   They burst and free a storm.

As hush'd as on a Sabbath,[42]
   The people homeward went ;

in about three hours, three hundred and forty chests of tea, being the
whole quantity . . . were emptied into the bay without . . . injury
to other property."—*Idem*, pp. 486, 487.
[42] "The people around . . . were . . . still. . . . After the work was
done, the town became as still and calm as if it had been holy time."—*Idem*.

Their eyes alone transparent,
  To show their souls' content.
But we, we met together,
  When all our work was done,
To toast the dawn of freedom,
  We boys of Lebanon.

Then, early stirr'd at morning,
  We left with Paul Revere,[43]
Who through the south went riding off
  To bear, from Boston, cheer.
We spread through all the country ;
  We told, how all was done ;
Till all the shoremen stored away
  A tomahawk and gun.
Throughout the land, no Tory
  Would brave their sworn attack ;
East India found no agent ;
  The tea that came went back.

But, better far for freedom,[44]
  There ran from mouth to mouth,
From soul to soul, a tide to roll,
  And flow from north to south.

---

[43] " The next morning the Committee of Correspondence . . . sent Paul Revere, as express with the information to New York and Philadelphia."—*Idem.*

[44] " The ministry had chosen the most effectual measures to unite the colonies. . . . Old jealousies were removed, and perfect harmony subsisted between all."—*Idem*, p. 488.

Beyond the power of local pride
　　Or envy to withstand,
It burst each colony's borders
　　To form one common land."
Before men talk'd of Union ;
　　But now was Union won,
When everywhere each village square
　　Held boys of Lebanon.

———

THE CROWN'S FIGHT AGAINST THE TOWN'S RIGHT.

LEXINGTON, APRIL 19, 1775.

"A GALLOPING horse is coming[1]
　　Across the field !—do you mark ?"—
We woke and flew to the window,
　　We peer'd away in the dark.

The cloud-black night was bringing
　　The stir of a storm to fear.
What flash'd and clash'd !—who brought it ?—
　　"I, I !" cried Paul Revere.[1]

[1] April 18, 1775. "Gage . . . secretly prepared an expedition to destroy the colony's stores at Concord. . . . Warren . . . at ten o'clock despatched William Dawes through Roxbury to Lexington, and Paul Revere . . . by way of Charlestown. Revere . . . five minutes before the sentinels received the order to prevent it . . . rowed . . . across Charles River . . . beyond Charlestown Neck . . . intercepted by two

"The British are off for Concord [1]
    To seize the colony's arms !
And Dawes [1] and I stole over
    The river and over the farms."

" Wait, wait," we cried, " a moment ;
    You trust our lead awhile !
A cross-cut here to the highway
    Will save you more than a mile !"

"Come quick ! " said Paul.   " Their plan is
    To bear the arms away,
And store them safe in Boston
    Before the break of day."

" Yet wait you, Paul, and, waiting,
    Tell how does Boston fare ? "
" Alas," he sigh'd, " no telling
    How many will breakfast there.

" You know that, since the Port-Bill [2]
    Laid up our merchant-fleet,

British officers . . . he . . escaped to Medford. As he passed on he
. . . continued to rouse almost every house on the way to Lexington."—
Bancroft's Hist. U. S., vol. vii., ch. 27, pp. 288, 289.
    [2] " The privilege of its harbor was to be discontinued, and the port
closed against all commerce . . . until the king should be satisfied that
. . . it would obey the laws."—This the Boston port bill.—*Idem*, vol.
vi., ch. 52, p. 511.
    [3] For contributions in food and money sent at this time to Boston, see
Lossing's Pic. Field Book of the Am. Rev., vol. i., p. 535.
    [4] " The second penal bill . . . abrogated so much of its charter as
gave to its legislature the election of the council, abolished town meetings

We had starved, unless the farmers'
    Had sent us food to eat.

" To stop this, chains of pickets
    Are strung on Boston Neck ;
Our bay is black with frigates,
    And all our trade they check.

" And thus they vow to treat us,
    Till, humbled by their might,
We hold no courts nor meetings,[4]
    And yield each charter'd right.

" Ay, ay, and let our leaders,
    For serving us too well,
Be borne in chains to Britain, [5]
    To fill some dungeon-cell.

" The men who call'd our Congress [6]
    They swear to seize to-day.—
High time to rouse the country !
    High time to save the prey ! "

. . . and . . . intrusted the returning of juries to the dependent sheriff."—*Bancroft's Hist. U. S.*, vol. vi., ch. 52, p. 525.

[5] " A third penal measure . . . transferred the place of trial of any magistrates, revenue officers, or soldiers indicted for murder, or other capital offense, . . . to Nova Scotia or Great Britain."—*Idem.* " Letters were written to Gage . . . to arrest . . . all . . . thought to have committed treason . . . that the Massachusetts Congress was a treasonable body. The power of pardon . . . did not extend to the president of ' that seditious meeting,' nor to its most forward members, ' who . . . were to be brought to condign punishment ' . . . either in America or in England."—*Idem*, vol, vii., ch. 26, p. 284.

" Off, off ! " we cried, and parted ;
　　Then dragg'd from under the hay [7]
The guns our goods had cover'd
　　When borne from Boston Bay.

Our wives pour'd out the treasure
　　They too had brought from town, [7]
The powder, flint, and bullets
　　Well tuck'd in box and gown.

We arm'd in haste, but hardly
　　Had left with pouch and gun,
Before the bell rang, telling
　　Of Paul in Lexington.

At midnight saw he Charlestown ;
　　Not two had struck the clock [8]
Yet here the trembling belfry
　　Was rallying all its flock.

They sought the green together ;
　　Set guards on every road ;
Then sought the inn to measure
　　The fate they might forebode.

[6] " Adams and Hancock . . . whose seizure was believed to be in-
tended."—*Idem*, ch. 27, pp. 291, 292.
[7] In anticipation of an attack from the British, the Americans had
been collecting stores for some time.　Cannon-balls, and muskets had
been brought from Boston into the country under loads of manure ; and
cartridges and powder by the women, in candle-boxes, baskets. etc.—See
Lossing's Pict. Field Book of the Rev., vol. i., p. 522.

Ten times their band in number
 Were those they watch'd before;
And here should they withstand them?
 Or fly to join with more?

"Stand here!" said Jonas Parker[19];
 "The law has arm'd the town."
"And here," said Clark,[9] their pastor,
 "Be right, and shame the crown.

"What, though they fire, and fight us?—
 Make every heart rain blood?
Their guns, if heard in Concord,
 May save it from the flood.

"And if the blood we give them
 Shall save the colony-stores,
Like fruit shall we be falling,
 Red-ripe to all our cores.

"And if the blood we give them
 Be given to make us free,
The court may learn a lesson
 And let our charters be.

[8] "At two in the morning about one hundred and thirty answered their names. . . . A watch was . . . set and the company dismissed. . . . Some went to their own homes, some to the tavern."—*Bancroft's Hist. U. S.*, vol. vii., ch. 27, p. 292.

[9] "Lexington . . . having for their minister . . . Jonas Clark, the bold inditer of patriotic state papers which may yet be read on the town records."—*Idem*, p. 291.

" We are few, but what are numbers ?—
    This church may proof supply
That right may move to triumph
    With only one—to die ! "

He paused—the door flew open ;
    All heard a watch call out :
" Full drive a horseman coming !
    Perhaps an **army-scout** ! "

And out they flew to face him ;
    But on the charger fleet
No enemy, only a neighbor,[10]
    Came galloping up the street.

" The foe are coming ! " he stammer'd ;
    " They capture all they meet ;
I dodg'd a man and musket ;
    And hark !—you hear their feet ! "

We hush'd and heard a tramping
    That well might bring despair,
And cause the nerves to tremble
    Their loads of fear to bear.

[10] One Bowman escaped, and on horseback notified Capt. Parker . . .
of the enemy's approach.—*Lossing's Pic. Field Book*, vol. i., p. 524.
    [11] " The last stars were vanishing . . . when the the foremost party
led by Pitcairn . . . was discovered . . . Alarm guns were fired, and the
drums beat."—*Bancroft's U. S.*, vol. vii., ch. 27, p. 292.
    [12] " The British van, hearing . . . halted . . . ; the remaining com-

" Sound drum [11] and gun," said Parker,[10]
  " And bell ! If they but halt,
Where time is all we plan for,
  We win without an assault."

They halted,[12] then drew nearer ;—
  What need of halting more ?
They came, a veteran army ;
  We never had fought before.

We stood but sixty farmers,[13]
  Our homes and wives between,
Whose hands, up waved or wringing,
  Seem'd fringing half the green.

"Be theirs the blame," said Parker [14] ;
  " Fire not till they fire first.
God's house is here, and heaven,
  If worse should come to worst."

Athwart the gray of morning,
  None knew how large a force
Came crowding against the common,
  With cries and orders hoarse.

panies came up ; and . . . the advance party hurried forward at double
quick time."—*Idem*, p. 293.
  [13] " Less than seventy, perhaps less than sixty . . . were paraded . . .
a few rods north of the meeting-house."—*Idem*, p. 292.
  [14] " The captain, John Parker, ordered every one to load with powder
and ball, but . . . not to be the first to fire."—*Idem*.

But yet across the common,
  And just beyond the church,
We form'd a line to check there
  The crown's illegal search.

At double quick, and onward,
  With bayonets fix'd, they came;
Then wide and wild their red coats
  About us burst like flame.

Before them rode their leader,
  And cried with many a curse:
" Lay down your arms, you villains ! "[15]
  You villains you, disperse ! "

But, true to law and country,
  Scarce one his musket dropt[16];
And then their column falter'd,
  Broke up, moved slower, stopt.

" You rebels ! " roar'd the leader,
  While up his pistol came—[17]
A hint his minions welcomed ;
  We saw them all take aim.

[15] " Pitcairn rode in front and . . . cried out : ' Disperse, ye villains, . . .; lay down your arms.' "—*Idem*, 293.
[16] " The main part of the countrymen stood motionless."—*Idem.*
[17] " At this, Pitcairn discharged a pistol, and with a loud voice [cried, ' Fire.' "—*Idem.*
[18] " The order was instantly followed, first by a few guns . . . then by a heavy close and deadly discharge "—*Idem.*
[19] " Jonas Parker (not the captain) . . . had promised never to run from British troops, and he kept his vow . . . he lay on the post which he took at the morning's drum beat."—*Idem*, pp. 293, 294.

We saw them, but we waited,
    Till "Fire!" their leader cried, [17]
And shot, and howl'd, "Surround them!"
    And round us turn'd to ride.

They fired and surged about us, [18]
    Ah me, a fiery flood!—
All overwhelm'd, our brothers
    Were falling, drench'd in blood.

"Serve God before the Briton!"
    Cried Parker, [19] where he bled;
And nine of us were wounded;
    And seven of us were dead. [20]

"Away!" a voice repeated, [21]
    "Away while yet we may.
To stay were now but murder!
    To wall and fence away!"

Off sped we then to shoot them,
    Like Indians, one by one,
But walls, in smoke between us,
    They deem'd it wise to shun.

[20] "Seven of the men of Lexington were killed; nine wounded."—*Idem.*
  [21] "In disparity of numbers, the common was a field of murder, not a battle; Parker therefore ordered his men to disperse. Then, and not till then, did a few of them return the British fire."—*Idem.* Behind stone walls and buildings. See *Lossing's Pict. Field Book*, vol. i., p. 524.
  [22] "The British . . . huzzaed thrice by way of triumph, and after . . . less than thirty minutes, marched on for Concord."—*Bancroft's U. S.*, vol. vii., ch. 28, p. 297.
  [23] "In Lincoln (after the affair at Concord) the minute-men of Lexington, commanded by John Parker, renewed the fight."—*Idem*, p. 305.

They cheer'd [22] and left for Concord.
  Our wounded home we bore :
Then we too left for Concord,
  To meet them there once more.[23]

THE RALLY OF THE FARMERS.

CONCORD, APRIL 19, 1775.

THE Concord men had warning,[1]
    And flew from all their farms,
Long hours before the daybreak,
    To save the colony's arms.

And, days before the warning,
    Our Salem Congress, too,
Had known their stores were menaced,
    And here had left but few.[2]

Yet these to drag and bury [1]
    Or hide in woods and rills,
Men flock'd to town and from it,
    Like ants about their hills.

[1] " There, at about two in the morning, a peal from the belfry of the
meeting-house " called the inhabitants.—*Bancroft's U. S.*, vol. vii., ch. 27,
p. 290.   " There, in the morning hours, men . . . were hiding what was
left of cannon and military stores."—*Idem*, ch. 28, p. 297.
[2] " The attempt had for several weeks been expected ; . . . in conse-
quence, the committee of safety removed a part of the public stores and
secreted the cannon."—*Idem*, ch. 27, p. 288.

But soon, when came the morning,
  The "red-coats" [3] rose in sight,
With guns above them flashing
  Like surf in seas of light.

Then, one by one, escaping
  What could but bode them ill,
The farmers cross'd the river,
  And climb'd, anon, a hill. [4]

To the hill there came from Bedford, [4]
  And Littleton, and Carlisle,
And Lincoln, Chelmsford, Westford,
  More men through each defile.

To the hill there came a rumor [5]
  How Lexington had fared,
But no one spoke of yielding,
  And all for strife prepared.

From the hill they watch'd the village, [6]
  Where every house to scout,
Like busy bees the red-coats [3]
  Went bustling in and out.

---

[3] "Red-coats," a nickname given to the British soldiers, who wore red coats.

[4] "About seven o'clock the British marched . . . under the brilliant sunshine into Concord. . . . The Americans . . . therefore retreated . . . till . . they gained high ground about a mile from . . . the town. . . . There they waited for aid. . . . Between nine and ten the number had increased to more than four hundred . . . from Bedford, . . .

Despite our wives protesting,
　　Their hostile blows would shower,
Till scores of barrels, bursting,
　　Beclouded all with flour.[7]

Ere long, they spiked our cannon,
　　And fill'd our pond with balls,[7]
And piled the cannon's wagons
　　To block the roads like walls.

And then this foe that fear'd it,
　　Our " liberty-pole " cut down,[7]
And burn'd it with the wagons
　　That yet might burn the town.

Soon seem'd our court-house burning,[7]
　　With none the flames to stay ;[8]
But " Justice," cried our leader,
　　" Will house in heaven to-day.

" Now wait we till these troopers
　　Of luck have had their fill,
And part of them drift hither,
　　Or all assault our hill.

Westford, . . . from Littteton, from Carlisle, and from Chelmsford."—
Idem, ch. 28, pp. 298, 299.
　⁵ " The Americans had as yet received only uncertain rumors of the
morning's events at Lexington."—*Idem,* p. 300.
　⁶ " The Americans saw before them . . . British troops . . . occu-
pying their town."—*Idem.*
　⁷ " Sixty barrels of flour were broken in pieces ; . . . five hundred
pounds of ball were thrown into a mill-pond. The liberty-pole and several carriages for artillery were burned ; and the court-house took fire."—
Idem.

" The hill, if they move up it,
    Their lines can never take ;
Like waves that dash at headlands,
    Their wavering ranks will break."

Just then, they most had started,
    Though some were plundering still,
To seize two bridges crossing
    The stream beneath the hill.[9]

To seize them was to sever
    Our women from our men,
Our homes from those who own'd them,
    And what would follow then ?

" The north bridge,"—argued Hosmer[10] ;
    " Keep back from it the foe !"
" No man of mine from Acton,"
    Said Davis,[10] "fears to go."

And then our leader Barrett[11]
    The order " Forward !" gave,
Where moved the men of Acton[11]
    Behind their captain brave.

---

[8] " At the sight of fire in the village, the impulse seized them ' to march into the town for its defence.' "—*Idem.*

[9] This is literally true.   See description of the circumstances.—*Idem.*

[10] " James Hosmer urged to dislodge the enemy at the North Bridge. . . . Capt. Isaac Davis, of Acton, said : ' I have not a man that is afraid to go.' "—*Lossing's Pict. Field Book*, vol. i., pp. 526, 527.

[11] " Barrett, the colonel, . . . then gave the order to advance, but ' not to fire ' unless attacked. . . . Davis, looking at the men of Acton, . . . cried : ' March.' His company . . . led the way towards the bridge, he himself at their head, and by his side Major John Buttrick, of

With arms beside them trailing,
   In double file and slow,[12]
Not daunted by the danger,
   These farmers faced their foe.

The British ran to ruin
   The bridge, and then retire.[13]
" Hold ! " cried our Major Buttrick [14] ;
   They answer'd but to fire.

Dead Davis fell, and Hosmer.[15]
   " In God's name," Buttrick [16] cried,
" Fire, fire ! "—and two fell dying
   Upon the British side.

Thus Heaven, where hung the purpose
   A grander man to mould,
Had Saxon hurl'd on Saxon,
   The new world on the old.

Concord, with John Robinson, . . . lieutenant-colonel, . . . but on this day a volunteer without command."—*Bancroft's U. S.*, vol. vii., ch. 28, p. 302.

[12] " In double file with trailed arms."—*Lossing's Pict. Field Book*, vol. i., p. 527.

[13] "The British began to take up the planks."—*Bancroft's U. S.*, vol. vii., ch. 28, p. 302.

[14] " Major Buttrick called on them to desist."—*Lossing's Pict. Field Book*, vol. i., p. 190.

[15] " A volley followed, and Isaac Davis and Abner Hosmer . . . fell dead."—*Bancroft's U. S.*, vol. vii., ch. 28, p. 303.

[16] " Buttrick . . . cried aloud: . . . ' Fire, fellow-soldiers, for God's sake, fire !' . . . Two of the British fell."—*Idem.*

[17] "The British retreated in disorder toward the main body."—*Idem.*

[18] " In . . . Concord, Smith . . . showed by marches and counter-

Our foe in haste retreated.[17]
    Their colonel, where they sped,
March'd forth to reinforce them ;
    Then all for Boston led. [18]

But now our men from Reading [19]
    And Sudbury hurried out,
And Woburn, wild to flank them :
    Their march became a rout. [19]

We had but half their number [20] ;
    But, wrongs avenging thus,
Their red coats had been safer
    With Spanish bulls than us.

Though guards at every turning,
    Would cover well their flanks ;
Our smoke, from ambush leaping,[21]
    Shot, ghost-like, through their ranks.

marches, his uncertainty of purpose. At last . . . he left the town, to retreat the way he came."—*Idem*, p. 304.

[19] "The minute-men and militia . . . ran over the hills, . . . placed themselves in ambush, . . . reinforced by men who were coming in from all around, and . . . the chase of the English began. Among the foremost were the minute-men of Reading, . . . of Billerica, . . . the . . . Sudbury company. The men from Woburn came up in great numbers and well armed."—*Idem*, pp. 304, 305.

[20] "Of the Americans, there were never more than four hundred together at any one time ; but, as some grew tired, others took their places." —*Idem.*, p. 308. The first detachment of British troops numbered "not less than eight hundred."—*Idem*, ch. 27, p. 288.

[21] "Every piece of wood, every rock . . . served as a lurking-place . . . 'the road was lined' by an uninterrupted fire from behind stone walls and trees."—*Idem*, p. 305.

From Dedham, Essex, Danvers,
  From Chelsea, Marblehead,
From Dorchester, and Brookline, [22]
  Our men to meet them sped.

Back slunk their line before us,
  A weary, wounded snake :
Up hill, down dale, round river,
  It wound and bled and brake.

The whole reserve in Boston [23]
  Pour'd out to help them back ;
But all the trees and houses
  Were haunting now their track.

They turn'd to shoot our mothers ;
  They turn'd our babes to kill ;
Our vengeance rose at Cambridge, [24]
  And raged at Prospect Hill. [26]

Down sweeping, Heath and Warren
  A charge to break them led ;

[22] " Two waggons, sent out to them with supplies, were waylaid and
captured by Payson, the minister of Chelsea. From far and wide minute-men were gathering. The men of Dedham, . . . from Essex, and
the lower towns, . . . The company from Danvers, . . . lost eight men.
. . . Below West Cambridge, the militia from Dorchester, Roxbury, and
Brookline came up."—*Idem*, pp. 307-9.
[23] Lord Percy reinforced them with " about twelve hundred men."—
Idem, ch. 28, p. 306.
[24] " West Cambridge, where Joseph Warren and William Heath, . . .
the latter a provincial general officer, gave . . . organization to the resistance, and the fight grew sharper."—*Idem*, p. 308.
[25] " The Americans pressed upon the rear of the fugitives, whose retreat could not have been more precipitate . . . had Pickering with his

Then Pickering's men from Salem [25]
    Burst, flood-like o'er their head.[26]

Full night had known its fullest,
    Ere all their fears were still'd ;
Full ninescore had we wounded,
    And more than threescore kill'd. [27]

Nor, till they touched the river, [28]
    And by the fleet had pass'd,
Our eyes that faced the danger
    Were once behind us cast.

And then, alas to view it !
    Hot, bitter tears we shed ;
Full thirty found we wounded,
    And wellnigh sixty dead. [27]

Our wives had lost their husbands ;
    Our mothers lost their boys ;
Our homes were fill'd with mourning,
    And gone were all our joys.

fine regiment from Salem and Marblehead been alert enough to have intercepted them in front. . . . they must have surrendered."—*Idem*, p. 309.

[26] See *Lossing's Field Book*, vol. 1, p. 528, etc.; also *Bancroft's U. S.*, vol. vii., ch. 28, p. 308.

[27] According to Lossing, the British lost sixty-five killed, one hundred and eighty wounded, and twenty-eight prisoners ; the Americans fifty-nine killed, thirty-one wounded, and fifty missing.—See *Lossing's Pict. Field Book*, vol. 1, p. 530. " The loss of the British in killed, wounded, and missing was two hundred and seventy-three. . . . Forty-nine Americans were killed, thirty-nine wounded, and five missing."—*Bancroft's U. S.*, vol. vii., ch. 28, p. 309.

[28] " The guns of the ships of war . . . saved them . . . while they were ferried across Charles River."—*Idem*.

Yet, when we clasp'd those corpses,
  As over Huns of old,
It seem'd the skies were filling
  With souls for ours enroll'd.

Our prayers when all were buried,
  Were vows to Heaven o'erhead,
From hearts that hail'd the glory
  Of joining there their dead.

Then, too, we held our weapons ;
  Had foil'd the British aims ;
And held our homes :—our women [29]
  Had quench'd the court-house flames.

Our men had met the army,
  And fought, and from that hour
They all had grown to soldiers,
  Who knew and felt their power.

And so, despite the anguish
  That fill'd the morrow's morn,
The voice that wept betoken'd
  A nation, newly born

[29] Mrs. Moulton extinguished the fire at the Concord court-house.
—*Lossing's Pict. Field Book*, vol. i., p. 526.

[30] " Heedless of his own danger, Samuel Adams . . . exclaimed : ' Oh!
what a glorious morning is this ! ' for he saw that his country's independence was . . . hastening on."—*Bancroft's U. S.*, vol. vii., ch. 27, p. 296.
" Adams and Hancock, whose proscription had already been divulged . . .
were compelled by persuasion to retire toward Woburn."—*Idem*, p. 292.

" And I," said Samuel Adams,[30]
  " Thank God this day to see ! "
" And I," came back from Hancock[30] ;
  " It makes the new world free ! "

ETHAN ALLEN.

TICONDEROGA, MAY 10, 1775.

THE bell that rang at Lexington
  Had call'd our men to arms ;
And but their wives and children now
  Were home to work the farms.

But soon, like words men whisper forth
  Near foes who plot their death,
From farm to farm bad news was borne
  On hush'd and trembling breath.

" Fill'd full of ' red-coats,' [1] Boston seem'd,"
  They said, " a wounded prey
That yet drank in fresh draughts of blood[1]
  From fleets that fill'd the bay ;

[1] The British forces, nicknamed " red-coats," were reinforced after the battle of Lexington.—*Lossing's Pict. Field Book of the Rev.*, vol. i., p. 537.
[2] " The provisional Assembly of Connecticut, after the battle of Lexington, concerted a plan to seize the munitions of war at Ticonderoga, for the use of the army . . . at Cambridge and Roxbury."—*Lossing's Pict. Field Book of the Rev.*, vol. i., p. 123.
[3] " Ed. Mott and Noah Phelps . . . committee to ascertain . . .

" To check their march, like mushrooms grew
    Our earthworks, night by night ;
But, if attack'd, our men would not
    Have arms with which to fight."

At Hartford our Assembly met,
    And heard this; nor in vain.
It sent men off to seize what fill'd
    The fort on Lake Champlain.

These pass'd to Pittsfield,[4] there were join'd
    By Easton, Brown, and more ;
Then on to Bennington,[5] and there
    Could muster full twoscore.

Too few were they to brave a fort
    Well mann'd at every gun ;
Yet those who slight the light of stars
    But seldom see their sun.

The sun that dawn'd before them here,
    And brought them help indeed,
Was Ethan Allen's [5] blade, that flash'd
    His mountain troops to lead.

strength of . . . fort and to raise men. . . . Sixteen men went with
them."—*Idem.*
    [4] "At Pittsfield Col. Easton and John Brown (afterwards Col.) joined
them. . . . Col. Easton by the time he reached Bennington had enlisted
forty of his men."—*Idem.*
    [5] "At Bennington, they found Ethan Allen . . . he sent the alarm
through the hills . . . about one hundred Green Mountain Boys and
near fifty soldiers from Massachusetts . . . rallied."—*Bancroft's Hist.
U. S.*, vol. vii., ch. 32, p. 339.

And thick as rills that rift in spring
　　Each bond the sun destroys,
Came pouring over all those hills
　　His grand Green Mountain Boys.

Two hundred [6] hardy men they were
　　As ever mountains rear'd ;
They fought with bears and frost at home,
　　And naught abroad they fear'd.

Erelong, a shout went ringing out ;
　　For all had made their choice,
And all had chosen Allen chief ;
　　And " Forward ! " call'd his voice.[7]

But one who heard his order, spurr'd
　　His charger from the rear,
And cried : " In me your leader see,[8]
　　For Cambridge sent me here."

"And Cambridge, Cambridge, what would she ? "
　　Cried Mott[9] and Phelps, "Nay, Nay!—
'T was Hartford sent us forth, and we
　　Bade Allen lead the way."

---

[6] Lossing says in all about two hundred and seventy men went on the expedition.—*Pict. Field Book*, vol. i., p. 124.

[7] " The men unanimously elected Ethan Allen their chief."—*Bancroft's U. S.*, vol. vii., ch. 23, p. 339.

[8] " Arnold joined them here with a commission from the Committee of Safety in Cambridge, and claimed the right to command. After Ticonderoga was taken, he assumed command, but his orders were not heeded. He then sent a written protest to Massachusetts, but this State sustained Allen.—See *Lossing's Pict. Field Book*, vol. i., p. 124, etc.

"And we," cried those Vermonters true,
  "We came with Allen here ;
And all agree that none but he
  Shall lead the mountaineer."

The other hush'd when this he heard ;
  And give them honor all :
They faced the traitor Arnold[8] thus,
  Who thus began his fall.

Give honor due to Allen too ;
  High compliment it is,
That, when the traitor train'd with him,
  He was no friend of his.

Three days they tramp'd, then Allen said :
  "We near the lake I see.
Let some go north and some go south,
  And some straight on with me.[9]

"Let those that push for north and south
  Row off with all that floats,
And make for Shoreham, where we all
  Will cross when come the boats.[9]

[9] "It was arranged that Allen . . . with the main body should march to Shoreham, opposite Ticonderoga ; that Capt. Herrick should push to Skenesborough, . . . seize all the boats there and join Allen at Shoreham, and that Capt. Douglas should go . . . beyond Crown Point and secure all boats that way."—*Idem.*

" And let the others fall in line
  Behind my lantern's glare.
Beyond, Ticonderoga waits ;
  At morn, we breakfast there."

Then, down the hunter's trail, our line
  Wound on as winds a snake,
And, late at night, prepared to spring,
  Lay coil'd beside the lake.

" Now off," said Allen, " north and south,
  And hail each coming oar."
Alas, to think that Heaven above
  Should favor man no more !

To north and south we scatter'd far,
  We listened o'er and o'er,
But not a sound, from north or south,
  The empty breezes bore.

A few there were could cross at last,—
  Alas, but all too few !
Night sped, and Allen, by the fort
  Could count scarce eighty-two.[10]

---

[10] " With the utmost difficulty . . . eighty-three men crossing the lake
with Allen, landed near the garrison. The boats were sent back ; . . . if
. . . waited for their could be no surprise."—*Bancroft's U. S.*, vol.
vii., ch. 32, p. 339.
[11] " As the first beams of morning broke . . . Allen addressed them,

" My men," he mutter'd,[11] "look—the dawn !—
　　Before can cross the lake
One boat again for other men,
　　The day in full will break.

" Yet note the wall.　You know it well ;
　　Ten times our force, if seen,
Though clad in mail, could never scale
　　Those cannon thick between.

" And here the boats.—What vote you all ?—
　　Your guns lift up,—no breath.[11]
The lake cross here ?—or weapons there ?
　　Face cowardice ?—or death ?

" Your guns all up ?[12] your hearts all true ?
　　How well !　Had one turn'd back,[13]
Yon mounts were his no longer save
　　To hedge and hide his track.

" He easier might have faced, at home,
　　When snows were all aflame,
The sun ! than wives and little ones
　　Whose cheeks would fire with shame.

. . . ' we must . . . quit our pretentions to valor, or possess this fortress.
. . . it is a desperate attempt, I do not urge it contrary to will.　You that
will undertake voluntarily, poise your firelocks.' "—*Idem.*
　　[12] " At the word, every firelock was poised."—*Idem.*
　　[13] Allen " drew up his men in three ranks on the shore, . . . and in a
low, distinct tone harangued them."—*Lossing's Pict. Field Book*, vol., i.,
p. 124.
　　[14] " The king in council had . . . dismembered New Hampshire, and
annexed to New York the country north of Massachusetts and west of Connecticut River . . . it was, therefore, held by the royalists that the grants

" How oft have you, when driven off
  The land you once had bought,[14]
Too poor to buy again a home
  For those for whom you wrought ;

" How oft, when all was torn from you,[14]
  And you had urged in vain
Your chartered rights, the common law,
  And all that God makes plain ;

" How oft then have you pray'd aloud
  That Heaven would send you down
A chance from off your country's brow
  To hurl the hated crown !

" That chance has come !   But once for all
  Can dawn a day like this.
And those who will not use their light
  Will all life's glory miss.

" But if one win it, yonder sun
  Sheds not a splendor fit
With which to rise above his name,
  Or earth that welcomes it !

made under the sanction of the royal governor of New Hampshire were an-
nulled.   Many of the lands for which the king had received the price . . .
were granted anew, and the former purchasers were compelled to redeem
them."—*Bancroft's U. S.*, vol. v., ch. 10., p. 214. "Sixty-seven families in
as many houses . . . had elected their own municipal officers; founded
three several public schools ; set their meeting-house among the primeval
forests . . . called their village Bennington.   The royal officers at New
York disposed anew of that town, as well as of others near it, so that the
king was known . . . chiefly by his agents, who had knowingly sold his
lands twice over."—*Bancroft's U. S.*, vol. v., ch. 14., pp. 291, 292.

" Yes, earth !   For they forgot, our lords,
    They dealt with Puritans,
True sons of those whom Cromwell led,
    Whose right means every man's ;

" Who take their individual ills
    For proofs of general pain,
And, where one prince has made them wince,
    Fight all, that man may reign.

" And they forgot, that mountaineers,
    High rangers, like the Swiss,
Would learn to value freedom's world
    By looking down on this !

"And yet should prove it !   Ay, my men,
    To-day they all shall see
How freemen, forced to care for self,
    Take care to keep it free.

" Now quick, but quiet ;   start with steel—
    Nor fire till sure to hit—
First through the gate, if through we may ;
    If not, then over it.

[15] Allen led the party, " Arnold keeping emulously at his side."—*Idem*,
vol. vii., ch. 32, p. 339.
[16] " They marched quickly but stealthily . . . to the sally port."—
Lossing's Pict. Field Book, vol. i., p. 124.

"I lead. You follow. Should I fall,
  Move on : my corpse may give
At least a vantage ground ! Move up:
  The cause, it is, must live ! "

Then Allen turn'd, and Arnold [16] too,
  His foremost rival still,
Then Brown and Easton,—all the line
  Stole softly up the hill.[16]

A startled sentry seized his gun,
  And aim'd at Allen's face [17] ;
The flint miss'd fire, and Allen rush'd,
  And wrench'd it from its place.

The sentry dodg'd, and darted down
  A passage through the mound. [17]
In pour'd our men ; you might have thought
  The sentry would be drown'd.

Swift, one by one, by Allen led,
  They plung'd along the gloom :
No fear of those who, just beyond,
  Might make the place their tomb.

[17] " The sentinel snapped his fusee at (Allen), but it missed, and he retreated within the fort under a covered way. The Americans followed,
and were thus guided . . . to the parade within the barracks. There
another sentinel made a thrust . . . but a blow upon the head from
Allen's sword made him beg for quarter."—See *Idem.*

On ran the sentry ; on, our men.—
  Their mountains gave no game,
Nor guide so quick to apprehend
  The grounds on which they came.

At last, uploom'd in dusky light,
  And choking all the way,
A man who poised his bayonet [17]
  To hold them all at bay.

" Take heed ! " he call'd.   " We take it, man,"
  Hiss'd Allen, where he sped ;
Whose clashing sword had glanced the gun,
  And gash'd the soldier's head.

" Have mercy ! " groan'd the wounded wretch.
  Said Allen : " Drop your gun.
Hist, hist, my men !   The walls are ours.
  Now seize the barrack—run ! "

No need to bid them !   In a trice
  Our boys had crown'd their race ;
And closed, with shouts like thousands, round
  The startled sleeping-place.[18]

[18] " The Americans rushed into the fort . . . and raising the Indian war-whoop, . . . formed on the parade in hollow square to face each of the barracks."—*Bancroft's U. S.*, vol. vii., ch. 32, p. 339.
[19] " Allen . . . went . . . to the door of the quarters of Capt. Dela-

Meantime, " The captain ! " Allen cried ;
   And scarce the word had said,
Ere on a door he pounded loud [19]
   To rouse his foe from bed.

It open'd partly, where behold !
   In robes as white as fleece,
The chief, beside his blushing bride,
   A picture stood of peace.[20]

" Surrender ! " [20] order'd Allen then ;
   " If not, by Him on high,
Your garrison—without a hope
   For quarter from us—die ! "

The captain's anger now had burst
   The spell of night's repose.
" Surrender ? " hiss'd he—then turn'd pale
   To hear loud shouts that rose.

" And who are you ? " he stammer'd out.
   " And whose is this ado ?
And whose the name in which you come
   And bid us yield to you ? "

---

place, . . . and giving three loud raps . . . ordered him to appear.
cr the whole garrison should be sacrificed."—*Lossings Pict. Field Book*,
vol. i., p. 125.
  [20] " Delaplace appeared in shirt and drawers, with the frightened face
of his pretty wife peering over his shoulder."—*Idem*.

"The name of Great Jehovah,[21] and "—
    Said Allen, drawing nigh,
"The Continental Congress!"—then
    He flash'd his sword on high.

"Jehovah?—Congress?" growl'd his foe;
    But, cow'd by Allen's eye,[26]
Jehovah, in the man, at least,
    He did not dare defy.

The day was won; the garrison
    Filed out across the green.
More generous welcome where they came,
    I think were seldom seen.

Not one who bore a cumbering gun
    Or lugg'd a weighty sword,
But we to ease him of his load,
    Would our relief afford.

Alack, we stack'd our shoulders full,
    Relieving them of care,
Then proved our good-will, Arab-like,
    By taking breakfast there.

---

[21] "'Deliver me the fort instantly!' said Allen. 'By what authority?' asked Delaplace. 'In the name of the great Jehovah and the Continental Congress!' answered Allen. Delaplace . . . at sight of Allen's drawn sword near his head . . . gave up the garrison." — *Bancroft's U. S.*, vol. vii., ch. 32, p. 340.

[22] "The garrison of forty-eight men were surrendered prisoners of

For days and days we never ceas'd
   Attending to them thus,
Until, as pride escorts a bride,
   We walk'd them home with us.[22]

And then the fort—ah me, to see
   The trouble rare it took
To clear the space, and give the place
   A less unfriendly look !

Tenscore of cannon, mounds of flint,[23]
   And tons of guns and balls—
We waited weeks, to find the means
   To cart them out the walls.

But first, we mail'd a message home ;
   And I have heard it said,
In many a place, the floor was wet
   With tears when it was read.

At Cambridge, at the news, the air
   With such a shout was rent,
It almost equal'd there the roar
   Of guns our fort had sent.

war, and . . . sent to Hartford."—See *Lossing's Pict. Field Book*, vol. i., p. 125.

[23] " 120 pieces of cannon, 50 swivels, 2 ten-inch mortars . . . 10 tons of musket-balls, three cartloads of flints . . . 100 stand of small-arms, 10 casks of powder, 2 brass cannon, 30 barrels of flour, 18 barrels of port, etc." —See *Idem.*

And Allen ?—Allen lived and thrived,
 And conquer'd all that tract,
Where Britain could not hold a fort [24]
 That once our boys attack'd.

But war has tricks ; and life has turns ;
 Misfortunes find the true ;
And Allen once, across the sea,
 Was borne a prisoner too.[25]

Yet heroes' homes are human hearts.
 And England's crowds would cling
About the form of him they felt
 Was grander than their king.

He came back home, and church bells rang—
 You might, in truth, have thought [25]
A second Christmas day had come,
 And Saviour's advent brought ;—

And guns were fired ; and, hail'd with cheers,
 Vermont bade all men call
This bravest, brightest of her sons,
 The General of them all.[25]

---

[24] " This success was followed by others; the capture of a sloop-of-war and St. John's Fort. . . . In the autumn of the same year, he was twice sent into Canada to excite rebellion against the English government."—*Appleton's Cyclopædia of Biography*.

And all the people while he lived,
　　They loved his eagle eye [26] ;
And when he died—ah, friends, you know
　　Such spirits cannot die !

To-day, go search those mountain woods
　　And valleys, humbly trod
By souls whose pure, strong faith holds on
　　To country, home, and God ;

Ask men who own those towering trees,
　　Or plant the hillock steep ;
The school-boys, bounding back from school,
　　Or watching well the sheep ;

The housewives, where in thrifty homes
　　The generous meals are spread ;
The sisters, gently handing down
　　The Book when prayers are said ;

Ask all, who value aught they own,
　　Whose fame all value most ?—
The flashing eye and flushing cheek
　　Will figure him they boast.

[25] " Allen was sent to Canada in 1775 ; was taken prisoner and carried to England, where his appearance excited great interest. On his return, he was received with great demonstrations of joy in Bennington, and made Maj.-Gen. of Vermont. He died in 1789, aged fifty."—See *Idem*.
[26] Allen is said to have had a remarkably keen and expressive eye.

HOW BARTON TOOK THE GENERAL.[c]

NARRAGANSETT BAY, JULY 10, 1777.

"LORD Prescott, down in Newport,"
  Brave William Barton[1] said,
"Would make all show his colors, though
  Their own blood dyed them red.

" Perhaps he thinks our natives,
  On England's footstool here,
Did they not feel his lordly heel,
  Might deem him not a peer."

" Say footpath here," said Potter[8] ;
  " Just now their doorsteps go
To pave the way[2] where, once a day,
  His lordship walks, you know.

"And then if those who meet him
  Go by, nor doff their caps,[3]
Aha, his cane will fall like rain,
  To make them mend their lapse."

---

[1] " Brig.-Gen. Prescott. . . . had been nurtured in the lap of aristocracy, and taught all its exclusive precepts. . . . He was a tyrant at heart, and, having the opportunity, he exercised a tyrant's plentiful prerogatives."— *Lossing's Pict. Field Bk. of the Rev.*, vol. ii., p. 74. "William Barton was a native of Providence, Rhode Island. . . . Lieutenant-Colonel in the militia of his State . . . when he planned and executed the expedition for the abduction of General Prescott," who commanded the British forces at Newport, Rhode Island.—*Idem*, p. 75. *Note.*

[2] " Prescott . . . had a fine sidewalk made for his accommodation along Pelham and up Spring streets ; for which purpose, he took the door steps."—*Idem*, p. 75. *Note.*

" Small spite ! and yet," said Barton :
   " A wrinkle shows the will.
A grazing ass that kicks but grass
   Has tricks that yet may kill.

" Who minds it, though a Quaker,
   Forsooth, lift not his hat ;
Yet one in town, he first rode down,[4]
   Then had him chain'd for that.

"And Tripp[5]—when spies had jail'd him ;
   And none knew what it meant ;
And when, half dead with fear, **they said,**
   His wife to see him went ;

" Said Prescott : 'Come and see him
   When hang'd[5] and no dispute.'
Who domineers o'er woman's tears
   Is less a man than brute !

" And I, for one, would enter
   This British lion's lair,
And volunteer to fetch him here,
   Or die beside him there."

[3] " His habit, while walking the streets, if he saw any of the inhabitants conversing together, was to shake his cane at them, and say : ' Disperse ye rebels.' He was also in the habit, when he met citizens in the streets, of commanding them to take off their hats, and, unless the order was instantly complied with, it was enforced by a rap of his cane."—*Idem*, p. 74.

[4] " He overtook a Quaker who did not doff his hat. The general, who was on horseback, dashed . . . him against a stone wall, knocked off his hat, and then put him under guard."—*Idem*.

[5] " Prescott caused many citizens of Newport to be imprisoned, some of them for months, without any assigned reason. Among others . . .

" Sure death ! " his comrades mutter'd ;
    " The troops guard every road.
A man to try your scheme should fly ;
    We know no other mode."

" He quarters now," said Barton,
    " At Overton's,[6] the Friend's,
Whose house is by the bay-road nigh
    Where by the bay it bends.

" The roads are block'd by soldiers ;
    We cannot reach him thus.
What then ?—A way across the bay
    May yet remain for us.

" I know three frigates guard it.[7]
    But when, some moonless night,
By clouds beset, the wind and wet
    Have swept the sky of light ;

William Tripp. . . . He had a . . . family, but the tyrant would not
allow him to hold any communication with them either written or verbal,
. . . His wife sought . . . a personal interview. . . . A captain, . . .
echoing his master's words . . . informed her, as he shut the door in her
face, that he expected her husband would be hung as a rebel in less than
a week."—*Idem.*

  [6] " General Prescott was quartered at the house of a Quaker, named
Overton."—*Idem*, p. 75.

  [7] " These were three British frigates with their guard-boats . . .
almost in front of Prescott's quarters."—*Idem,*

  [8] " With a few chosen men, Barton embarked in four whale boats with
muffled oars at Warwick Point at nine o'clock in the evening.—*Idem.*,
p. 75. " Mr. Barton, by request, furnished me with the following list of
the names of those who accompanied his father on his perilous expedition.

" And when the breeze and breakers
  Out-sound a rowlock's beat,
Amid the roar a muffled oar
  Might safely pass the fleet."

His comrades hush'd and heard him ;
  Then swore to try the feat ;
And soon with more each held an oar
  To row him past the fleet.[8]

The night was dark and stormy ;
  The bay was wild and wide ;
And, deftly weigh'd, each paddle-blade
  Like velvet stroked the tide.

They near'd the English frigates,
  They heard their sentries' feet,
They heard a bell, and then " All 's well "[9]
  Re-echo'd through the fleet.

OFFICERS.—Andrew Stanton, Eleazer Adams, Samuel Potter, James Wilcox. NON-COMMISSIONED OFFICERS. — Joshua Babcock and Samuel Phillips. PRIVATES.—Benjamin Pren, James Potter, Henry Fisher, James Parker, Joseph Guild, Nathan Smith, Isaac Brown, Billington Crumb, James Haines, Samuel Apis, Alderman Crank, Oliver Simmons, Jack Sherman, Joel Briggs, Clark Packard, Samuel Cory, James Weaver, Clark Crandall, Sampson George, Joseph Ralph, Jedediah Grenale, Richard Hare, Darius Wale, Joseph Denis, William Bruff, Charles Hassett, Thomas Wilcox, Pardon Cory, Jeremiah Thomas, John Hunt, Thomas Austin, Daniel Page (a Narraganset Indian), Jack Sisson (black), and —Howe or Whiting, boat-steerer."—*Idem*, p. 76. *Note*.

[9] " They heard the cry : ' All 's well,' from the guard-boat of the enemy as they passed silently."—*Idem*, p. 76.

They pull'd around a guard-boat[9] ;
    They struck the land, and then
Filed softly out, and moved about,
    Like shadows more than men.

They split in three small parties[10] ;
    And each stole softly round,
A sentry near a guard-house here,
    And there a camping ground.

At last the three were guarding
    The house on every side,
With six or eight before the gate[12]
    They just had open'd wide.

"Your countersign !" a sentry[11]
    Call'd out ; and Barton said :
"Have none to-night ";—his tone was light—
    "Have here deserters fled ?"

"Ah, from the boats ?" the guard said.
    "Yes," Barton hiss'd, "from one !"

---

[10] "Barton divided his men into several squads . . . The main portion
passed . . . between a British guard-house and the encampment of a
company of light-horse, while the remainder was . . . to approach Prescott's quarters from the rear."—*Idem.*
[11] "As Barton and his men approached the gate, a sentinel hailed them
twice, and then demanded the countersign. 'We have no countersign
to give,' Barton said, and quickly added : 'Have you seen any deserters
here to-night ?' The sentinel was misled by this question, supposing them

But as he hiss'd he clutch'd, nor miss'd,
    The sentry's throat and gun.

The sentry gasp'd and gave it ;
    Lay gunless, gagg'd, and bound.
Our men had pass'd the door, at last,
    Nor yet had roused a sound.

The Quaker sat there reading[12]
    "What would you have ?" he said ;
Then, when they ask'd for Prescott, cast
    His eyes up o'er his head.

As whist as cats the captors
    Crept up each tell-tale stair,[13]
And cross'd the floor to where a door
    Was lock'd, nor time to spare.

Then one of them—Jack Sisson,[13]
    A burly, patriot black—
Bent down his frame, and, taking aim,
    Burst through, and flung it back.

---

to be friends . . . until his musket was seized, and himself bound and menaced with instant death if he made any noise."—*Idem.*

[12] "Barton entered the front passage boldly. Mr. Overton sat alone
reading . . . Barton inquired for Gen. Prescott's room. Overton pointed
upward, signifying that it was directly over."—*Idem*, p. 77.

[13] "With four strong men and Sisson, a powerful negro . . . Barton
ascended the stairs, and gently tried the door. It was locked; no time
was to be lost . . . the negro drew back . . . and using his head for a
battering-ram, burst open the door at the first effort."—*Idem.*

They saw the general starting,[14]
  And bounding forth from bed,
And seizing hold his watch of gold
  That hung beside his head.

"Let darkness take you robbers
  From sword," he cried, " and shot ! "
" No robber harms ; put up those arms,"
  He heard, nor left the spot.

" We came to take you captive,
  Alive," he heard, " or dead.
If you alarm the camp, the harm
  Will fall on you," they said.[14]

" Move on."—" I dress," he told them.[15]
  But they, in tones polite,
Replied : " Not so.   We came, you know,
  Without our wives to-night.

" Your cloak is all you need now,
  The night is black and hot.
Your last resort—our time too short !—
  Thank God you were not shot."

---

[14] " The general, supposing the intruders to be robbers, sprang from his bed, and seized his gold watch that was hanging upon the wall.   Barton . . . told him he was his prisoner, and that perfect silence was now his only safety."—*Idem.*

[15] " Prescott begged time to dress, but it being a hot July night, and time precious, Barton refused acquiescence, feeling that it would not be

Down stairs they march'd their captive.
  But hark ! In some far room
A window crash'd—and Barton dash'd
  Out doors and through the gloom.

No harm was done ; for others
  Had swiftly caught and bound
The general's aid, just where he made
  A leap to reach the ground.[16]

So now they held three captives ;
  And these, by daggers led,
They slipt about the camp and out,
  As needles flit with thread.

At last they reach'd the water,
  At last, row'd o'er the tide ;
None heard their oars upon the shores,
  Or boats by which they hied.

They pass'd the English frigates,
  They heard their sentries' feet,
They heard, " All 's well ! " call'd out to tell
  How fool'd had been the fleet.[9]

cruel to take him . . . where he could make his toilet . . . at his
leisure. So, throwing his cloak around him . . . the prisoner was hurried to the shore."—*Idem.*
  [16] " Prescott's aid, hearing the noise in the general's room, leaped from
a window to escape, but was captured."—*Idem.*

And then their stroke was bolder :
  For Warwick Point [17] they bore.
A coach and pair were there to bear
  Their captive far from shore.

Here [17] Prescott broke the silence :
  "Your push was boldly plann'd."
Said Barton : "Yes, and with success";
  And took the reins in hand.

Success it was for Newport.
  The foe knew all it meant ;
They lock'd no more a prison door
  Against our innocent.

Success it was for Barton.
  In days like those of old
No envy rife, nor party strife,
  Would slur a deed so bold.

Through all our homes in Newport,
  Through all our camps afar,
Men praised his name, and hoped he came
  As victory's morning star.

[17] " At Warwick Point . . . Prescott first broke the silence by saying to
Col. Barton : ' Sir, you have made a bold push, to-night.' ' We have
been fortunate,' coolly replied Barton.   Captain Elliot was there with a
coach to convey the prisoners to Providence."—*Idem.*

Where Freedom's day was dawning,
   The man, whose light so shone
To bless the land, appear'd more grand
   Because he rose alone.

Erelong, a grateful Congress
   Chose one that for him brought
A sword on which inscriptions rich
   Recorded all they thought.[18]

In green Vermont they gave him
   A generous land-grant too.[18]
A part of what we all had got
   By fighting, seem'd his due.

But what by far was fittest,
   And cheer'd in every tent,
Were words that raised this man we praised
   To lead our regiment.[19]

Where few and frail the forces
   Our land could call its own,
All felt that he would steadfast be,
   And fight, though left alone.

[18] " For that service Congress honored him by the presentation of a sword, and also by a grant of land in Vermont."—*Idem*, p. 75. *Note.*
[19] "And on the 24th of December following he was promoted to the rank and pay of colonel in the Continental army."—*Idem*, p. 77.

MISCELLANEOUS.

A SONG ON SINGING.

A SUPPOSED IMPROMPTU.

THE board is bare, the lights are low,
  My songs are sung, but, ere we go,
One more I bring, and answer so
  Your kindly plaudits ringing.
No wealth and rank belong to me,
But yet, where thought and word are free,
The voice alone a power may be,
  And rule the world by singing.

How oft, of old, when reign'd the wrong,
And rare and regal rose in song,
The call sublime that roused the strong
  From hut and hamlet springing,
Like avalanches launch'd in might,
Where thunder shakes an Alpine height,
Resistless down its path of white,
  Has right been led by singing.

How oft, when sounds of war awoke,
And wide as earth a vision broke
Of sword and gun in flash and smoke,
  And flags o'er freemen springing ;
Where few escaped the foeman's power,

As fail'd the chief and fell the tower,
The land has yet survived the hour
    When nerved anew by singing.

All else, at last, with death may meet,—
Brave hearts whose hopes had made them beat,
Like moats beneath the soldiers' feet,
    When victory's cheers are ringing;
But e'en the dead whose deeds inspire
The minstrel, o'er the grave or pyre
May rise, like Israel's cloud of fire,
    And lead their race through singing.

Nor less the power of song, when peace
Has dawn'd apace, and hopes increase,
As men in thrall have found release,
    Their fetters from them flinging.
Oh, what could make their thanks complete,
Did crowds exultant fail to meet
In great Town Hall, or village street,
    And shout their joy in singing!

Or when sad souls the wine would quaff
Of mirth brimm'd bubbling o'er with laugh,
What sparkling draughts in their behalf,
    The comic bard comes bringing!
And ever, round the social board,
As full the foaming pledge is pour'd,
See how good-will the heart could hoard
    Is lavish'd with the singing.

How blest are homes, all fill'd with song,
The mother's hum, the choral strong,
The hymn that bears great thoughts that throng
 Where all pure hope is winging !
How heaves the breast in air so sweet,
How thrills the blood it fills to meet,
While all the spirit bounds to greet
 The joys of life in singing !

There let sweet love a pair ensnare
With dainty dreams of visions fair,
Wherein, like wings athrob the air,
 Rare wedding bells are ringing.
Then, stirr'd by moods that move the heart,
What tunes upon the lip will start,
As if true love could not impart
 Such sweets except through singing !

The cares may come that track success,
Or storms of swift and full distress
May make of life a wilderness,
 A flood of anguish bringing ;
The sorrows of the soul will rise,
And pour their woe through weeping eyes,
And drain at last the source of sighs,
 When hearts o'erflow in singing.

If doubt and vice with cloud and tide
Surround a wretch whose father's pride

And mother's love have wellnigh died,
  And sister's hands are wringing,
Ah, then, beyond the waves that roar,
He too may heed the friendly shore,
Where others, won from woes before,
  Their heartfelt praise are singing.

Through mists that, like a shroud around,
In densest folds the soul had bound,
My life has known a song to sound,
  Nerve dying hope by ringing
As clear as tolls a lighthouse bell
Where ghost-like rush the breakers fell—
The soul they would have borne to hell
  Was warn'd from it by singing.

A shadeless waste, a mist-hid sea,
Were earth that knew no songs of glee ;
And what would heaven beyond it be
  If anthems ne'er were springing
From voices there, where funeral knells
Are sweeter far than marriage bells
To love call'd hence that ever dwells
  Within the sound of singing !

The wise who once thought heavenly spheres,
As all unroll'd their store of years,
Woke music through their atmospheres
  That soft and far was ringing ;
Heard subtler music, it may be,

Where love rules all, yet all are free,
And though not thoughts, yet hearts agree,
  For all beat time in singing.

Ah, when no lights of life remain,
As dimly death's cold draft we drain,
How sweetly then will sound the strain
  From heaven through darkness winging,
Where choirs above through endless years
Praise love that ransoms all from fears
Nor asks for aught, save what to seers
  Appears to be glad singing!

But stay—to keep below with men
The minstrel knows not how nor when.
Here end I then—yet once again
  Let echoes answer, ringing
To that which lulls the babe at birth,
And voices all the good of earth,
Gives God His glory, heaven its worth,—
  Eternal sway to singing!

THE MUSIC OF LIFE.

MUSIC round the world is ringing,
    Sweeter ne'er is heard by man;
Music angel hosts were singing,
  Ere the morning stars began;
Sweeter 't is than dreams of music,

Music one awakes to hear
Trailing on a train of echoes
   O'er a mild and moonlit meer ;
More it moves than martial marches,
   More than gleams of long-lost hope,
More than suns to glory lifting
   Dew they draw from plain and slope ;
Music 't is that thrills us only
   In the art that hearts control,
When the breath of ardor holy
   Softly stirs a sighing soul.

Music in the breast is bringing
   Every soul its own reward,
Like the lute's that tunes to singing
   Only tones that with it chord.
Let the heart devoid of pleasure
   Throb as throbs its rhythmic beat,
Soon will joys that none can measure
   Round it and within it meet,—
Joys without in those about it,
   Joys within, that pulsing come,
Firm of tread as warriors marching
   Where before them rolls the drum ;
Known by inward senses only,
   Only known like bliss above,
Life of life and order holy,
   Sounds the music soft of love.

MY IDEAL.

SHE came : she went : 't was all a dream,
  A groundless hope, a barren scheme ;
And yet a dearer dream did seem
  Than ever made a dawn seem drear.
She tuned sweet music in my breast,
Till every sad or joyous guest,
That sway'd it once, with wondering rest,
  Grew hush'd as hate when heaven is near.

She came : she went : a beam sublime
That, straying toward a sunless clime,
Trembled along the edge of Time
  And then in fright sped back amain.
Ah, wherefore came she if to go !
I had not known the half of woe
Had I not felt that heavenly glow,
  And, match'd with it, found earth so vain.

She came : she went : I know I dream'd ;
Nor dared to test fond hopes that gleam'd ;
But yet how dear the future seem'd,
  And, though it was the world, how real !
Ah, wherefore did she leave so soon,
And change to night what had been noon !
Did Heaven sufficient deem the boon
  To grant to me a form ideal ?

CAGED.

OUR jest and gossip ceased at last ;
    It seem'd as if my lips were fast.
Ah me, such holy hopes loom'd then ;
My mind could only think, " Amen."
But soon she cried out, " How absurd ! "
And laugh'd, whereat her little bird
Caught up the music of the word,
And trill'd an echo, loud and long,
Till, deafen'd quite, she check'd the song.

" That bird," said she,—" Hush, hush, you thing !—
Flew in the window here, one spring.
We caught and caged him, and he grew
The sweetest pet that ever flew ;
I hold my finger toward him so,
And down he flies and lights, you know,
And pecks my hair and lips, and oh,
How jantily—you ought to see—
He perks his head and chirps for me !

" Last year, he flew away, one day,
And then, the scene we had ! the way
We wept for him ; and search'd the town !
And how it made the neighbors frown
The twentieth time we ask'd for him !
But, just as day was growing dim,

He lit on yonder ash-tree limb ;
And ' Dick,' I call'd, and back he flew ;
Now, did n't you, birdie ?—naughty you ! "

With this again she laugh'd at him ;
And I,—I thought the room grew dim ;
And then, I whisper'd : "Dear, a word,—
For I—I know one other bird
That longs and longs to fly to you ;
And, dearest, you may cage it, too ;
'T will sing, and serve, and be so true."
And then she blush'd, and then she wept,
And then this bird of love she kept.

WHATEVER THE MISSION OF LIFE MAY BE.

WHATEVER the mission of life may be,
    Let love keep true, and let thought keep free,
And never, whatever may cause the plan,
Enlarge the calling to lessen the man.
            The cut of a coat,
            Cant chatter'd by rote,
A priestly or princely state remote
            From the ties that bind
            A man to mankind,
Are a clog and a curse to spirit and mind ;

For God, who made us, made only a man,
No arms of a snob, no shield of a clan.
Far better a friend that is friendly to God,
Than a sycophant kissing a ribbon or rod.

Help on no ways nor words that extol
The vise of a bias that binds the soul ;
No rank held up by holding down
True worth as an underling stript of his crown ;
            No cause with a lie
            For a party-cry
To catch the low or to court the high ;
            No life with a creed
            That ends all the need
Of knowing or growing in thought or deed.—
Weigh well their worth ; true dawnings of light
Can abide your waiting and grow more bright.
Weigh not, you prove the trend of my thought :
Your soul is a slave to be sold and bought.

THE DESTINY-MAKER.

SHE came ; and I who linger'd there,
    I saw that she was very fair ;
And, with my sighs that pride suppress'd,
There rose a trembling wish for rest.
        But I, who had my own design

For destiny that should be mine,
I turn'd me to my task and wrought,
And so forgot the passing thought.

She paused; and I who question'd there,
I heard she was as good as fair;
And in my soul a still, small voice
Enjoin'd me not to check my choice.
    But I, who had my own design
    For destiny that should be mine,
    I bade the gentle guardian down,
    And strove to think about renown.

She left; and I who wander, fear
There comes no more to see or hear;
Those walls that ward my paradise
Are very high, nor open twice.
    And I, who had my own design
    For destiny that should be mine,
    Can only wait without the gate
    And sit and sigh—" Too late ! too late ! "

DRAMATIC.

HAYDN.[1]

I.

HARK, sister! hear we not the vesper hymn?
And is it not the hymn that Haydn wrote?
Why not push wide the window? Rob we God,
If, while our praise to Him be passing by,
Some air, made sweeter, tarry here with us?
There, there—it dies away.—Why say "it dies"?—

[1] This poem was suggested by the tale entitled "A First Love," in the "Musical Sketches" of Elize Polko. Her authority for the narrative was the historical fact that the wife of Haydn had a sister who was beloved by him, and who entered a convent. My own authority for the imagined connection indicated in the poem between the marriage of Haydn and the influence of the father and the priest, is derived from such passages as these, which may be found in every biography of the musician: "Forced to seek a lodging" (*i. e.* when a boy in Vienna), "by chance he met with a wig-maker, named Keller, who had often noticed and been delighted with the beauty of his voice at the Cathedral, and now offered him an asylum. This Haydn most gladly accepted; and Keller received him as a son. . . . His residence here had, however, a fatal influence on his after life. . . . Keller had two daughters; his wife and himself soon began to think of uniting the young musician to one of them; and even . . ventured to name the subject to Haydn. . . . He did not forget his promise to his old friend Keller, of his marrying his daughter. . . . But he soon found that she . . . had . . . a mania for priests and nuns. . . . He was himself incessantly annoyed and interrupted in his studies by their clamorous conversation. . . . At length he separated from his wife, whom, however, he always, in pecuniary concerns, treated with perfect honor." *Biographical Dictionary of Musicians*, 2 vols., London, 1827.

Such facts, taken in connection with the well-known piety of Haydn, are a sufficient warrant, as I think, for my supposing that "priests and nuns" who so annoyed him had had something to do with drawing into a convent that member of the family whom he had loved the most. In the poem I have endeavored to bring the personality of the musician before the mind of the reader by using the name Haydn, rather than his baptismal name, Joseph.

Because it lived?—Ay, ay, my body here,
Because it moves and throbs and tells of thought
And wakens thought in others, thus you know
My body lives.   And music, while it sounds,
Does it not move and throb and tell of thought
And waken thought in others?—Then it dies.—
But ah, the music, it has never sinn'd,
No wish has ever known save that of heaven,
And need not linger long here.   Yet to eyes
That scan eternity, time cannot be
The measure gauging vital force ; nay, nay :
Then heavenly lightning were a weaker thing
Then earthly smoke.—Ah, sister, I have thought,
If there may rise, high up in halls of heaven,
Sweet echoes of our earthly lives, re-lived,
Yet not as here they lived, that there may rise
From earthly music, echoes just as real.
At least, my Haydn's music throbs with life.
The sounds are sentient as his own dear soul ;
They make me thrill, as if a power should come,
And touch, with hands below these fleshly robes,
And clasp, as loving spirits do, the spirit.
They woo me as a god might, owning heaven.

Why should I not talk thus?   Go bid the flowers
Keep back their perfume ; then, perchance, may
        souls,
All sweet with blooming love, keep back sweet words.

I love him.—Shrink not, sister.   Hear you must.—
And say not I am weak.   Should I not grow
Far weaker, holding in a love so strong ?

II.

For years he lived there in my father's house,
My elder brother and my lover too,
My helper, and my hero : all my youth
Was one bright dawn about that sunny face.
Four years my senior was he ; yet, withal,
So delicate in blunt and boyish ways,
And young in all things but in being kind,
He seem'd more near me.   Ere I knew of it,
In budding girlhood even, he had pluck'd
My blushing love, and wore it on his heart ;
And all my life took root where sprang his own.

III.

Once I remember now our strolling far
Down through that glen, whose deep gorge un-
          announced
Heaves all its bordering plains to sudden hills.
The time of year it was, when nature seems
In mood most motherly, with every breath
Held in a mild suspense above a world
Of just born babyhood, when tiny leaves,
Like infant fingers, reach to drain warm dews
From palpitating winds, and when small brooks

Do babble much, birds chirp, lambs bleat, and then,
While all around is one sweet nursery,
Not strange it seems that men ape childhood too,
And lisp—ah me !—minute the syllables,
Yet still too coarse for love's ethereal sense !

IV.

As was her wont, at that time walk'd with us
Doretta fair, my sister, such an elf !
My pride and Haydn's pet, whose merry tones
Would ring out, if our thoughts turn'd far from her,
Like bells that homeward lure the wind-blown bees,
And bring our flighty fancies back again.

But Haydn liked this not, would ward it off,
And turn her chafing overcharge of nerve
From tongue to foot, with " Here, Doretta, imp !
You cannot climb the ledge," or " leap the brook,"
Or " find the flowers " ;—then bending down to me,
Say : " I abhor our German prudery.
We too should walk alone, or else have four,
Or six.   When two agree they make a match.
A third is but a wedge with which to split
The two apart."

     And once he paused with me ;
And while Doretta linger'd, hid from view,
We two sat languidly upon the turf.
"Who feel like springing in the Spring?" he said,—

" Yet all life may spring on as bodies do
That draw first back, or down, and then leap up.
To feel relax'd, perchance, prepares one best
To leap the hedge of each untested year ;
First action, then reaction—eh, not so ?—
And think—The same may form the law of souls :
They stoop, then rise ; they kneel, then know of
    heaven,—
And say, Pauline, if once there rose in view
An aim sublime, to make one proud, so proud,
Say, would he not do thus ? "—

                " Ha ! " laugh'd a voice ;
And soon Doretta's curls a shade shook down
Between his face and mine. She smooth'd his
    brow ;
And with a wreath of heart's-ease crown'd it then.
" There, there, my sweet heart, be at ease," we
    heard.
" You take my head then for my heart," he said.
" Nay, nay," she answer'd, " nay—would crown
    them both ;
Your music with your muse ; your head, the home ;
The mistress there, your heart."

                  " With all one's heart
But mistress of his head alone, would love
Gain much ? " he ask'd.

              " Immortal fame," said she ;
" Not so ? "

"And do you think," he sigh'd, "that this
Could set the heart at ease ?—or think you none,
If set at ease, can thrill with drum-like throbs
That marshal on the spirit to success ?—
You may be right.   In life's unending strife,
The wrestler the most fit to win the palm
May be the strong soul's restlessness, while rest,
Like sweetmeats, all too sweet, when served ere
          meats,
But surfeits appetite before it acts.

"But look," he added, starting suddenly ;
"The sun has touch'd the earth.   See how its
     disk,
Red-hot against the river, starts the mist,
Like steam, to drive us home."   With that we all
Walk'd home together ; nor a chance was given
For him to say the thing he would have said.

Yet, sister, I have lately often thought
His lips, thus closed, were making ready then,
When came Doretta there, to breathe to me
What might have roused me, like a Gabriel's trump
When rise dead hearts at resurrection-time,
And open'd for me here a life of love.

V.

Nay, do not bid me cease.   I must confess.
It is not discontentment with my lot.

My heart, it suffocates.   This feeling here,
It stifles me.   I think that one might die,
Forbidden speech.   Ah, friend, had you a babe,
A little puny thing that needed air,
And nursing too ; and now and then a kiss,
A mother's kiss, to quiet it ; and arms,
Warm arms to wrap and rock it so to sleep ;
Would you deny it these ? And yet there lives
A far more tender babe that God calls love ;
And when He sends it, why, we mortals here,—
I would not say we grudge the kiss, the clasp,—
We grudge the little heavenling even air.
The tears will come.   It makes me weep to think
Of this poor gentle babe, this heir of heaven,
So wronged because men live ashamed of it.
Not strange is it that earth knows little love
While all so little dare of love to speak.
For once (I ask no more) you must permit
That I should nurse the stranger, give it air,
Ay, ay, and food, if need be ; let it grow.
God's child alone, I have no fear of it.

VI.

Long after that, our Haydn found no chance
To talk with me ; and this, I know not why.
My father—I could never find out why
My father aught surmised : we walk'd alone,

Doretta, Haydn, I—my father though
From this time seem'd less trustful ; not that he
Loved less his favorite, Haydn ; but we both
Were still so young.   And he, poor man, who earn'd
With all his toil not much, had form'd a plan
(As one might form a rosary, stringing beads,
Then spending all his hours in counting them),
Where hung bright hopes, but strung on flimsy
    thread,—
Mere lint, brush'd off a worldling's flattery,
That I for wealth should wed.   So, like a gem
For future pride, he lock'd me up in school.

VII.

And there strange faces drove my lonely thoughts
Back into memory for companionship ;
And there imagination moved anon
To fill the void love felt in earth about,
Invoking fancies where it found no facts,
Beheld an earth about that seemed bewitch'd.

If Haydn's presence had my love call'd forth,
His absence, thus conjured, (could it do else ?)
Call'd forth my worship.   You remember, friend,
Those heroes of old Rome appear'd not gods
Till all were dead and veil'd from mortal eyes.
And so with Haydn was it, and his world,—
These never had appear'd so fill'd with light
As when so far from me.   The slightest hint

Of home, that made me think this home was his,
Made all things there as bright as heaven itself ;—
Yes, yes, though heaven so very bright must be !—
For even here the past is bright ; and there,
Up there, we faith shall have, such perfect faith,
That none can longer fear the future. No :
As restful shall it seem as now the past ;
And then with all things bright, behind, before,
Where could a place for gloom be ? Even here,
Could gloom be found if only men had faith ?

VIII.

A year pass'd over me. Can I forget
That wondrous April day that set me free?
At first, as though I own'd no soul at all,
I seem'd myself a part of that wide air,
And all things else had souls. The very earth
Beneath me seem'd alive ! its pulse to throb
Through every trembling bush ! its lungs to heave
Where soft-blown wind-sighs thrill'd the wooded
    hills !
And then, this great life broke in many lives,
All one through sympathy. In lieu of clouds,
The gusty breeze caught up the fluttering lark
And shook down showers of trills that made bare
    rocks
More sweet than fount-spray'd flowers, while all
    the leaves

Went buzzing on their boughs like swarming bees.
Then reverence hush'd the whole; for, greeting me,
Our dear church spire seem'd soon to mount the hill,
Our home to reach around a slow-turn'd rock,—
And all stood still with Haydn.   Chill as ice,
My hot cheek felt my sister's kiss then, then my
  father's,
And then bewilder'd, as from out a dream,
At last I woke.

    And what a dawn was that !
As if the sun had drawn the earth to itself,
I dwelt in central light ; and heaven, high heaven—
Could feel some rays, perhaps, was touch'd by
  them,
At star-points in the sky, but own'd no more.

IX.

Doretta in the year had grown so fair
That, in her first ripe flush of maidenhood,
I did not wonder, while I watch'd his eyes,
My Haydn's eyes, that he could crave the fruit.
And intimate they were.   Right merrily
Through all the house I heard their voices chime.
But me our Haydn did not seem to know ;
So quiet was he, and reserved with me.
Yet all my heart would flutter like a bird's
At his approach ; and all my will fly off,

And, as if poised in air and not in me,
Leave half my words and ways without control,
Until I seem'd as if I prized him not.

X.

But this he little mark'd.   Doretta's form
Had cast a shade, perhaps, that dimm'd his view.
Then, too, within the year, still subtler charms
Had cast their spells about him : work had come.
He needed now no more to earn his bread
By joining us wig-makers while we plied—
My sister and myself—our father's trade.
The church that had dismiss'd him, when from
      change
It could now keep that voice, whose tones, of yore,
Had touch'd my father so that heart and house
Had both sprung open that the sweet-voiced boy
Might find a home,—the church had called him
      back
To aid again, but in the orchestra,
The fresher singing of his younger mates.
With this had pupils fill'd his vacant hours ;
And, far away, an organ, play'd at Mass,
Besiren'd all the Sundays.   Thus cheer'd on,
His brighten'd prospects had renew'd the charms
Of music rivalling all things else with him.
Full often, could we watch him, listless, gaze,

Ay, even toward Doretta's voice and form ;
Then turn, like one bewildered by a dream
Fast-closing every sense to all besides,
And seek our small bare attic, where anon,
For hours together, pausing not for aught,
The ringing strings within his harpsichord
Would seem to call toward form that formless force
Enrapturing so the spirit.   When his moods
Would note Doretta not, nor waiting meals,
Nor sunset hues, nor moonlight at its full,
Nor e'en the striking of the midnight bell,
What could I think that he could care for me ?

XI.

At last his illness came.   How pale he lay !
We fear'd for him, lest life should slip its net :
The fleshly cords were worn to film so thin !
But how the soul would shine through them !   Its
        light,
I would not say that it could gladden me,
Yet—strange is it ?—while sitting near him then,
The fresh air fanning toward him, which his lungs
Were all too weak to draw there for themselves,
For that so gentle, babelike sufferer,
I lost all fear ; and, true to womanhood,
I loved him more for low and helpless moans
Than ever I had loved him when in health.

XII.

How oft I thank'd the Power that gave me power
To think and do for him what he could not.
I knelt : I gave my body to his needs :
Brain, hands, and all things would I yield to him.
And was I not paid back ?—His dear, sweet heart,
Each slightest beat of it, would seem to thrill
Through all my veins, twice dear when serving two.
And this was love ! You know the Master's words,
That they alone who lose it find their life.
'T is true.   No soul can feel full consciousness
Of full existence till it really love,
And yield its own to serve another's life.
"To serve Christ's life," you say?—But part of
     that
By Christ's humaneness is to serve mankind.
I speak a law of life, a truth of God :
To heaven I dare as little limit it
As to the earth ; whatever be our sphere,
We know not life therein until we love.

XIII.

True love has life eternal, infinite.
Complete within itself, and craving naught,
It needs no future far, nor outlet vast,
Nor aught to feel or touch in time or space.
A sense within, itself its own reward,

It waits not on return.   For it, to love
Is better than to be loved, better far
To be a God than man.

                  At least, my love
More further'd me than Haydn.   With all I long'd
And all I toil'd, Doretta was the one
Who could the best succeed in aiding him.
For she at home had dwelt, knew household ways ;
And I was but a bungler, knew them not.
And so to me was mainly given the task,
To fan him while he slept.   But, when he woke,
Although his lips would move with no complaint,
Nor eyes would glance for other than myself,
I could not do for him as then could she.
For she would turn his pillow, tell him tales,
Bring books and pictures, just what pleas'd him
    most.
But, ah, to me those patient eyes of his
Appear'd such holy things !   My deeds were
    hush'd :
I did not dare disturb the silence there.
It could not all have been mere selfishness ;
Yet I to look at him was all content.

XIV.

And my inaptitude my sister knew.
And partly since as well as I she knew it.

And partly since as well as I she loved,
Whene'er she heard him waking, she would come
And by him sit till fast asleep again ;
And only when there thus was little left
That could be done, would I be left to do it.

At times then I would lean above his couch,
And grieve to think that I could do no more ;
At times would rise in thankfulness that God
Would let me do so much.   A thought like this
Perhaps He chose to bless.   I came to think
That even though I might not have her art,
Doretta's art, that I at least might have
As much, perhaps, as guardian angels have,
Without our hands or voices, keeping watch
In spirit only.   Still, when sister came,
The thought would come that, if their souls un-
     seen
Could envy, sometimes they might envy men.

XV.

How hard I strove against this jealousy !—
Would plead with Mary, and would kneel to Christ ;
And seek the priestly father and confess
The feeling all to him.   Nor would he chide
One half as much as I would chide myself.
How would he shame me that I dared to love

" A man who had not ask'd me for my love !
A man who loved my sister and not me ! "—
Then bid me count my beads for hours and hours :
A week or more I slept not, counting them ;
But, while my thought was fixt but on my sin,
It seem'd my sin but grew.   It grew in fact :
For on this voyage of life, not seas alone,
But skies—all things about us—mirror back
The souls that they surround.   With each to him
That hath, is given back more of what he hath :
One smiles at aught, it gives him back a smile ;
He frowns, it gives a frown ; he looks with love,
He finds love ; but without love, none can find it.
Alas, that men should think one secret fault
Can hide itself.   Their sin will find them out.
Before, behind, from every quarter flash
Their moods reflected.   Let them tell the tale,
Nay, let them whisper, glance, or shrug one hint
Of what they find in earth about, and lo !
In this, their tale of it, all read their own.

XVI.

I wander much.   There came a change at last.
Our charge was better ; and, one afternoon,
Almost before I found that he had waked,
Upon my cheeks arose a burning heat,
While, past a mist of tears that flow'd, there dawn'd

The light that waited in his clear, blue eye.
"Pauline," he murmur'd then, "Pauline, my
    friend—
And what?—You weep for me! I shall not die.—
Nay, do not rise, nor call Doretta yet.
Hist, hist!—nor let her hear us. Why is this,
That you stay never with me when I wake?

"You think you 'cannot do for me'?—do what?
And have I ask'd you any thing to do?—
I pray you stay: do not do any thing,—
What pretty cuffs!—There, there: it still shall lie,
The little hand; I like to look at it.—
Who said I wish'd for books, and prints, and tales,
And bustlings all about?—Who told you this?
Your sister?—She a good, kind nurse has been:
And you, you too, have been a good, kind nurse.
Think you that I have never lain awake,
Nor known the long hours you have watch'd with
    me?—

"What say?—'Done' but 'your duty'?—Say not so.
A friend most pleases when, forgetting due,
He seems to do his pleasure; but a foe,—
Who does not shrink to feel him near enough
To freeze one with a chill though duteous touch?
Mere duty forms the body-part of love:
Let love be present, and this body seems

The fitting vestment of a finer life :
Let love be gone, it leaves a hideous corpse!
Pauline, I crave the life, I crave the soul :
Would you content me with a skeleton ?

" I 'meant' your 'sister'? Why ?—who named her ?
   —I ?—
Name her, did I, as being duteous ?—
Who 'mean' I then ?—You little fluttering bird !
Suppose you were some actual little bird,
How would you tell whence came or whither went
The wind that ruff'd your feathers ?—Do you
   know,
You women always will match thoughts to things ?
You chat as birds chirp, when their mates grow
   bright :
You love when comes a look that smiles on you.
We men are more creative.   We love love,
Our own ideal long before aught real :
Our halo of young fancy circles naught
Save empty sky far off.—And yet those rays
Fit like a crown, at last, about the face
That fortune drives between our goal and us.

" Yet, all may fail of truth ; none fail like those
Who deem themselves the most infallible :
None more than men who, fallible in proof,
Yet flout the failure of a woman's guess.

And your guess?—it went right.   I thought of her,
Your sister.   We both honor her, and much.
And yet I fear her, lest her will so strong
Should overmatch by aught your strength of will.
For God has given you your own moods, friend ;
And are you not responsible for them ?
And if you yield them up too readily,
Not meaning wrong, yet may you not mistake ?
Our lives, remember, are not sounding-boards,
Not senseless things, resounding for a world
That nothing new can find in what we give.
If one but echo back another's note,
Can he give forth God's message through his own ?
Yet,—Nay, I would not chide, I caution you.
Wit heeds a hint ; 't is dulness questions it.

" And so you thought I wish'd my pillow turn'd,
And books, and tales, and bustlings all about ?
Does not the world, then, worry life enough,—
That one should crave for more to worry him ?
Do I so lack for exercise ?   Ah me !
Some nervous mothers—bless them !—shake their
      babes.
I never deem'd it wise ; oh, no—am sure
The friction frets the temper of the child.—
Not natural, you see : God never shakes
The ground with earthquakes when we wish for
      spring.

He does not drive life from its germ, He draws
By still, bright warmth.　Pauline, but look at me.
Too weak am I now to be driven to life ;
Nay, nay, but must be drawn.—And ah ! could tell
Where orbs there are more bright than suns could
　　　be—
Nay, do not blush nor turn that face away.
You dream, aha, that I want sunset ?—what ?—
The colors come right pretty, but—there, there—

"What say ?—I ' dare not face ' you now ?—Those
　　　eyes,
Too bright, are they ? or loving ? Love, like God,
So brightly dear is it, that lives like ours,
Poor vapory lives, mere dews before the dawn,
Dare not to face it lest we melt away ?—
Then be it so.　Then look, Pauline, I dare !
Am I not yours ? Should you not use your own ?—
Ay, darling, draw me all within yourself."

XVII.

Then, while he spoke with hands there clasping mine,
And eyes that tired mine own with so much light
Their trembling lids were vext by feeble tears,
Doretta came.
　　　　　　　But startled, seeing me,
She only smiled ; said : "Haydn, what ! awake ?—
And you, Pauline ?—You good have been, so good ;

Nor call'd me ; no.   How very kind in you !
Why, after all, some little training thus
Might make you like, perhaps, to be a nurse,—
Or housekeeper.—To-day, how wreck'd it look'd,
Your room ! Our father just now came from there ;
So vex'd, you know."

    I flush'd, and thought, at least,
That she to speak of it had not been kind.
And could have told her so, but check'd the words,
And went my way ; and sought my father first,
And told him what the cause had been, and then
I sought my room, and pray'd that I might know
If it were well to tell my father too
Of Haydn's love ; or tell my own to Haydn ;
Or if he loved me, since my sister's words.
If only he could know my soul in truth,
I felt that I could suffer all things then ;
Could die, if so the veil about my heart
Withdrawn could be, and show him how I loved.
Alas, I did not know then, had not learn'd,
That love may more endure than even death.

XVIII.

The sunset brought Doretta to my room ;
And she began, and chided me, and said :
"How dared you talk ! and what were Haydn's
  words ?—

He lay so ill, with fever high, so high.
He could but rave.   How dared you lead him on ?
He worse may grow,—Who knows, Pauline ?—may
    die ;
And all the cause may be your nursing him !—
When will you learn to learn what you know not ? "

XIX.

And then she told me such a long, sad tale,
Of how great store she placed upon his life ;
And how they two had thought the self-same thing :
She knew each inner chamber in his heart,
And what key could unlock it ; and she named
First one and then another of our friends,
Whom she could never love as him she loved.
Then sigh'd she : " Ah, Pauline, had you explored
The world about, with all its barren wastes,
And found one little nook ; and had you work'd
And till'd it well, and form'd a garden there ;
And had you watch'd the plantlets grow until
Their dainty bowers bent over you with shade,
All sweet with bursting buds and carolling birds,
What could you think of one who came and stript
Your life of this, the thing that so you prized ?—
Alas, and what could I,—if any power
Should wrest from me my Haydn, all that soil
Where spring all hopes that bless my lonely hours,

And make it sweet for me to live my life,—
What could I think of her ? Though you, Pauline,
You have not known and tired of many men.
You have not search'd, as I have, through the
      world "—

" Nay, sister, I have not," I said.

                  Then she—
" Quite right : and cannot yet know love, true love.
Kept close at school you were, and hard it was ;
And harder still to-day that you must wait,
As I have done,—at your age too. But yet
Right love is ripe love. Life must be exposed
In sun and storm—to frost and bruising too :
The fruit grows mellow by and by alone."

" Why, dear," said I, " I think that I can love !
You know what Haydn sings,—that maids, like
      flowers,
Are sweetest, pluck'd when in the bud ? "

                     " There now,
You always will be quoting him ! " she cried,—
" Because, forsooth, a man, your first man-friend !
Yet, not compared by you with other men,
How know you him, what sort of man he is ?—
Girls unsophisticated are like bees :
They buzz for all, and yet sip all their sweets
From the first flowery lips that open to them."

XX.

"Nay," answer'd I, "I like him not for that,—
Because a man !"

        "What ?—not for that ?" she said :
"Aha, have shrewder plans ?—I know, I know
It would be well if you, or I, could feel
That all were settled for our wedded life ;
So many ifs and ifs, it vexes one ;
It would be better, were we done with them.
But we, poor girls, too trusting natures have.
Weak parasites at best, each tall stout man
Seems just the thing that we should cling about.
But, dear, I think that half these trunks give
    way :—
The wonder is we dare to cling at all !"

"But Haydn," said I, "Haydn "—

              "As for him,"
She sigh'd, "may be he is not trustless all ;
Yet if he be, or be not, how know you
Who know not human nature, nor have learn'd
The way to work it, and bring out its worth ?
A friend grows grain and chaff.   Sift out the first
And cultivate it well, some gain may come—
Some profit from your friendship."

              "But," said I,
"If you should change yourself who change your
    friend,

Or change but his relations to yourself,
Or, some way, make a new, strange man of him?"—

"Then would I make," she said, "what pleases me;
And with what pleases me preserve my love."

XXI.

"And I," replied I, "not for future gain,
For what he may become, would prize my friend;
I prize the thing he is; nor wish him changed.
I would not dare disturb for aught besides
The poise of traits composing sympathy,
Which, as they are, so balance my desires.
Ah, did I chiefly look for gain to come,
For him or me, where were my present joy?—
Nay, nay, that love I, which I find possess'd."

"Pray, how much can you find possess'd?" she
ask'd.

"Enough to love," I said.
                              "What holds enough
For that?" she laugh'd.
                              "Enough," I answer'd her,—
To make his presence here a boon to me;
To make his wishes a behest for me;
To make me feel an instinct seeking him,
And, finding him, a consciousness of all."

" ' A consciousness of all,' is vague," she said.
" I ask for reasons and you rave alone.
This very vagueness, while you answer me,
Proves all your love a myth, or immature,"

" Ah, dear," replied I, " there is higher love,—
A love of God, a love all worshipful ;
And that love should you ask me to define,
I might an answer vaguer still give back :
The finite only can be well defined."

" The finite ! " she repeated ; then exclaim'd :
" Oh, you wish worship ! We must find you then
An idol ! and I know a golden one ;
And so do you—nay, nay, deny it not.—
And father's heart is fix'd on him ; besides
Your lover could fall down and worship you ;
So father says.   Two idols you could have,—
Your home a very temple ; only, dear,
Be not so backward.   Had but I your chance—
To you our suitors all present their best.
You get the diamonds as if you were noon ;
While I, I get but coals.   They never touch,
Unless to burn or else to blacken me."

XXII.

She spoke, then left abruptly.   Strange it was,
With what abhorrence I would shrink from her

While speaking thus.   Not selfish seem'd she all,
But so insensible ; and these, our tastes,
These dainty despots of desire, our tastes
The worst of tyrants are ; nor brook offense.
I wellnigh hated her.   Yet minded thus,
While musing on her moods that seemed so hard—
Have not you noticed at the arsenal,
At times, when watching those grim helmets there,
All suddenly, upon their polish'd brass
A wondrous brightness ? then, within the disk,
Your own face hideous render'd ?   So with me :
Amid her harsher traits that there appear'd,
Shone soon the brighter metal ; out of it,
Leer'd back to greet me my own hideousness !—
For I, it seem'd, had been the selfish one.
Had I regarded her, my father's wish,
That suitor's choice ?—Nay, I had thought of none,
None saving Haydn.

           Then I ask'd again,
Could this be true—the thing my sister said,—
Could aught so sweet as Haydn's love exude
From moods, all mushroom'd by disease ?   I thought
How marvellously throng'd with strange weird
     shapes
Deep halls of fancy loom, when lighted up
By fires of fever ; how, with trust complete,
The weak lean oft on all beside themselves,
And soon I blamed my heart that it could dare

To lure his poor, weak, crazed confession on ;
And then I flush'd, and broke in passionate sobs,
To think Doretta dared to hint such things.

XXIII.

Three days my woes alternated, and then
I went to my confessor for relief.

" What, child," he said, " love troubles you again ?
The rest of us poor mortals here, we fret
Because we have too little of it, you
Because you have too much.   All girls are prone,
Young girls, to deem their own love great and grand;
But you, my child, find yours a very monster !
It taxes all your powers to get it food ;
Yet nothing does unless to tramp on you.
Now tell me, think you God it is, or man,
Who makes our earthly love so troublesome ? "

" Why, man," I said, " of course."
                                    " Of course," he said ;
" Then think you not it might be wise to get
Some less of man in you, and more of God ?—
How fares it with your prayers ? "
                                    " But yet," I urged,
" It scarcely seems my fault, this woe of mine."

"Seems not your fault ? " he answer'd ; "weigh the
      sides :

One for you—three against you—which should
    yield?"

"No; two for me," I said,—"myself and Haydn;
Besides, the other three have no such love."

"No love?" he said. "Is that a Christian mood?
A modest, humble mood?—'Have no such love'?
How test we love, my child? It seems to me
That love, like light, is tested by its rays.
The halo crowns the saints, our lights of life,
Just as the love they shed surrounds their souls.
Where one is God's, the strong soul serves the
    weak ;
The mother yields her powers to bless her babes ;
The man his powers, for her ; and Christ for all.
Ah, child, if you were strong ! had love like
    theirs ! "

I sigh'd, " But how can one know whom to serve ? "

" How ?—Put it thus :—your own wish ? or your
    father's ?—
How reads the decalogue ? "

                    " But," answer'd I,
" It seems as if some higher power there were
That first should be obey'd—some power like
    God."

"Yes, child," he said, "there is, of course, the
　　Church :
Of course, of course."
　　　　　　　　　　"Who is the Church ? " I ask'd.
And then he laugh'd : "Who ?—What a question,
　　child !—
Why, read your prayer-book.　Why, of course, the
　　Church,
Speaks through its ministers."
　　　　　　　　　　　　"If you speak then,"
Inquired I, trembling,—"give advice to us,
Is that the last resort ?—must one obey ? "

"Why, that depends," he said ;—"but, dear me,
　　child,
You must not think us bears ! We growl at times
In sermons, eh ?—But then, dear me, dear me,
We would not eat our flock up, little lamb !—
But come," he added, " come ; enough of this ;
How fares it with your prayers ? "

XXIV.

　　　　　　　　　　Soon after that,
One day, while troubled much, I met by chance,
My Haydn, half restored, outside his room.
For once, he sat alone ; and, seeing me,—

"Why, friend, what accident is this?" he ask'd.
"In tears, too, tears?—Tell now, what sullen storm
Has left such heavy drops? Did it not know
That these too tender lids might droop? if droop,
What rare views they might close to some one
    here?—
What can have happen'd?

                "Why not speak to me?—
You seem the very statue of yourself.—
Why, what has chill'd you so?—Not I?—Not I?—
Pauline, I know, if I to you were cold,
A certain rosy face with opening lips
Could come with power to bring me summer air,
Dispelling sweetly my most wintry wish,
Despite myself!—Why will you trust me not?"

And then I spoke to him. I hinted first
My moods were odd; not moods for him to mind.

"Odd," answer'd he; "I knew a family
Where all the children grew so very odd,—
Like fruit when tough to touch and sour to taste.
Not ripe nor mellow. Too much spring had they,
And not enough of summer in their home.—
I know that you are not so very odd
That you would keep apart from one you love.
And I, can I not hope that I am one?"

XXV.

At these words then (how could I help myself?)
My heart-gates flew wide open; emptied all,—
The whole the priest had told me of my sin;
And how we should not talk together more.

How wild it made him!   Never had I seen
One shaken so.   His anger frighten'd me.
"This crafty priest," he said, "you ask'd of God:
He answer'd you about the Church, 'of course.'
And of the Church about the priests, 'of course,'
And of the priests about himself, 'of course.'
I tell you this is cursèd selfishness;
I tell you it is downright sacrilege!—
To strain the oceans of the Infinite
Down through that sieve, man's windpipe, wheezing
        out,
'I deal the voice of God, I, I, the priest'"

"O Haydn," said I, "How—how can you dare?"

"How dare?" he cried out, "dare?   Am I a dog,
A dog or woman cringing to a man,
Because of kicks or curses?"
                              "Nay," I sobb'd,
"I kneel before his office, not to him."

" Poor girl," he said, " forgive me—stop—I beg—
What ? can you think that I would make you weep ?
Not, darling, not of you, I meant to speak,
But of the system."

           " System," I replied ;
" Why, Haydn, are you not a Christian, then ? "

" And wherefore not ? " he ask'd.
            " Because," I said,
" You speak so of the Church.
            " But I," said he,
" Was arguing not of that, but of the priest."

" And he has been ordain'd," I said : " And you,
You reverence not the ministers of God ? "

" **Of God**," he mutter'd,—" yes, when that they are.
I reverence the princeship ; not the prince
Who doffs his regal robes, and leaves his throne,
And lowers his aims and slaves it with mere serfs."

XXVI.

" What can you mean ? " I ask'd.
            " I mean that priests
Are not ordain'd for work in every sphere.
A prince dispenses, does not mine, his gold.
A priest administers the truth reveal'd ;

What power has he to delve divine designs,
Or minister dictation, in the spheres
Where God, to train our reason, leaves us free?
Your priest who tampers with our home-life here,—
What warrant holds he, human or divine?
Whatever move him—if he serve your father,
Or deem that gifts like those he fancies mine,
May worthier prove, devoted to the Church,
Is he in this our final arbiter?—
Have I no judgment?—are not you of age?
Pauline, but heed me; let no power, I beg,
Succeed in sundering us.   Heaven hears my words.
I fear some plot may crush, or make your soul
(God save you if you yield) a mere bent truck
To bear some weight of meanness on to ill."

"But I," I said, "had ask'd the priest's advice."

"He handled ill th' occasion," answer'd he.
"I would not dare to mould another thus.
Nay, though I knew that I could model thence
The best-form'd manhood of my mind's ideal.
Who knows?—My own ideal, my wisest aim,
May tempt myself, and others, too, astray.
If I be made one soul to answer for,
And make myself responsible for two,
I may be doubly damn'd.   How impious,—
The will that thus would manage other wills;

As though we men were puppets of a show,
Not spirits, restless and irresolute,
Poised on a point between the right and wrong
From which a breath may launch for heaven or
      hell!—
You dare submit to this impiety?"

" But, Haydn," said I, " you, too, heed advice."

" Advice?" he answer'd.   "What?—is this the
      ground
On which these base authority?—Nay, nay,
Base where they may, their ground is wilfulness,
Years back invested ; not disrobed, because
Old forms are reverenced.—Yes, but are they right?
Think you God gives to strength of will the right
To say what is right?   And if not, what then?
If one obey then, how can he be sure
That he obeys not sin?"

                              "They may have will,"
I said, "but you forget ; the priests are wise."

" About what life?" he cried.   "In every path
Experience is the warrant for advice.
But life for them—what know they real of life?—
Naught, naught ; and if they give you their advice
They give you naught, or else they give you
      whims ; —
A bachelor teaching dames about their babes !

Or matrons how to guide their grown-up girls!
Alas, their counsels ignorant, partial, false,
Repel toward infidelity the wise;
And half of those they hope will follow them
Make hypocrites or hypochondriacs."

XXVII.

What could I say?   I rose to leave him then.

"And have they really separated us?"
He ask'd.
    And I, "What mean you?"
        "Are you then
My friend or not?" he went on, mournfully.

"What is a friend?" I ask'd.
       "What else," he said,
"But, in a world, where all misjudge one so,
A soul to whom one dares to speak the truth?"

"Ah, Haydn," ask'd I, "must we speak all truth?"

"Why not?" he said, "is ill less ill when hid?—
Is not the penitent a sinner frank,
The hypocrite a sinner not so frank?"—

"But yet," protested I, "the truth may harm."

"How so?" he ask'd.   "If one show naked sin,—
Who knows?—it then may shame men from the sin.

And could the naked good accomplish more?
Must not we Christians here confess our faults?
Why should we not? Has wrong such lovely smiles
And loving tones, that men should long for it?
The harm is in the lie that masks the sin."

"And yet," I said, "the young—the prejudiced"—

"For their sake," said he, "wisdom may be wise
In what it screens from folly.—Yet you know
The crime of Socrates,—'corrupting youth'?
The tale is old; this lying world wants liars,
But what of that? The Christs lie not: they die.
Our God is great. I deem Him great enough
His truth to save without subverting ours.
True sovereignty has truth: 'tis not a sham
That holds high rank because we courteous men,
Considerate men, allow it seeming rank.
Who lies to save the truth, distrusts the truth,
Disowns the soul, and does despite to God.
Who strives to save his life thus, loses it,
In evil trusting and the Evil One,—
Salvation through the Devil, not through Christ!"

XXVIII.

Then while he sat there, with his flushing cheeks,
Himself defending thus,—I, charm'd the while,—

The door flew open, and behind it stood
My father and the priest.
                    Then had they said
But one harsh word, it had not been so sad.
But kind they were, too kind.   Ah, sister dear,
Have you not felt how much more pain it gives,
This pain from kindness?   Love is like the sun :
It brightens life, but yet may parch it too.
And wind may blow, and man may screen himself ;
And rain may fall, and he may shelter find ;
And frost may chill, and he may clothing wear ;
But what can ward off sun-stroke ?—Love,
Its first degree may bring fertility ;
Its next one barrenness.   It lights ; it blights.
The flames of heaven, flash'd far and spent, turn
    smoke
To glut the gloom of hell.
                    Words kind as these
(We could have braced ourselves against them
    else)
Threw wide, like spells, each passage to our hearts
That caution should have guarded.   "We knew
    not
Our own minds, poor young pair," they said.   "At
    least,
Our love could wait :   meantime, whose love could
    claim
Our trust, like theirs whose treasure lay in us ?"

XXIX.

And then to me alone they spoke of Haydn :—
" He passionate had been :—how knew I when
His passion might be turn'd against myself ?
And he had sinn'd, so sorely, sorely sinn'd :—
How could one thus defame the Church and
    priest ?
And did my love for him suggest such words,
Or should my love hereafter sanction them,
Might not his wrong prove mine ?—If I should yield,
Be won by his unbridled words, might not
My act confirm his trust in thought uncheck'd ?
And thought uncheck'd,—it oft more danger fronts
Than does the uncheck'd steed, whose frenzied flight
Defies the rein, and, dashing down a road
Straight deathward, trails his luckless driver on,
Whirl'd powerless to prevent all as a babe."

I spake of Haydn's love.

             They bade me think
" How often love that loses earthly friends,
Comes back from all things outward toward itself ;
And finding self, finds heaven's design within ?
Did not I know that loss and gain are both
Sent here to aid the worth of inner traits
And change the phases of the spirit's growth ?—
Each passing season circling round a tree

Leaves, clasping it, a ring ; the rings remain,
So seasons past remain about the soul :
And men can trace its former life far less
By tales the tongue may tell, than by the range
And reach of that which circumscribes the mood,
Including or excluding right or wrong."

XXX.

And then they added : " Might it not be found
That loss of my love was the very means
Design'd by Providence for Haydn's good ? "

To this I could but answer that " his love
Seem'd Providential too, a holy thing."

They only frown'd, and said : " The Prince of Ill
Came oft robed like an angel of the light ;—
Why not like love ?—The only holy thing,
Such proven to be, was Christ.   And what of Him
When moved by love ?—of His great sacrifice !—
And did I really prize this Haydn so,
Would love prompt naught in me ! "
　　　　　　　　　　And thus they talk'd,
Till, welcoming doubt, my faith succumb'd to it ;
And all the love once making me so proud,
Whose growth, I thought, would be so sweet and
　　　fair,

Stung like a very thistle in my soul ;
Each breath of theirs would blow its prickles keen,
And sow its pestering seedlets far and wide
O'er every pleasing prospect of my life.

XXXI.

And I recall my calling out in prayer,
How long, how toilfully, how fruitlessly !
At last, my doubt had made me leave my beads,
And, moved as if to cool a feverish faith,
Pass out, the night air seeking.   There I saw
The moon.   It soothed me always with strange
    spells,
The moon.   But now, as though all things would
    join
To rout my peace, I seem'd this moon to see
Caught up behind an angry horde of clouds,
Chased by the hot breath of a coming storm
That clang'd his thunder-bugle through the west.
When once the rude gust hit the moon, it tipt—
Or so it seem'd—and with a deafening peal
It spilt one blinding flash.   Then, where this lit,
Just in the path before me gleam'd a knife !
Held o'er a form of white !   To see the thing
I scream'd aloud.   It seem'd a ghost !

                        My scream
Awoke no echo save Doretta's voice :—

" Pauline ?—and were you frighten'd ? "

                          Then to this,
In part because the shock had stunn'd me much,
In part because I felt me much provoked,
But most because my ears were deaf to sport,
I answer'd naught.   Whereat, as now I think,
Though then in that unnatural, nervous mood
My mind surmised more horrid inference,
Her voice, in still more mischievous caprice,
Went on to vex me more.

                     " What ?—Fear you me !
And have you done so much against me, then !
And if you have, why fear you here a knife ?—
You think the blade might draw some little blood ;—
Would that much signify ?—the body pain'd ?
Suppose that one should wield some subtler blade
And draw some tears, mere watery tears, weak
     things ;—
Would they much signify ?—a soul in pain ?
And did you never now do that ?—draw tears ?—
And think, is not the soul much worse to harm
Than is the body ?—Fy ! why fear a knife ?
If I supposed that through a lifetime long
My soul should bleed its dear strength out in tears,
Why would it not be mercy to myself
For me to check the longer, stronger woe
By shedding here some drops of weaker blood,
Now, once for all ? "

"O dear Doretta mine,"
I cried, and still more anxious, "do you mean"—

"This," answer'd she ; "I mean that I would cut
My body's life in two parts, rather than
My soul's life."   "Sister," I could only gasp,
"Cease—do ;—put by that knife"—
                "Why?" answer'd she ;—
"For what?—Your wish? Do you so often yield
When I wish aught?—Say now what would you
    give?"

"Give?—Any thing!" I answer'd.
                        "Be not rash,"
Came then. "It scarcely seems your way ; besides,
The light is dim.   How know you? may not ears
Not far off overhear us here?   Beware!—
But stay!" she added, "I will go my way,
And you go yours.   Who cares what either does?"

XXXII.

"Doretta, nay ; but stop," I cried again,
"Put by the knife!—and if you will, then I—
Then I and Haydn will not—
                        "You?" she laugh'd,
"And Haydn?—Humph!—Who cares what you
    may do?—
But ah—if planning thus to vent your thought,

Could I have chosen, eh, a shrewder way?—
Ha! ha!—to murder me, or you, or him!
It starts all madness, yes, to tap your moods.
But go in, simpleton,—the rain has come,—
And trust the knife to me.　It meant no harm
Except to this beheaded cabbage here."

And, shaking this aloft, she flitted off,
While I walk'd vaguely back, to find my room
Still sadder than before.　I could not think
That my surmise was just; yet could not think
That all her strange demean was meaningless;
To this day yet, I pause and puzzle oft
That scene to ponder; then, to moods confused,
It seem'd the final blow, unsettling all.

XXXIII.

What comes as direful as the direful night
A spirit spends in trouble?—fill'd with fears
That sleep may bring distressful nightmares now;
And now, that morn may come before we sleep;
Until, betwixt the two, distracted quite,
Awake one dreams, and dreaming seems awake,
And evermore does weep at what he dreams,
And then does weep that he should dream no more.
In darkest fancies all that night I lay,
A murderess, guilty of Doretta's death.

XXXIV.

Alas ! and after those long hours of woe,
More woe awaited me when morning came.
Our Haydn's bed-worn frame, so frail before,
New-rent by throes of passion yesterday,
Once more lay prostrate in the arms of death :
So thought we all : I, ere the fact I heard,
Could feel its cold shade creeping over me.
The shutters closed, the silence everywhere,
The very coffin of our lively home,
The sadden'd looks, the voices all suppress'd,
The kind physician's face, that wore no smile,—
I did not need to ask the cause of all.
I sought and saw my Haydn.   How his face
Gazed forth, a ghost's, against my sense of guilt !
For I, perhaps, had made his last thought sin ;
And I, perhaps, had lured him toward his doom.
I thought then of my father, of the priest,
What they of love had said, of genuine love,
Such love as Christ had had.   I ask'd myself
If there was naught that I could sacrifice ?

XXXV.

Ah, friend, do you recall that afternoon
When first we met ? How sad yet sweet it seem'd !
So many kindly sisters with me spake,
And for me prayed, and when the dusk had come,

And hardly any eye but God's could see,
We knelt before the altar ; and I rose,
Content if like that light before the shrine
Within my heart one light alone could burn ;
Though all the earth beside might loom as dark
As those chill, shadowy chapels down the aisle.

I felt another life when walking home.
Such conflicts come but seldom ; storms of spring,
Uprooting much, and wracking much the soil,
They find it frost-bound, and they leave it green.
Alas, if grain or chaff grow then, depends
Upon the germs their rains have wrought upon.

XXXVI.

When Haydn grew less ill, could talk once more,
And proved our prayers for him were not in vain,
The kind physician urged that he and I
Be kept no more apart.   My father then,
At first, would not consent.   I went to him.
" My father," said I, " do not fear for me.
If God will give our poor friend health once more
Then have I vow'd that never will I take
A veil, save one that weds me to the Church."

" My daughter,—what ? " he ask'd " you never
      take—

Ay, what is this you say?—you wed the Church?—
In God's name, child, explain yourself."

                                      "A vow,"
I said, "A vow that I have made the Virgin."

"What strange, what thoughtless deed is this?" he
    ask'd.
"You take a vow, one not to be recall'd,
That you will thwart our hopes, our plans for you?—
And shut away, away from all of us,
This face, this form, so cherish'd all these years?—
True?—Is it true?—I would not frighten you:
Poor girl, God knows that you will have enough
To shudder for.—Yet, it bewilders me:
How could you, you who had been wont to be
So trustful and considerate and calm,
How could you do a thing so rash, so wrong,
Nor once consult me?—Tell me this, my child:
What false inducement could have tempted you?"

"Woe me!" I sobb'd, "I marvell'd when you said
I could do so, the time I told you here
That I would rather be a nun than be
That rich man's wife."

                        "You dear, poor girl," he sigh'd,
"Those words were but a whiff, whiff light as
    breath
One blows at flies that come to trouble him.
And can it be that they?—I half believe

(My words have conjured cursèd deeds before)
The very atoms of the air, like pools,
Hold spawn-strown vermin-eggs ! If one but speak,
But break the silence ; if his breath but bear
One faintest puff from passionate heat within,
Lo, breaking open some accursèd shell,
It hatches forth foul broods of venomous life
That come, blown backward by the changing wind,
To haunt him who provok'd their devilish birth !
By day they sting our eyes, and make us weep ;
By night steal through unguarded gates of sense,
And sting our souls in dreams !—My heart ! and
    you ?—
How could you deem my thoughtless words to be
The voice of so deform'd a wish as this ?"

"But father," said I, " he, the priest, your friend,—
At least, it seem'd—so thought."
                      "The priest ! " he cried,
"Has he been meddling with your malady ?—
My friend ?—My friend is he no more."
                           "Nay, I,"
I said, " had sought his counsel ; even then
He said but little."
                   " Little ! " he rejoin'd ;
"That little was too much ! Nay, never more—
Yet hold."— And here he paused.—" The priest
    has power—

Yes, now I think of it, it need not all
Be darkness ; no.—The priest—one clew there is
May clear this labyrinth.—The priest, he may,—
He shall an absolution get ; yes, yes,
An absolution, that shall make us right."

And then my father, in his hopeful way,
Recover'd somewhat.   And he fondled me.
" I see, my child, you love this Haydn, yes.
Why, here you stand a woman when I thought
You only were my pet, my little girl.—
But do not cry : no, no ; I honor you,
My little woman ! — There, forgive me now ;
Forgive my words.   And when it comes, my child,
The absolution, then, we then shall see,
If your old father can be kind or not."
With this he kiss'd me.   And at that, I wept ;
Nor could I tell him that his hopes were vain.
I scarce could think myself that they were vain.

XXXVII.

From this time onward no one check'd me more,
Attending Haydn.   All the household heard
My sire " could trust his child to be discreet " ;
And e'en Doretta too had something learn'd
That made her caution more than half relax.

Then days and weeks and months pass'd quickly
    by

In which, when Haydn's prison'd love would start,
E'en while I heard the trembling of its bars,
My lips would check him, saying, gently, then,
" But not now, Haydn ; nay, but we will wait."

And thus a habit grew that our two lives
Dwelt there like friends, made separate by war,
Who out from hostile camps, wave now a hand,
And now a kerchief, but who never speak.
And yet I cannot say love never spoke.—
We did not mean it ; but I think that love
May tell its tales, unconscious of the fact,
For who is conscious when God touches him ?—
But littlest acts there were ; yet spirits read
From signs too fine for measurements of space ;
Love heeds no measurements.   But hints there
        were ;
And yet what words of love yield more than
        these ?
They hit the sense of love, but fail of sense
Where nothing loving waits to take the hint.

This learn'd our souls at last ; I wot not how.
And kitten-like, at play beside the hearth,
We told our secrets, and none knew of them.

XXXVIII.

How swiftly sped the hours in happy nights
When, after work, he rested there at home !

Such winning ways he had to lure my trust !
Such sweet pet names would call me, till I felt
So fondly small, he well might be my lord !
Would tease me so, anon to comfort me !
Or rouse my temper that he mild might seem ;
Or tell such tales, that in my dreams I laugh'd
At wit reflecting, though distorting, his ;
Or better still, would play for me,—such strains !
The very thought of them would seem like sleep,
While half the night I linger'd still awake,
Half-conscious of the call of early birds
And sparkling spray of light dash'd o'er the dews.

XXXIX.

At last, one night, when no one else was by,
Some new impatience moved him ; and he spoke :
"Pauline, my friend, allow me only once ;—
And say not, now, say not we still can wait :
Have I not waited long ?   Pauline, my own,
What forms the substance of this mystery
Whose dark shade rests about you ? Surely, friend,
The slightest will on your part would have power
To bid it off."
　　　　　"Not so," I answer'd him
(I felt that I should tell him all at last) ;
"Not if the shade that so you speak of fall
From something you and I could not remove."

"That cannot be," he cried. "How can it be?
Of old your father would not brook our love;
But lately much has done to forward it."

"And know you then," I asked, "what wrough
his change?"

"His wiser judgment," answer'd he; "not so?"

"Are there not times in life," I ask'd, "and paths
Where conscientiousness and love may cross?"

"There," he exclaim'd, "the same old plea again!—
Your weakness is your wickedness. Why, friend,
Does not our conscience come from consciousness?
And when, then, are we conscious? When un-
well:
Hot, swollen blood frets limbs that feel inflamed:
A sound man lives unconscious of its flow.
And so a morbid train of foul ideas
Will vex a soul diseased. But if in health,
Its aims all true to God and self,—what call
For conscience, which we wear but as the curb
Whereby God reins the thought that love reins
not?—
If right I be, then nothing needs to cross
Pure love. It may have freedom.—
                              "Or at most
Our conscience is the leven of character;

And just enough of it may sweeten life,
But too much keeps in ferment moods that work,
Like brewings, flung to froth and sediment :
The froth flies up and off to vex our friends ;
The rest sinks down in self, embittering
Our own experience."

           " And yet," I said,
" Our conscience, in religion "—

                  " There," he cried,
" This too much conscience, overbalancing
All wiser judgment, has wrought worse results,
Made men crave heaven and fear for hell, so much
That, in the gap betwixt the two, was left
No charity with which to do good here
While on the earth."

         " I hope that mine," I said,
" Will prompt to some small good in present life.
What would you say, some day, were I a nun ?"

" 'Say !'" answer'd he—and scorn was in the
    tone,—
" What say ?—why this: that if those blooming looks
Hid wormy fruit like that, I ne'er would trust
Sound health again !

         " Pauline, I half believe
The conscience of a nun is consciousness
Of mere unrest—no more.   In natures framed
Of spirit, mind, and flesh, the cause may be

Some sin that clogs the current of the soul ;
But, just as likely, thought that puzzles one ;
Yes, yes, or indigestion, nerves diseased—
No trace of sin whatever;—moods cured best
By sunshine, clean clothes, larders full, good
    cheer."

XL.

His words I styled "irreverent, unjust ! "—

" I might be both of these," he said, "in case
I blamed the poor souls for the life they lead.
But did I blame them ? Nay, for in this world,
Between youth's immature credulity,
That dares to think but what some guardian thinks,
And manhood's faith mature that thinks for itself,
A realm there is where will must learn to act
Through doubt and danger ; where the character,
First wean'd from oversight, must learn to choose.
Then, like a tottering child it yearns to cling
To one whose greater power can for it act.
Its moods determine that to which they cling.
Some girls are giddy :—they embrace a lover.
And some are gloomy:—they beset a priest.
He, like the first, may ply his own designs,
May take advantage of their weaker state,
And capture them for veils, if not for vice."

"But marriage is a capture, too," I said.

"If so," he answer'd, "yet a natural state,
Made statelier through authority of law,
That, otherwise, might authorize the wrong ;—
A state to which, as not to convent life,
All social instincts prompt ; may prompt the more
The more one's years. Who then can it for-
    swear ?—
Think you a maid, with half her moods unform'd
At twenty, can conceive what thoughts may come
To turn or torture her at thirty-five ?—

"But what, Pauline, Pauline,—you turning pale !—
In earnest, were you !—Had you really thought ?—
In God's name, darling, this could never be !—
Think only—Wherefore now ? "

                  "Because," I said,
"I hoped some good to do."

                  "And do you deem,"
He ask'd, " that then the Virgin did no good,
When nursing her sweet babe ?—and was no saint ?
And what of Christ, who ate and drank with all,
Call'd glutton and a bibber, yes, of wine ?—
Was He no saint ?—What think you mortals need—
To learn of life that never can be theirs ?
Nay, nay, to learn of life, inspired by love,
Which all can live, made better by its power.

If you a saint would be, oh, do not seek
For truth so sunder'd from the common thought,
For love that knows no common sympathies."

XLI.

"Are some," I said, "not call'd in special ways
To nurse and tend the aged, sick, and poor?"

"Are some not call'd," he ask'd, "in special ways
To tend like this the men they love the best?—
Whate'er old age may need, needs it the most
The young who old have grown before their time?—
Need sick men nurses pale?—or poor men, those
Whose moods have never stored the rich results
Mined from a world the world's heir should ex-
    plore?—
Nay, nay, these all would be more ably served
By spirits free to live their own love's life.
Who gains aught where the spirit is not free?
Think you the veil, too hastily assumed,
May never change the hues and views of life,
Perverting them?—or cause beclouded love
That might have bloom'd in light, to fade in gloom?
'T is only when those knowing what they leave
Turn calmly from all else to convent walls
That love should not dissuade them.   Let them find
Large, sunny, healthful halls; and dwell therein:

From thence deal forth that gentle charity
So potent coming from a woman's hand.
Not strange it were if sickness, tended thus,
Enliven'd by her smiles of light, should flush
Or blush to perfect health ! if wickedness,
Beneath incrusted woes of years of wrong,
Should feel the earlier faith of childhood waked
By woman's voice, and thus be born again !—
And find a life renew'd within the soul
As well as body.   Let the convent thrive.
But rid it of all circumscribing vows."

" Of all its vows ? " I ask'd.

                   " Why not ? " he said :
" No character, I think, grows wholly ripe
Save that which grows as nature guides its growth;
And nature made us pairs.   I know some say
The soul should conquer nature ; but this means
That spirits all should claim their rights,—be lords
Of forms that spring from earth.   But are they so
When by a vow they swear to serve a form,
And don the life and livery of a slave ?
Would men look'd Godward more ! 'T would save
     their souls
From many a hell that their own hands have made.
One time when young I stood before a tree,
And vow'd that, till an hour had pass'd away,
My eye should see it not.   What came of it ?—

The vow in misery kept me through the hour.
And had it been a maid and not a tree,
The vow had caused me more of misery.
Yet God's laws never bade me turn my back
On tree or maid : nay, were my nature framed
With any touch of truth, these both were made
For souls like mine to look at and enjoy."

XLII.

"But, Haydn," said I, "your strange convent, fill'd
With age and vowless maids—you banish thence
Christ's life, self-sacrifice."
　　　　　　　　　　"And sacrifice
But sates the worst of vanity," he said,
"Unless our yielding yield to higher good.
Christ's work here glorified humanity—
I must believe that souls, not when outside
The world but in the world, though not of it,
And in the body acting bodily,
The lives transfiguring our common lives
And common cares, the most resemble His.—
The one who seeks to glorify herself
In feigning burial to human cares,
Humiliates rather her humanity.
She hints—not so?—that truest womanhood
Is maidenhood?—By Eve and Mary, false !—
The mother lives the model of her sex,

And not the maid.   And she who seeks to lower
The mother's rank that she may lift her own,
Yields less than she bids others yield to her."

" But she serves God," I said, " and others men."

" How serves one God in doing this ? " he ask'd.
"God made our nature.   Who make way with it,
Make way with manhood, turn to suicide.
He made the world where works His Providence
To train our life.   Who leave the world, leave
    Him—
May add but more damnation to their woe."

" But if men leave the world," I said, " for this,—
That they may serve the Church, how leave they
    God ? —
They rather go to him."
       " What is the Church ?
He ask'd.
     " The kingdom of the Lord," I said.

" Yes, yes," he cried ; " and add the Master's
    words :
' The kingdom is within you.'—And, if so,
I own some right to heed the voice within ;
And none can rightly bid my spirit bend,
A passive slave to laws outside of me."

XLIII.

"O Haydn," begg'd I, "say not this.   Here speaks
The same rebellion that was once my own.
We must not judge for self, but reverence
The words of men ordain'd to teach the world ;
The words of men so learnéd in the truth ;
The words of councils fill'd with just such men.—
No reverence have you for authority ? "

" Mere common courtesy would teach me that,"
He said.   " And how could common piety,
If awed before the Power above the sky,
Deny a kindred awe to power on earth ?
The Church has power—and more.   I reverence
        it.
It may be God's own storehouse of the truth.
But ah, some truths have never yet been stored !
Infinity is broad, and broad enough
For truth to grow within me and without,
In self as well as in the best about it.
And I believe that all things God makes grow,
Unfold in ways that work in harmony.
And, when I love a soul as you I love,
Did all the priests on earth assemble here,
In front of them the pope, in front of him
A shining form put forth by them as Christ,
And tell me this pure love could lie to me,

I would not "—

     " Haydn stop !—dare not !" I cried ; —
"And I have pray'd to God so much, so much,
To make you more submissive."

              " I submit
To God," he said ; "but with my love to God,
How can I yield the godliest thing I own ? "

And there he sat, so firm and yet so kind,
I could not help but sigh, " You make me doubt."

"Would God," he said, " I could do that for you !
Then might you have true faith.   Where springs
    from will
One wise effect that does not follow doubt ?
One choice that does not weigh alternatives ?
Doubt comes with waverings of the balances
Before the heavier motive settles down.
Let those who feel so sure their views are right,
Dissolve my doubt :—I dare to doubt if they
Walk not by knowledge rather than by faith.
I read that Jesus answer'd him who pray'd,
' Lord, I believe, help thou mine unbelief ' ;
That on the cross itself even He could cry :
' My God, O why hast thou forsaken me ? '
And so I think, at times, these doubts of ours
May only rise like minor preludes here,
Ere that triumphant cadence, ' It is finished.'

But come, Pauline," he added then with warmth,
" And promise me that you will yield them up,
These dark, sad thoughts.   Why, they could make
     of me
An infidel outright !   Could faith destroy
Our love, what good then might it not destroy ? "
A wonder is it, that to moods like this
I could not say the thing I would ?

XLIV.

                              Months pass'd.
My time drew nigh.   My vows must be fulfill'd.
I told my father of it, and he wept.
Poor man, he spent his hours alternately.
At times he urged ; at times he chided me ;
At times he kiss'd my cheek and look'd at me ;
At times he took me by the hand, and said :
" My daughter, dear, we will defer the deed " ;
At times he moaned : " My daughter will do
     right."

XLV.

Then slowly dawn'd on Haydn's mind the fact,
Though not, as yet, the reason of my vow.
And all the household grew so mild with me ,
And all the neighbors gazed so piteously :

If they had clothed my body in a shroud,
And I had loiter'd round it there, a ghost,
Life scarce had seem'd more lonely or more chill.

But yet more sad than all it seem'd for me
To shun poor Haydn.   To his attic driven,
Who knew his grief ?   Alas, who knew it not ?
Did ever harpsichord so crave a voice
To utter forth a cry of full despair ?
Did ever aught that human hands could touch
So tremble to reveal such agony
As wrung the frame of him whose fingers wrought,
Along the sympathetic key-board there,
The counterpoint still pointing out his woe ?

XLVI.

Through all those days how heeded I each sound,
That broke the stillness in that room of his !
Would hold my breath between the notes to feel
His own suspense before the impending strain
When fell, anon, the spirit's overflow.
I never so had trembled at the peals
Of thunder as beneath the chords he struck ;
Nor felt my cheek so moist by rains as there
By tears that flow'd as flow'd his melodies ;
While all the air about appear'd surcharged
With dangerous force electric, touch'd alone

To flash keen suffering from his heart to mine.
And yet, each day, his music sweeter swell'd.
Ere that, it may have lack'd in undertone,
The pleading pathos of half-utter'd grief :
Since then, I never hear it but it seems
As if the heavens had been bereaved of love,
And pour'd their sad complaint on earth beneath ;
And I who listen to the sweetness of it
Can never tell if I should smile or weep
To think that it has come so far below,
Or feel that it has left so much above.

XLVII.

One night I found my father still more sad
Than was his wont.   I knelt before him then,
And " O my father, why is this ? " I ask'd.
But he said nothing.   Then I question'd him :
And found the cause out.   Haydn was the cause.
My father loved him so, as men love sons ;
And long had hoped he might a son become.
But they had talk'd in confidence, and talk'd
About Doretta.   " Ah," my father sigh'd ;
" My plans for all of you are vain !—
　　　　　　　　　　　　　　　　" Why now ? "
He cried, " in this my old age, now, too late
To be replaced again, should I have lost

My aims, my home, my hope, my happiness ?—
And who has brought it on ? has done such wrong
His deeds deserve it ?—Here am I, myself,—
I loved you, loved you both, but plann'd your
    good :
The priest loved (so he says) the Church and you :
Doretta loved ; sought only love's full fruit :
And Haydn loved ; wish'd but to show his love :
And you, child, loved, were but obedient :
We all of us were loving, were we not ?
Yet working outward, wisely, as we deem'd,
We all have done the thing to doom us all.
Alas what power has wrought to thwart us thus ?
I do believe, though long I doubted it,
There lives a Devil ! Hell-scorch'd hands alone
Could weave such death-black shrouds from thread
    so bright,
Drawn from sleek skeins of love. That spider-
    fiend,
Feeding on our sweet plans, emits this web,
To trip and trap us in like flies !—Ah me,
It may be well that one should suffer here
Until a wish bereaved shriek prayers for death ;
But through what fearful pangs earth peels away
This withering flesh from off the worthier soul !
The scales about my own grow thin, how thin !
Pauline and Haydn gone, and home, and hope,—
What further shred invests the love so stript !—

Is this, then, being freed from earth ?—Yet where
Are signs of heaven ?—My God, I see them not."

"O father, rave not thus," I cried.   "O if—
If Haydn,—if I had some power with him."—

"Nay, daughter, nay," he said.   Yet o'er his face
Flush'd hope like hues at dawn.   I kiss'd his
    brow,
Said, "Father, I will try," and went my way.

XLVIII.

And Haydn then, when found, appear'd so sad.
"Ah," sigh'd he, "we two souls were fitted so
To match each other.   Here, where jars the world,
And all goes contrary, where every sun
That ripes this, withers that ; and every storm
That brings refreshment here, sends deluge there,
We two, exceptions to the general rule,
Like living miracles (is love fulfill'd
A miracle indeed ?), seem'd born to draw
The self-same tale of weal or woe from each.
I saw but last night, darling, in my dreams,
Our spirits journeying through this under gloom :
And hand in hand they walk'd ; and over them,
As over limner'd seraphs, did there hang
A halo, love reflected.   By its glow

The gloom about grew brightness : while far off,
In clearest lines, the path passed up and on.—
Pauline, but heed me : once again, I pray
(If ever once I pray'd to God above),
Blot not this light from all my future life."

XLIX.

" Ah, Haydn," said I, "would you have me change?
What soul shall dwell on God's most holy hill
But he 'that sweareth to his own hurt,' yes,
' And changeth not '?"

    " But yet," he said, "but yet
If you were wrong to swear ? How can it be
That any project so against the soul—
Each instinct of one's nature—should be right ? "

" Yet nature," said I, "may be but corrupt.
What is this instinct, that it should not lie ?
If one should feel the instinct of the lamb
While skipping to welcome the butcher's knife
That waits to slaughter it, would he be wise
To follow instinct ?"

    " Why not ? " answer'd he :
" The lamb was made that it might die for man :
It follows instinct and dies easily.
The soul was made that it might live for God :
It follows instinct and lives happily.

The cases differ thus.   May there not be
Some depth, beyond the reach of mortal sight,
Within whose grooves unseen our spirits glide
Unconscious of the balancings of will?
God's touch may be too subtle to be sensed.
May it not stir beneath all conscious powers,
A spontaneity that moves the soul
As instinct moves the body?—Ah, to me,
Love seems an instinct that impels them both."

"How so?" I ask'd, in hope to guide his thought
Toward sacrifice.

     "You wish me then," he said,
"To turn philosopher for you?—I will.
This love, in morals based on faith in man,
And in religion on our faith in God,
Seems, in its essence, an experience
Not wholly feeling, yet not wholly thought,—
Not all of body, yet not all of soul,
Of what we are or what we are to be,—
But more akin to marriage, within self,
Of our two separate natures, form and spirit.
God meant them to be join'd: when wedded thus,
One rests content, the other waits in hope."

"To rest, to wait," I said to this; "and if
Such ends displaced were, would there not remain
The work that forms our earthly heritage?"

"And may not God," rejoin'd he, "grant us
 more
Than that which we inherit?"
        "He may grant
His rest," I said. "Yet rest, the Paradise
Of work, is yet the Purgatory, too,
Of indolence."
     "The soul's true Paradise
Is nothing earn'd," he said. "It is a gift.
With Eden lost, insolvent made by sin,
Work, as I view it, is a loan from Hope
With which man pays the debt of Memory.
But if I reckon right, a pauper still,
He scarce can earn enough to pay them both.
And so our rest, I take it, is a gift
That crowns our strife, yet is not won by it;
Which, as we live not conscious how 't is earn'd,
We live not conscious how it may be lost.
Things out of consciousness are out of care.
We rest not as in death that furthers naught;
We rest as in a dream, in sleep,—a state
Wherein God watches while the soul regales.
We rest not from the healthful stir of work,
But from the slavery proportioning
Our pleasure to our pain—a law for serfs,
But not for sons. Our rest is peaceful, hush'd,
The very church of choice, as different
From other joy as prayer may be from sport."

"And does not choice," I ask'd, "feel often moved
To spurn a lesser for a greater good?
For greater good, too, may not Love on high
Unseat some idol of our ignorance?"—

L.

With this, I pictured for him brightest life;
And, like a blot on every scene, myself;
I claim'd my character was not the one
That best could aid his own; show'd how my sire,
The priest, Doretta, all agreed in this.
And then, in contrast with myself, I sketch'd
A nature all deem'd fitted for his moods.
I may have sinn'd in it; but, grim as fate,
My father's face, recall'd, would urge me on:
I noted all Doretta's nobler traits;
And when I thought he must my aim surmise,
And while he held his gaze upon the floor,
As though he gave assent, at last I spake
Doretta's name.
     And if the solid earth
Had quaked, he had not started more. O God,
Why did I not accept his instinct then!
He look'd at me, first pale, then flush'd, then firm;
And then with tremulous, painful breath, he
  said:—
"And this device from you? from you, so pure?

So free from guile ? You should have spared me
    this.
That Jesuit has train'd you well ! Ah, now,
I know how Adam grieved that Eve could fall ;
How Eve herself, when round her soul first crept
The serpent's cautious coils of smooth deceit,
To strap her inch by inch ! I read it now,
That tale : 't is all an allegory, ay ;—
That serpent means the world. The world steals
    round,
Intent to seize and own each heir of heaven.
Not long are souls allow'd ideal life,
Not long unfetter'd sense or hearts unbound :
Our smiles grow stiffer, till, some fatal day,
The last is clutch'd and held, a hideous grin.
Then, when the body stirs not with the soul,
The last nerve wrested from the Spirit's rule,
Naught in us left of love, the world unwinds :
Our capturer dissolves in mist or dust :—
And we, for its embrace, have lost our God !"

LI.

His mood alarm'd me, yet could I protest :
"Nay, Haydn, nay ! I do not love the world :
I long to leave it ; yes, all thought of it."
"How much less worldliness is found," he ask'd,
"Within the Church than in your world so call'd ?—

The Prince of this World is not nice in choice
Of equipages ; where he cannot check,
He mounts the car of truth and grasps the rein ;
And when the Devil drives, he drives for home.
'The world,' what means this, but the world
    alone,—
The mass, devoid of mind, truth, spirit, love ?—
But holds no church the same?—A mass?—ay, ay.
Devoid of mind ?—Why not ?—But show the place
It crowds not reason out to edge in faith.—
But 'faith,' say you, 'is reasonable ' ?—Ay,
When in it there is reason ; when the thing
In which it trusts is truth.   But ah! too oft
Just prick the forms, and back of them you find—
What ?—truth ?—nay, nay, a priest—a man, for-
    sooth,
Who differs from the rest of men in clothes,
In wearing worn-out habits, which the need
And progress of our times have cast aside ;—
Ay, wearing them o'er body, mind, and soul ;
Though all who think know well that moods,
    whose range
Is girt by customs past, (which could alone
Prejudge thought's present range) fit prejudice ;
And this is in behind your Church's forms.

"You say, perhaps, 'the Spirit formed the forms
To fit the life ' ?—they fitted life that was ;

But life, if life, will grow ; the life of love
Has not yet fill'd the scope around, above,
Of heavens that for it wait. What form'd the
    forms
Can still be forming them.—If forms exist
Wherein no Spirit works, no present life,—
The things are hollow ; and a hollow form
The Devil flies for, like a flying squirrel
For hollow tree-trunks ; and when once within,
But half disguised inside his robes of white,
Loud chanting out mere ceremonious cant,
He tempts toward his hypocrisy an age
That knows too much of Christian life, at last,
For heathen life to tempt it.

                  " Judge by fruits :
Here you—God gave you beauty—to be seen !
And grace to bless this dear, sweet home. What
    power
Would snatch you from us ? make a very hell
Of what might else be heaven ?—Think you 't is
    love ?
Not so ; it only hates love ; plays the part—
Not of the Christ who yielded up his life,
But of the world that made him yield it up ;
It only trusts in force, in force that lies ;
And now that it can hold you with a vow
Which but deceit could claim that God enjoin'd,
It seizes you to plunge you down, down, down,

To feel the full damnation of a faith
That can believe the voice within the soul
A lying guide which cannot be obey'd
Without foul consciousness of inward sin,—
To plunge you down, and hold you till the cells
Of your pure, guileless heart, all stain'd and
    steep'd,
Drip only dregs of stagnant viciousness!"

LII.

"You terrify me, Haydn!" I exclaim'd.
"And you have done far more to me!" he cried.
"You were—Ah me, what were you not?—so pure,
Transparent as the mid-day atmosphere.
Should some red thunderbolt from sunlight burst
And burn all torturing blindness through my eyes,
The night came less foretoken'd! I, who dream'd
That here I gazed on truth, here bent these knees
Upon the very battlements of heaven,—
I to be tript thus from my dear proud trust,
Sent reeling down by such foul-aim'd deceit!—
Strange is it if my jolted brain should slip
The grooves of reason?—if I rave or curse?—
You, who had known my heart, and after that,
And after I had warn'd you of the thing,
And simulating all the while such love,—
You, vowing to abjure me! more than this,

To-day with such cold-blooded, soulless tact,
Soft-stealing, through the door-ways left ajar,
Within the inmost chambers of my heart,
To snare,—as though the victim of a cat
That could be play'd with, trick'd with, kill'd, cast
    off,—
This heart of mine which, as you might have
    known,
Was throbbing but to serve you !—Yes, once more,
You gain your end ! Once more, your wish is
    mine.
How can I love ?—God help me !—Go you free."

LIII.

How fiercely then did Haydn's music storm !
And soon he would have left our home in haste :
My father spoke to stay him. Long they spoke ;
And sometimes wrathful were the words they
    used.
But then, at last, my father told him all,—
Why I had vow'd, that I his life might save,
And he broke down before it.
                  Never more
May God permit me to behold again
A broken man ! Alas, how pleaded he !
And pray'd me for my pardon o'er and o'er,
Till wellnigh I believed he heard me not ;

And in the end sigh'd out : " It might be so,
My plan be wisest ; nay, he would not yield
His manlier judgment, to fulfil my wish,
To make me happy, or my sire or me :—
Doretta surely was a housewife wise :
It seem'd the older custom, thus to wed :
He young had been, had whims.—God bless us all."

LIV.

Oft, after that, I urged him ne'er to wed
One whom he could not love.   He only sigh'd :
" This heart of mine that once loved you, Pauline,
How could it love again with love as true ?
Yet what, if not ?   My soul was immature,
Romantic, young.   It must be manly now.
A man has breadth.   I take it manly love
Is love that yields most blessings to the most.
And mine shall bless yourself, your father, her."—
And so he calm'd my doubt and cheer'd me much.

LV.

And oft I spoke with him about the Church.
" Can I forget its holding you ? " he ask'd.

" Ah, Haydn," said I, " I remember once
When young you were, when music scarce had lured
Your soul, so thrill'd ! to test its energies :
Then Gluck your master was ; you follow'd him,

And far beyond your own, as then you deem'd,
Flowed forth the full perfection of his chords.
Now men see Gluck behind you. Yet, e'en now,
Before you still, sweet chords allure you on.
Ah, friend, Gluck only happen'd in the path
That open'd then beyond you. But those chords?—
Those you can reach not, Haydn, till you reach
The choirs of heaven !

        "And thus, at times, I think
That I too may have happen'd in your path ;
And this, your love, now looking toward myself,
May gaze, when I am gone, on holier things,
Ideal all."

        " When you—alas," he sigh'd,
" When you are gone, then life will all become—
I fear it much—one lonely wail for you."

"And yet a lonely wail, breathed forth," I said,
" From one with spirit sweeten'd, sweet may seem
To earth that hears it."

        " Ah, I take the thought,
You mean my music," answer'd he. " O God,
To save one's art must love be sacrificed?—
Redeem'd at that price, art would be too dear ! "

LVI.

One thing he promis'd me. I urged it much.
" In secret convent-prayers," I said to him,

"My soul must know if it should praise or plead.
A year from now, we two must meet once more.
We cannot talk, and yet we may commune
While I stand silent at the cloister bars.
Then if your wedded life afford you joy—
I doubt it not, — bring with you fresh-pluck'd
  flowers ;
If else than this, bring but the wilted stems
Of these I give you now."

      Then soon had pass'd
The last vague hours that saw me part from all.
I stood before the shrine. I feel it yet :—
The organ moaning sweetly far away ;
The people whispering low amid the aisles ;
My heart so loud, nor hush'd in sermon-time ;
The multitude with wide eyes fix'd on me ;
Doretta, and my father, still and sad ;
And Haydn's face upon his pale, pale hands.

LVII.

And two months after that I saw them wed,
My Haydn and Doretta, in the church.
And, since then, I have pray'd for him long days,
And longer nights ; and I have oft had hopes
That my faint life new strength would gain from
  God.
But now so white, so thin, my body seems,

With scarce enough of substance left in it
To be a ghost ;—ah, what if, like a ghost,
It soon should vanish ?

                  So I thought, to-night,
If I could tell you this, confess my fault,
Unload my heart of all her sweet, sad love,
That God might give me rest.   I did not, nay,
I did not mean it, to excite myself.
They told me it might bring my death ; but oh !
Have I not borne enough to merit life ?
How had I counted all these weeks and days,
Up to the hour we two should meet again,
And I should find how all my prayers were heard,
And heaven had made my Haydn blest !—

                            He came,
Last week : and what, what, think you, can it
    mean ?—
He brought the wilted stems.—

                        I do not know.
I only know that I can earn no rest :
And all our household so much else have earn'd.
And now how can I?—I can try no more;
But all my pathway has been block'd for me.
They say such words are infidelity,—
O Christ!—yet I can try no more.

                      Hark ! hark !—
Is not that Haydn's hymn we hear again ?—
How faint it sounds !—or I, I faint may be.

The window—move me.　There—look out—those
　　clouds—
The sunset ?—Ah, what comes on earth so bright,
So beautiful as clouds ?—There were no clouds
Where one could always look and see the heaven.
The music, hear it—hear how sweet !—Say, say,
Did I sing then ?—Not so ?—and only dream'd ?—
I thought that music mine, and then myself ;
And Haydn's heart, it beat here, beat in me,—
Ah me, so tired !—Yes, let me rest on you.
O God, for but one hour to live !—For what ?
Have I not loved then ?—Yes, and tell him so,
Tell Haydn ; thank him.—God, praise Him for it.
Life, life—I did not know it—has been sweet.—
Hark ! music !—Does it not come from above ?

SKETCHES IN SONG.

Third Edition, Revised.

Sketches in Song.

A FISH STORY

FOR THE LITTLE CRITICS.

A STRANGE fish came from an inland home
  On a journey down to the sea.
He split the ripples, and ript the foam,
  And danced and dived in glee.
"Ho, ho!" cried the fry where the sea grew near,
  "Hurrah for a fresh-water fool!
One gulp of our salt when he comes out here
  Will send him back to his pool."

The fish was fleet, but the bar was high,
  And the low tide roil'd and dim;
And he groped, as he slowly pass'd the fry,
  And to and fro would swim.
"Ho, ho!" cried they, as they shook their scales,
  "The muddled one misses his way!"
And they fann'd their fins, and slash'd their tails—
  "Aha, he here will stay!"

The fish paused not till the way grew clear;
    Then launch'd out under the spray;
And shower'd his fins in a white-cap near
    That rivall'd the rays of the day.
" Ho, ho, showing off to the sharks ! " cried the fry;
    " And look—a gull on the shoal.
Yon surface-shiner would better be shy;
    The bird will swallow him whole."

The fish pass'd on, till the sea grew deep,
    Then, plunging down through the blue,
A flash came back from a parting leap,
    As at last he sank from view.
" Ho, ho," cried the fry, " we can all do that,
    If we only go out with the tide."
But the tide had gone, so, left on the flat,
    They fried in the sun, and died.

UNVEILING THE MONUMENT.

I.

THE monument stands, no longer the care
        Of mallet and chisel and plummet and
            square.
With a flourish of trumpets and rolling of drums
        The glad hour comes

When the statue above it will loom unveil'd.
  Lo, now the crowds that are under it sway;
  The bugles are sounding; and look!—away
The veil is dropt!—and afar is hail'd,
With wild huzzas and hands that fly,
The form of the man that stands on high.

II.

  How the crowd are cheering! but, ah, their
       cheer
    Recalls a day
    When few were here;
And the most of them daintily shrank away,
  Afraid a foot or a frill to smear
In the mire of this place, while deep in the clay
  The soil was dug for the monument here.

III.

And was there not, when his course began,
  While clearing the ground for the life he had
       plann'd,
A time this crowd would have shrunk from the man
  Whose image is now enthroned by the land?
Alas, how oft in youth's chill morn
Their tears alone are the dews that adorn
    The natures that wake
To the light of a day beginning to break!

And oft how long, ere the light will burst,
The mists of the valley surround them first!
And oh, how many and many a tomb
Of a dead hope, buried and left in gloom,
Must mark the path of the man whose need
Is taught through failure how to succeed!
And oft how long, ere he knows of this,
  Will hard work doom
His heart that in sympathy seeks for bliss
To a life as lone as death in a tomb,
  Where sweetness and light
  Are all shut out,
  Nor a flower nor a bird
  Is heeded or heard,
Nor often, if ever, there comes a sight
Of a friend who cares what he cares about,
  Or is willing to soil
A finger with even a touch of his toil!
For our race are too ready to turn with a sneer
From arms that are brawny, and hands that smear.
While a man is dependent, in need of a friend,
 The world is a snob, and shuns its own peer.
When a man is a master, his need at an end,
 The world is a sycophant, cringing to cheer.
Cheer on, wise world, but, oh! forget not,
Whatever encouragement each man got
When in gloom and doubt his course began,
But little he heard from the lips of man.

IV.

But the monument knew a different day,
    When masons with mortar and mallet
        wrought here
The firm and deep foundation to lay.
Still few would turn from the well-trod way
To climb the mounds of marble and clay
    Which hid the work ; or, if some drew near,
They only came with a stare of surprise,
Or a shrug or sigh for its form or size.

V.

That man, too, now on the monument resting,—
    How long and hard life's basis to lay,
Strove he, while about him was nothing suggesting
    The meed that the present is proud to pay !
When all sailing is over, the shouts of a state
That hail a Columbus may name him great.
Before it is over, that isle of the west,
        The goal of his quest,
Is merely, for most, the point of a jest.
Nor a few, the while he turns to his mission,
Will deem him moved by a mean ambition.
Ay, often indeed, the nobler the claims
        Inspiring his aims,
        The more earth deems
        They are selfish schemes
Of a Joseph it hates for having strange dreams.

Alas, where hate
  Is a normal state,
Who serves the world with a love that is great
Is rated a foe by those who refuse it,
Nor always a friend by those who use it;
For he, forsooth, he knew of their need
In the day they knew not how to succeed !—
And thus this man in the marble wrought on,
  Life's fruit fell off, and the fall frost froze,
And the winter of life came, weary and wan,
  Ere words to welcome his worth arose.
Wise world, the one who is now your boast
Heard few of your cheers, when needing them most :
The pride of his youth in his life or its plan,
It came not then from the praise of man.

VI.

But the monument grew, anon to display
  Above its foundation,
Those fair white sides that rose to their station,
All cunningly wrought into tablet and column.
Then children, and others, as childlike as they,
Would delight in its beauty ; but, doubtful and
    solemn,
The wise were all wary. "A man cannot
    rate
A work till complete," said they, "so we must
    wait."

VII.

And thus the man grew,
And thus did a few
Find, thoughtfully plann'd for the wants they di-
vined,
His work that is now the pride of his kind.
Who prized it at first ?—
Ah, those little verst
In the codes that are current turn first from them all
To the herald that comes to trump a new call.
Those nearest their youth
Live nearest the breasts that glow with the truth,
And welcome it gratefully warm from the heart.
Earth's elders and sages,
Far off from the place where the springs all start,
Scarce ever can prize
A stream that supplies
A draft less far from its font than their age is.
No deeds can course from as grand a source
As the life of which they in their youth form'd a
part.
Naught sparkles as bright
To them as the light
Of an old, cold, frozen, and crystallized art.
But, ah, if you ask them what was true
When the words or the ways of their art were new,
If you ask them what were the traits it would show
Ere the form now frozen no longer could flow,

Or how it differ'd in nature from those
That spring in the present, when first it rose,—
All this their critic cares not to know.
He is nothing if not the dog of his day,
  Who barks or who licks
As his master, the world, may make him obey
By throwing him bones or swinging him kicks.
Pray, what can he know till all the world know it !
  If currents in view
  Are to crystallize too
Like things of the past, the winter will show it.
  The future must rate
The fruit of the present : so shrewd men wait,
  And but of the dead
  Are their eulogies read.—
Good souls, they never will let one rest
Until he is borne to the land of the blest !
  No heart is aglow
With the burning zeal of a holiest mission,
But makes them fearful of heat below,
And tremble in dread of a fiend's apparition.
For Satan has toils that, no matter whether
Come evil or good, trap all men together.
  Whenever one spies
  Light coming, he cries
"'T is naught but a will-o-the wisp to the wise."
Half trust him, and half, not duped by his lies,
Begin to dispute them ; and then, at the quarrel,
The seer of the light has thorns for his laurel.

Ay, rare, indeed, in that day is his fate,
If the eye of the prophet—so noble a trait—
Escape from censure and gibe and hate.
For an eye like his will a goal pursue
So far in advance of his time and its view,
That only the march of an age, forsooth,
Can o'ertake the vision he sees in his youth.
But, oh ! in that age, when it comes, the earth
Will live in his light and know of his worth.
And many and many will be the men
   Who move on then,
   And about them find
The scenes that he in his day divined,
Who, sure of his presence, will know he is nigh,
And feel he is leading, and never can die.
This man of the monument lived like that.
Men cheer him now ; but of old they sat
In judgment against him ; while, far away
From the place where they had chosen to stay,
He push'd for the light ; and grew old and hoar
Ere one whom he knew had begun to explore,
Or seek what he sought.   Alone in the van,
He had fail'd of aid had he thought it in man.

VIII.

Yet now are justice and judgment one.
That statue glows in the gleam of the sun,
Amid drumming and trumpeting, chorus and
  song,

The praise of the speaker, the shout of the
    throng,
Throned white o'er the waving of plumes and
    of flags
That surge to its base as a sea to her crags.
Now cheer we the monument, capp'd and
    clear'd,
So cheer we the man for whom it is rear'd.

IX.

What ? cheer we the man ?
    No doubt, in youth
There were times when the joy in his heart overran
At a smile from one who knew him in truth ;
There were times, years later, when merely a tear
    From a grateful eye
    Would have seem'd more dear
Than all the glitter that gold could buy ;
But, alas ! in age, when character stands
As fix'd as yon monument, then it demands,
Ere aught can move it, far more, far more
Than the cheer or the sigh that had stirr'd it of
    yore.
Not oft, nor till ages of suns and storms
Have wrought with the verdure in earthly forms,
Are these turn'd into stone, no more to decay.
    But often on earth
    The owners of worth

That men image in marble grow stony, that way.
Ah, man, whom in hardship you might make a
    friend
And turn from—beware, beware in the end,
Lest he whom you harden grow hard unto you.
  O world, when ready your hero to cheer,
How heeds he your welcome? say, what does
    he do?
  His eye, does it see? his ear, does it hear?
His heart, does it throb? his pulse, does it thrill?
Or his touch, is it cold? his clasp, is it chill?—
O world, you have waited long; what have you
    done?
O man, you have wrought so long; what have you
    won?—

X.

    That monument there,
      So high, so fair,
  That throne of light for the man who led,
  Is only a tomb.   They are cheering the dead.

XI.

  And he himself—did he know it all?
      Had he look'd, in his youth,
Past the shadows of form to the substance of truth?
Had he learn'd that all life turns to seasons, and
    shifts
  From winter and spring into summer and fall?

Or divined that eternity, balancing gifts,
Grants honor like heaven, a state after strife,
And a glorified name to a sacrificed life ?
Did he know that sighs, when yearning for love,
Best open the soul to breathe in from above
The air immortal, and make it worth while
   That art should chisel in marble clear
The lines divine that temper a smile
   Beyond the sway of a mortal's cheer ?—
Did he know it or not, perchance for his good
His work was lonely and misunderstood.
Perchance it was well, the best for the soul,
Its nature, its nurture, that aught to control
The aims inspiring his life or its plan
Had gain'd but little from earth or man.

UNDER THE NEW MOON.

THE hills rang back our parting jest ;
   The dear, dear day was over ;
The sun had sunk below the west ;
   We walk'd home through the clover.
Our words were gay, but thought astray
   Our parting kept regretting,—
" The old old way ! " would seem to say ;
   " The suns are ever setting."
Then, gazing back with longing soon,
   At once my step grew bolder ;

For, bright and new, I spied the moon
   Just over my right shoulder.

I turn'd about and bade her look ;
   We were not superstitious ;
We jok'd about that shining hook,
   Bright bait, and skies auspicious.
We joked, but, oh, I thought with woe,
   "This bright bait lures me only,—
Like more before it, comes to go,
   And leave life dark and lonely.
Past yon horizon, things are strewn
   With broken moons," I told her :
" Each bore a bright hope, too, each moon,
   When over my right shoulder.

" Alas to trust in each new light,
   A man were moonstruck, surely,—
A lunatic ! "—We laugh'd outright,
   And then look'd back demurely.
Lo, dimly shown, the moon's old zone
   Made full hope's crescent new one.
I thought, " Would my old love, made known,
   Prove hope of love a true one ?
What would she say ? "—I ask'd her soon,
   And took her hand to hold her.
" Ah, love," she sigh'd, " to-night the moon
   Is over my right shoulder."

ALL IN ALL.

BE calm, O Wind, and gently blow,
   Nor rouse the waves' commotion.
Ye Clouds, veil not the bay so low :
   My love sails o'er the ocean.

Out, boatman, out !   The wind will rise ;
   The yawl will find it stormy.
Ay, thrice thy fee.—Her signal flies.—
   My love is waiting for me.

Blow on, ye Winds, your prey is flown ,
   Who cares for wave or weather ?
My love, my own ! no more alone,
   We walk the shore together.

NOTHING AT ALL.

SO many eyes that dim tears fill,
   That a glance of love could clear ;
So many ears, all sad and still,
   That a sigh of love could cheer ;

So many hearts that are beating to greet
   Love that will heed no sign ;
So many lips that are parting to meet
   Love that is air, like mine ;—

Dykes that fashion has bank'd so fast,
　　Burst from our souls apart !
Burst ! and let the truth flow past,
　　Filling each unfill'd heart.

———

THE IDEALIST.

I HEAR fair Fancy call'd a guide
　　Who smiles when one is youthful,
But oft in sudden shades will hide,
　　And prove at times untruthful.
　　　"When through the skies,"
　　　They say "she flies
And leaves behind each earthly care ;
When round about her in the air
　　No danger seems attending
　　The light we find her wending,
Beware ! amid the brightest air
The storm may burst, the lightning tear,
　　　Beware and fear !
　　　With earth so near
None can be free from care."

I hear fair Fancy call'd a guide
　　Of rarest grace and beauty ;
But prone to lead the soul aside

From irksome paths of duty.
   " Man is but man :
   He cannot scan
Too high delights, and highly rate
The lowly joys of earth's estate.
   A soul to fancy turning,"
   They say, " is fill'd with yearning ;
And lives in dreams and idle schemes,
That with their lure of rival gleams
     Make dim the light
     About the sight
The working soul esteems."

I hear fair **Fancy** call'd a guide
   Oft rendering life distressful,
With views that loom too high, too wide,
   To make a man successful.
     They say, "We err
     Who soar with her.
Earth only shoos or shoots a bird ;
To draw its wealth, it yokes the herd.—
   But few are those not tiring
   Of natures too aspiring.
The common leaders of the day
Amid the common people stay,
     Who but confide
     In those that guide
Along the common way."

And yet my dear and dangerous guide,
 I prize thy peerless beauty.
I chose thee long ago my bride
 For love and not for booty.
  How much is wrought
  By risking naught?
When I behold a path of bliss,
Tho' bordering on the worst abyss,
 My fears of falling under
 Will not restrain my wonder.
And, from what thou hast found for me,
Full many a truth my soul can see
  That earth must know
  Ere it forego
Its need of knowing thee.

A PHASE OF THE ANGELIC.

I WONDER not that artists' hands,
 Inspired by themes of joy
To picture forms of angel-bands,
 Paint, first of all, the boy.

I know if I were set the task
 To lure a man's desire
By traits the heavenliest one could ask,
 When most our souls aspire,

I would not take a blushing bride,
    For she may wed for pelf ;
Nor him who stands the bride beside,
    He may but love himself ;

Nor matron, with her thoughts confined
    To maxims meant for youth ;
Nor man mature : too oft his mind
    Will close to others' truth.

But I would blend the purity
    Of her whom I adore
With manly power for mastery
    And promise yet in store.

So I would take the boy who roams
    Toward life, half understood,
From thresholds of those holy homes
    That face alone the good ;—

A boy who has not reach'd the brink
    Where vice will cross his track,
Whose wish that loathes the wish to drink
    Still keeps the tempter back ;—

A boy who hardly knows of ill,
    Or ill can apprehend,
With cheeks that blush, with eyes that fill,
    And faith that fears no end.

And oh, I know that those who love
  The purest part of joy,
Would choose with me from all above
  The heaven that held my boy.

———

THE BELLE.

A SMILE—could it be meant for me?—
  Yet there she stood before me.
But she had charm'd so many eyes
And I was neither rich nor wise,—
The belle of all the county, she :
      I seem'd a child,
      She only smiled
Because she knew her mien was mild,
  While mine confusion bore me.

And praise—could it be meant for me?—
  Ah, how could I suppose it ?
The rarest minds I knew about
Had held her gauge of them in doubt.
A prize past all I hoped for, she ;
      But young was I ;
      And this was why
She thought my pride to gratify ;
  Yet I could but disclose it.

A blush—could it be meant for me?—
   Yet so she met no other.
A face that all with joy would meet,
   Could it have blush'd my own to greet?
A belle whom all had sought for, she;
     Yet I could see
     Heave but for me
A sigh that strove and would be free.
   I spoke to free another.

She answer'd—All was meant for me
   Whom rivals off were shoving;
And all my love had burst in flame
   To feel her ardor while it came.
" A woman, whosoe'er she be,
     Is nothing more,
     O loved of yore,
Than just a woman, nothing o'er,
   And can but love the loving."

THE POET'S REASON.

I LIVE to write; and write, good friend.
   In part, I know, for you;
Though, while I do so, in the end
   Myself it pleases too.

"The world," you think, "may prize my rhymes."
　Of old, I hoped it would.
But many and many have been the times
　I only deem'd them good !

I "love to write"?　You near the truth.
　I love to talk, as well ;
And poems breathe a part, forsooth,
　Of what the soul would tell.—

Ay, ay, the soul.　For it how meet
　That those we love should see—
Not poems—but the poem sweet
　That all one's life would be !

AMONG THE MOUNTAINS.

MY mountains, how I love your forms that
　　stand
So beautiful, so bleak, so grim, so grand.
Your gleaming crags above my boyhood's play,
Undimm'd as hope, rose o'er each rising day.
When now light hope has yielded place to care,
O'er steadfast work I see you steadfast there.
And when old age at last shall yearn for rest,
By your white peaks will each aspiring glance be
　　blest.

How bright and broad with ever fresh surprise,
The scenes ye brought allured my youthful eyes!
Now, when rude hands those views of old assail,
When growing towns have changed the lower vale,
When other friends are lost or sadly strange,
Ye stand familiar still, ye do not change.
And when all else abides as now no more,
In you I still may see the forms I loved of yore.

Ye mounts deserve long life. Your peaks at dawn
Catch light no sooner from the night withdrawn,
Than those ye rear see truth, when brave men vow
To serve the serf, and bid the despot bow.
In vales below, if tyrants make men mild,
The weak who scale your sides learn winds are wild,
That beasts break loose, and birds awaken'd flee,
As if in deepest sleep they dream'd of being free.

High homes of manhood, human lips can phrase
No tribute fit to echo half your praise.
By Piedmont's church and Ziska's rock-wall'd
see,
By Swiss and Scot who left their children free,
By our New England, when she named him knave
Who, flank'd by bloodhounds, chased his fleeing
slave,
Stand ye like them, whose memories, ever grand,
Tower far above earth's lords, as ye above its land.

Ay, stand like monuments in lasting stone
To souls as lofty as the world has known.
Ye fitly symbol, when with kindling light
The dawn and sunset gild your summits white,
The glories of their pure, aspiring worth
Who aim'd at stars to feed the hopes of earth ;
And fitly point where they, in brighter skies,
View grander scenes than yours where your heights
    cannot rise.

MARTIN CRAEGIN.[1]

UP, thou Warden gray of Honor,
    Swing thy temple's rusted door ;
Hither from the mine of Pittston,
    Hies, at last, one hero more.

*   *   *   *   *   *

[1] " Martin Cooney," [I have found, upon making inquiry at Pittston, that the boy's name was Craegin, not Cooney] " is the name of the boy who, deep down in the horrid depths of the Pittston mine, performed a deed of heroic self-sacrifice which shames into insignificance the actions by which many happier men have climbed to fame and honor. Cooney and a companion stood at the bottom of the shaft as the car was about to ascend for the last time. High above them roaring flame and blinding smoke amid the crash of falling timber were fast closing up the narrow way to light and life ; below them in the gloomy pit were a score of men working on, unconscious of their deadly peril. Cooney, with one foot upon the car, thought of his endangered friends. He proposed to his companion that they should return and warn the miners of their threatened fate. His companion refused to go, and then Cooney, without a moment's hesitation, but with full consciousness that he had chosen almost certain death, leaped from the car and groped his way back through the growing darkness. It was too late ; the miners had closed the ventilating door before he reached them ; and standing there between the immovable barrier and the shaft, the hot breath of the fiery pit poured in upon him in a pitiless blast, and so he died."—*Philadelphia Evening Bulletin*, June 5, 1871.

While he toil'd amid the miners,
    Came a cry that startled him ;
" Fire !" he heard, and o'er him quickly,
    Saw the smoking shaft grow dim.

" Now for life !" a comrade shouted,
    " Mount this car ! no more cars go ! "
" Nay for life," replied young Martin,
    " Call the men at work below ! "

Cried the first : " No time to tarry !
    Look !—The flames !—We must not stay ! "
" Time for them to close the smoke out ! "
    Martin cried, and rush'd away.

" Fire ! fire ! fire !" he shouted shrilly,
    Groping down the passage dim.
" Fire !" those heard, and closed the passage,
    Closed it on the smoke and him.

" Stop the smoke !" cried men above him.—
    Still the ghastly fumes crept on ;
Caught the boy, and, crawling round him,
    Choked his corpse they clung upon.

" Woe on woe !" cried those above him,
    " All will die ; the fires descend ! "

By the coal-pit, by the coal-boy,
  Never light like that was kenn'd.

Whence, O whence that blinding brightness?
  What had touch'd the boy afar?—
For the chariot of Elijah
  Had he spurn'd his comrade's car?

"Stop the fire!" cried all the village,—
  Ah, but none could now keep down
Martin's love, there marshal'd heavenward,
  Haloed by a martyr's crown.

Not the flood that men set flowing
  Faster than the fire could spread,
Now could quench the flame eternal
  Burning in the soul that sped.

Not the cloud of smoke that gather'd,
  Not the dark, sad funeral pall,
Now could dim the boy's devotion,
  With its glory gilding all.

      *   *   *   *   *

Up, thou Warden gray of Honor,
  Wheels immortal sweep the sky,
Swing thy gates!—another hero
  Love incites to do and die.

OF SUCH IS THE KINGDOM.

WHAT has a child that a man has not,
　　When "of such is the kingdom" on high?
At play in the home, at work in the school,
Oh, what does he care for the soul, or its rule,
　　Or for aught that hints of the sky?
Ay, what does he serve but his own desires,
Impell'd by a fancy that toils or tires?
His moods flow on like currents in brooks,
Or ruffled or smooth, to answer the crooks.
All things that are sweet or fair to see
He buzzes and bustles about like a bee.
He would work his arms at ball and bow,
Though he never had known it would make them
　　　grow.—
What virtue is his?—While a man can doubt
The truth within him, nor show it without,
The child holds fast, unfetter'd by lies,
A faith that he never has dared to despise,
Expression that knowns no other control
Than that of the Maker who moves the soul,
A beauty of wisdom that works to obey
A holy, because a natural way;
　　And that may he have that a man may not.

　　What has a man that a child has not,
　　　When "of such is the kingdom" on high?

Oh, he has been train'd by the **world and the**
    school
To curb his character in by rule
  Till the rule of his life is a lie.
A man like that would spurn to find
In God's designs the quest of his mind.
He crams and drams for an appetite
That nothing on earth can sate or excite.
His words are as dry as the words of a book,—
Your sentence is ready, wherever you look.
His views—he never saw any thing strange:
If he did, some fellow might question his range.
And all of profit he tests by pelf,
And all of manhood measures by self,
Forgets that God rules the world he is at,
And stars himself as its autocrat.
Alas for reason with such a judge!
If ever you whisper or smile or budge—
You may study and ponder and prove and pray—
But he has a sneering, cynical way;
    And that may he have that a child has not.

  What has a man that a child has too,
    When "of such is the kingdom" on high?
He knows that life is better'd by rules,
But he knows how split the wise and the fools
    When judging of rules they apply.
He feels that life worth living proceeds

From nature that prompts the bent of deeds;
And he lets the reins of his being go,
Whenever the soul moves upward so.
If he look to God through self or His Book,
Or leading the way through a bishop's crook,
He welcomes whatever has worth in the new,
Though it grew outside of his Timbuctoo.
For modest he is, and loves to find
Earth blest by minds that differ in kind.
In short, to the simple, the frail, and the few
He is fill'd with charity through and through;
And, waiving your reason its right of control,
Trusts God for enough truth left in your soul;
And though he may tell you he doubts your way,
He has much to love in spite of his "nay";
    And that may a man and a child have too.

MY LOVE IS SAD.

M Y love is "fill'd with gloom," you say;
        Yet think! when I had spied her,
The flowers that made her bower so gay
        Had lost their light beside her.
Ah, could my darling see it so,
And gloomy seem?   No, no; no, no.

My love is weary, wandering;
        Yet I, who sped to find her

With worlds of fancies on the wing,
   Saw all fall far behind her.
Ah, could my darling see it so,
And weary seem ?   No, no ; no, no.

My love is lone and weeps, I see ;
   Yet here I wait to win her,
For what is all the world to me,
   My arms are clasping in her.
Ah, could my darling see it so,
And lonely seem ?   No, no ; no, no.

MY DREAM AT CORDOVA.

I.

NIGHT bade me rest.   I left the street,
   Its faces fair and banter sweet ;
And oh, how human seem'd the town
Beside which I had laid me down !
But, ere I slept, the rising moon,
From skies as blue as if 't were noon,
Pour'd forth her light in silvery streams,
Eclipsing all my light of dreams.
And soon, as if some power would shake
My drowsy eyes, and make them wake,
The walls were spray'd with showers of **light,**
Whose flickerings left a fountain bright

That toss'd the moonbeams in its play,
And dash'd and flash'd their gleams away.
I just could see the fountain flow
Within a marble court[1] below.
It seem'd a spirit, clothed in white,
But half reveal'd to mortal sight,
Whose glancing robes would lift and glide
O'er dainty limbs that danced inside,
And touched the ground with throbbing sweet
As if the tread of fairy feet;
While round about the fount-sent shower,
That strung with pearls each grateful flower,
Rare fragrance rose from bush and bower.

II.

Ere long across the marble court
Soft laughter rang and calls of sport,
And maidens pass'd the entering gate,
Whose voices rose in sweet debate,
So clear, so pure, they might have sprung
From moonlight, not from mortal tongue.
I lay there charm'd, my eyelids closed,
My limbs enchain'd; but, ere I dozed,
Gave one look more.   Alas for me!
The moon had moved, and made me see,

[1] "A thoroughly national hotel . . .   I look down from my window through marble colonnades . . . perfumed with the scent of . . . trees, which bend . . . over a richly sculptured fountain."—*Hare's Wanderings in Spain*, pp. 93, 94.

In dreamlike light where slept the day,
Vague forms that join'd those maids at play.
They linger'd there, half hid by trees
And sprawling cactus ; now at ease,
Now whirling off in shadowy sets
Where urged guitars [2] and castonets. [2]
Anon, this music rose and fell,
As if, because, all fill'd so well,
So laden down with sweets before,
The languid air could hold no more.
" Ah, how could it or I ? " I thought ;
" This land of lasting spring is fraught
With charms that pale by living truth
The brightest dreams that lured my youth."
Then, while the music heaved my breast,
The thought it cradled sank to rest.

III.

I slept and dreamt.   To you it seems
No censor, swung to souls in dreams
Before the mind's most holy shrine,
Rear'd there to memories most divine,
Could incense hold whose fumes could rise
And dim what bless'd my closing eyes.
You think my soul most surely thought
Of Cordova in dreams it brought.
You think that once again it calms

[2] Instruments found everywhere in Spain.

My mood to watch beneath the palms
The ancient river [2] freshly lave
Rome's ruined bridge [2] that naught could save.
You think, once more, my wonder wends
Across that orange-court [4] and bends
In that cathedral-mosk, [5] in which
A thousand [5] shafts with sculptures rich
Surround the soul like ghosts of trees
Beyond the touch of time or breeze,
While all the shafts to all bespeak,
In jasper, porphyry, verdantique,
The skill that train'd their artist's hand
In grand old times that blest this land
Before the Moor's glad suns had set
On days that earth can ne'er forget.
Nay, nay, I dreamt with joy intense,
But did not heed a hint from thence.

IV.

You think my spirit rose to flights,
Aspiring past all present sights,

[2] " The bridge over the Guadalquivir . . . composed of sixteen arches
. . . very picturesque . . . built by Octavius Cæsar."—*O'Shea's Guide to Spain.*
[4] " What spot can be more delightful than the grand old court, surrounded by flame-shaped battlements . . . beneath huge orange trees planted some three hundred years ago."—*Hare's Wanderings in Spain*, p. 88.
[5] " From the court you step with bewilderment into a roofed-in forest of pillars . . . amid the thousand still remaining columns of varied color, thickness, and material, which divide the building into twenty-nine naves one way and nineteen the other. Into the midst of all a cathedral was engrafted in 1547." (It was built originally for a mosk.)—*Idem*, p. 89.

Invoking from the grave of time
The heroes of that city's prime,—
The great Gonsalvo [6] marching on,
Or Ferdinand [7] of Aragon ?—
You think I saw, by camp-fires bright,
The turban bow beneath the sight
Of chieftains marshall'd, far and near,
With drifting plume and flashing spear,
Like cloud and lightning sent to sweep
Abdillah's [7] Moors across the deep ?—
You think I trod these lanes in days
When Califs vied to sound their praise,
And term'd the town that seem'd so blest
" The grander Bagdad of the west " [8] ;
Or trod them, when it gave the Goth
His " Home of holiness and troth " [8] ;
Or, long ere through its children's veins
Flow'd Roman [9] blood to richen Spain's,
Beheld it named by every mouth,
" The matchless gem of all the south " ? [8]—
Nay, nay, I dreamt with joy intense,
But did not heed a hint from thence.

---

[6] Gonsalvo de Cordova, called " the great captain," born 1443.
[7] Ferdinand of Aragon, whose forces, setting out from Cordova, drove Abu-Abdillah, or Boabdil, the king of the Moors, from Granada in 1492.
[8] Titles applied to the city in different periods of its history,—when inhabited by the Moors, the Goths, and before the Romans conquered it.
[9] Referring to the " blue blood " of the Spanish aristocracy, supposed to be indicative of Roman ancestry.

V.

It must have been Spain's year-long spring
That gave my winter'd fancies wing;
And brought to life a long-lost love
That these had come to brood above.
How throbb'd my heart to see once more
That face, that form, that friend of yore!
Again my arms were round that neck;
And cheek to cheek without a check
Our souls had met.   O Love, long cold,
What frame could hope to feel, when old
And numb from long bound loads of pain,
Such warmth and life thrill every vein!
The gone delight was all too dear.
With heart aglow, as dawn drew near,
To him who slept amid the past,
A Spanish sky seem'd overcast.

VI.

Bright Sun, I sigh'd, no light can gleam
Beside true love and shine supreme!
Fair Spain, no realm so fair may be;
But love recall'd unsexes thee.
Nay, no land shows one sunlit scene
That rose-like bursts from earth's wide green,
But brings an image swept away

When eyelids close at close of day.
'T is but the impress mind receives,
That, sunn'd or sombre, never leaves.
Ah, if the past must always cope
With future joys for which we hope,
How vain the aims that make their quest
A life that merely shall be blest,
And slight earth's meed of lowly sweets
For purple heights and golden streets !
Faith fails that merely waits below.
Dreams after death would bring but woe
Without remember'd love that blest
The soul before it found its rest.

VII.

Keep, Cordova, thy rare renown.
The veils of twilight, falling down,
Could fold around no fairer town ;
Yet many a sight, where came the night,
To this, my soul, had seem'd as bright.
I left thee sad ; but bore away,
With light to linger night and day,
And charms divine as thine to me,
The dream that came to rival thee.

THE FLOWER PLUCKED.

"YOU say you leave forever?
     Our walks and talks have had their day?
You say this flower blooms not to stay,
     Nor friendship ;—we must sever ?—
Alas, to think my favorite flower,
That so delay'd its blooming hour
     Through all the stormy weather,
Through March and April, May and June
Has open'd now to shut so soon !
Nay, nay ; it shall not fail me so.
It yet shall feel—though but my blow."
She spoke, and smote with all her might
The fragile stem and blossom bright ;
     And both flew off together.

"Not so," he cried ; "nay, never.
Forgive it ! Spare the flower ! alas !"
And knelt and pick'd it from the grass.
     "What, did she love thee ever?
If so the blow she gave to thee
Has made thee doubly dear to me.
     Ah, Flower, in sunny weather,
And not in March, nay, nay, in June
Thy leaves in opening brought this boon ;
Nor so shall close !   There waits for thee
One mission more, thy best, I see !"

He spoke, and placed the fallen flower
Against his heart—and so that hour
  The maid and flower together.

THE ARTIST'S AIM.

IN candor, my friend, you seem too much at home
  With nymphs of Olympus and gods of old Rome.
The world has advanced, and the artist, if sage,
Will seek to give form to the thoughts of his age.
The curve of a limb and the pose of a head
May be all the same in the living as dead ;
But she that you woo, must have life and be young
And speak, ere you love her, and speak your own
      tongue.

Truth only is lasting, and only the face
Transfigured by it has a lasting grace.
And truth is in nature, nor dealt second-hand
Through art, though most artful to fill the demand.
So think of the present, its deeds and its dreams,
As Raphael thought, but not Raphael's themes ;
Nor be a Venetian to picture like Titian
A woman to worship or goddess to kiss.
You are a new-world's man : model from this.

Ay, let the dead bury their dead, and pursue
The aims of a people that push for the new.

The proudest ambition, the readiest hand,
Might wisely embody ideals less grand ;
No sweeter Murillo's divine designs,
Whose purity rivals each thought it refines,
While the dreamy intent of a life-brooding haze
Throngs thick with the beauty of immature praise.
Conceptions immaculate still may be
In the pure white light that he could see,
Inspired to incarnate a soul in each plan,
The life of a picture as well as of man.

The wants of the present, one never can gauge
By the heathenish tastes of a heathenish age.
The mummy lived once, and spoke as it ought.
We moderns, forgetting its life and its thought,
For lost art sighing, too oft re-array
What is only a corpse, and ought to decay.
E'en if it were living, long centuries fraught
With progress in action and feeling and thought
Outgrow the old charms, and make the world crave
New phases of art that the past never gave.

So I fear, when I see men striving to mold
The forms of the new after those that are old,
While all true life grows better and better,
That classical models a modern may fetter.
Small virtue has one with no hope in his heart,
And little of merit, if none in his art.

While only the light of a coming ideal
Lures those to the good who imagine it real,
No work can ever inspire the earth
That embodies no promise of unfulfill'd worth,
And naught that the world accounts worthy of
    fame,
In art as in act, but is rank'd by its aim.

MUSICIAN AND MORALIZER.

WHAT am I " doing," night and day,
    Loitering here with the flute ?—
Doing ?—why blowing my plaints away,
    Off, till I blow them mute.

" Foolish " am I ?—It may be so.
    Who, forsooth, are the wise ?
I to the wind my sorrows blow :
    Others hoard up their sighs.

" Useless " am I ?—The while I play,
    Many another one's heart
Throbs to my melody, till, they say,
    All of his woes depart.

Nothing of sweetness can fill the air,
    Nothing of beauty bloom,

Save as visions of life more fair
  Over the spirit loom.

Listen to this now—mine and thine.
  How could I show more worth,
Than as a reed for a breath divine,
  Blowing from heaven to earth?

" Music-mad " am I ?—Have your say,
  Whether you blame or applaud,
I the behest of my soul obey,
  Just as it came from God.

WHAT THE BOUQUET SAID.

FOR one who would himself be here,
    And for ourselves who hold you dear,
We come, fair maid, to welcome you.
For sun-bright eyes like yours we grew,
For cheeks like yours, with ardor meet,
Would flush, aglow their glow to greet ;
And up to you, our fragrance rare
Is breathed from lips that burst in prayer.
Our goddess dear, our sister sweet,
This meeting leaves our lives complete.
Now dew may fail, or frost may sear,
We fade, we die ; but have been here.

WITH THE YOUNG.

OUR struggles with the world, I know,
  Are blessings in disguise.
No honors that elsewhere earth can show
  Outshine its victor's prize.
Yet, when, with naught their course to guide,
  My feelings freely well,
My thoughts will turn to souls untried,
  And with the young I dwell.

Why ask a feeling the reason why?—
  One's lot may have been too hard.
Those loved in youth, as years go by,
  May rouse no more regard.
Who knows how many in age may fall
  Whose feet all deem'd secure?
Who knows how many can trip at all
  And ever again be pure?

Perchance through each fair childish face
  I seem to see, as of yore,
A form whose young and tender grace
  Beside me moves no more;
And yet a form that waits for me,
  Where still, as hope maintains,
What has been, is, or is to be,
  In a state unchanged remains

Perchance, I share in heaven's delight
    Whose hosts recall the past,
And guide, at times, in robes of white,
    Earth's young through gloom and blast.
But leave the cause yet undivined,
    When feelings freely well,
The young have claims no others find,
    And with the young I dwell.

A TRANSLATION.[1]

O'ER Santiago's happy homes
    The parting sun delay'd,
And brightly o'er its roofs and domes
    In gleams of sunset play'd;
And toward the dome most bright came throngs
    Of maidens hastening there;
And from them words more sweet than songs
    Went pulsing through the air.
They sought that dome because the home
    Of God where sins were shriven;
Now under it with splendor fit
    Should prayer to Him be given.

[1] In 1864, the Immaculate Conception of the Virgin was celebrated with unusual splendor in the Church de la Companiè of Santiago, Chili. In the midst of the ceremonies the draped image of the Virgin caught fire. Almost instantly the flames were communicated to ropes suspending along the ceiling upward of twenty thousand colored lamps. These fell in a rain of fire upon the audience below, burning with the church itself as many as two thousand persons, chiefly young ladies from the higher grades of society.

Within, a thousand banners bright
  Would wave o'er walls ablaze ;
And priests, array'd in gold and white,
  Like seraphs chant their praise.
Within, the organ's ardent strains
  Would rise with incense rare ;
Ah, then, how sweet would be their gains
  Who breathed that sweeter air !
Sent upward so their prayers would flow
  Like fountains heavenward driven,
That far away would break in spray,
  And fall in blessings given.

And soon those thousand banners bright
  Did wave o'er walls ablaze ;
And priests, array'd in gold and white,
  Like seraphs chant their praise—
When up there flared a flame that glared
  Athwart the lamp-strung dome ;
And hot as hell its red lights fell
  To fright their victims home ;
And, o'er and o'er, was heard : " The door ! "
  And cries where fright had striven.
But oh, no more would swing that door,
  On throngs against it driven.

Red lips of fire flew to and fro,
  And kiss'd each maiden's cheek ;

They blush'd, but oh, too deep the glow !
    They kneel'd, but oh, too meek !
Death wrapt them round in robes of flame,
    Let loose their streaming hair,
And, when their souls were won, became,
    Ash-white, their couch-mate fair.
Anon, the fire was raging higher.
    But these to rest were given,
Long ere the bells had wail'd farewells
    When out the belfry driven.

To Santiago's mourning homes
    At morn a stranger stray'd,
And found, where once of all those domes
    The brightest sunn'd the shade,
Four hundred carts of corpses charr'd
    Two thousand nameless dead,
And scores of thousands weeping hard
    For life so sadly fled.
And all around the smoking ground,
    Whence all hope else was driven,
With lifted eye, their dome the sky,
    Their prayers to God were given.

FARMER LAD.

FARMER lad, in the morning gray,
    Blest may seem the town, and they,
Slumbering late, who, void of blame,
Seek at their leisure wealth and fame ;

But how many there, thy race would run
To know thy rest when the day is done!

Farmer lad, when the herd's faint bells
Clink far off o'er the sunburnt fells,
Better may seem the coin that calls
Ringing and bright from the town's cool halls;
  But how many there, would give all its gleams
  For the golden light of thy guileless dreams!

Farmer lad, where the herd will drink
Waits a maid that bathes by the brink
Bare brown feet; and the rill, made sweet,
Thrills to touch her who thee would greet.
  There is more for thee in the blue of her eye
  Than in all the towns that are under the sky.

THE WIFE.

ABOUT her fair sweet face, all bright,
  Is a constant halo of calm delight;
    And her smile attracts
    To genial acts
All those who live in the sunny sight.

She moves in a sphere not wholly obscure,
With ways that are not wholly mature,
    But ready to go

Where friend or foe
May point the way to the wise or pure.

Her mien by every grace refined
With a welcome bends to all things kind ;
    But something true
    To duty too
Remains unbent in her inner mind.

Her soul seeks not the name of wife,
To sit by a plume, or the prize of a strife.
    She longs to share
    Not the outward glare,
But the inward glow of her husband's life.

Ah, like the sky encircling the sea,
Embracing his thoughts wherever they be,
    She rests above
    His life with a love
That binds him fast, yet leaves him free.

Toward her his thoughts in fancies rise,
Like mists aglow in the sunset skies,
    And like nights here
    When the stars appear,
His gloom gives way at the glance of her eyes.

Through her his hope like a morning dream
Attains a day of love supreme,

Suffused with a light
That makes earth bright,
And life what it otherwise could but seem.

Would God her heart could ever abide,
A heaven for his heart's heaving tide,
Still calm above
His restless love,
And all the storms that over it glide!

NOTHING TO KEEP UNDER.

YOU envy those whom all men greet
With favors never ceasing,
The men whose ways are so discreet
Their friends go on increasing,
Whose moods get more than they deserve,
Because not oft they blunder;
But, even when unkind, have nerve
To keep unkindness under.

You envy those whose lips imply
A smile for every neighbor,
Though all his deeds may give the lie
To truth for which they labor,—
Good, easy souls, who never need
To fret in wrath or wonder,

To feel how hard is life, indeed,
　With so much to keep under.

You envy those whose calm consent,
　Amid all earth's mutations,
Can sail the sea of life content
　With others' observations ;
Who entertain no wish for strife
　Near shores where breakers thunder ;
But hold a cautious helm to life,
　And keep ambition under.

Hold friend—the good for which men yearn
　Makes ill to them provoking ;
And zeal it is, on fire to burn,
　That fills its air with smoking.
If this be so, some day, your soul
　A worth world-wide may sunder
From those who have—their self-control,
　But nothing to keep under.

OUR DAY AT PISA.

WE took the train at Florence,[1] we,—
　　The day was warm and pleasant.
The town of Pisa would we see.
　No time was like the present.

[1] The poem is supposed to be written by an American "doing" Italy.

Anon we climb'd the Leaning Tower,[2]
Dropt something down, and sat an hour ;
And then the grand Baptistry[2] door
They swung for us ; and, o'er and o'er,
We made its domed rotunda roar,
     To echo back our joking.

We set our pockets jingling, we,
     To make our guide a crony,
Saw the cathedral, paid a fee,
     And ate some macaroni,
Then feasted on an outside view
Of all three buildings,[2] yet so new ;
Then bought, in alabaster[3] wrought,
Some models of them ; then we sought
The Campo Santo,[4] where we thought
     About the dead, while smoking.

We took the train at sunset, we,
     And while we left the station,
Extoll'd the land, " How much to see !
     How grand this Roman nation !
Our own, how mean !—no works of art ! "
We strove to sigh, but check'd a start

[2] The Leaning Tower, the Baptistry (under the dome of which may be heard, by those who care for it, an echo, repeating itself many times), and the Cathedral are all found in one square.
[3] Alabaster worked into articles suitable for gifts is one of the chief commodities of Pisa. Great quantities of it are purchased for presents.
[4] Campo Santo or cemetery, the most famous in Italy.

And cried, " How home-like ! " o'er and o'er.—
What thrill'd us thus ?—alas, it bore
No hint from art ; we heard once more
   A frog, near by us, croaking.

———

THE HIGHEST CLAIMS.

I WOKE and found my dream withdrawn,
   And, with it, each weird guest,
Whose urgency, from eve to dawn,
   Had robb'd me of my rest.
One call'd me ruler of the land ;
   One chief of hosts enroll'd ;
One brought me wealth ; one bade my hand
   A pen immortal hold ;
But none spake aught of aims I thought
   More blest than theirs could be ;
And, leading on to all I sought,
   Still claim'd the most from me.

" To hold a sceptre in the state,
   Like Moses o'er the sea,
Controlling thus a rival's fate,
   Who overwhelm'd will be ;
To wield a sword in dangerous times,
   Till foes yield up each aim,

While hope with firmer footstep climbs
   The crumbling ledge of fame,—
All this I know were well, but though
   Each foe should bend the knee,
An homage grander still, I trow,
   Would claim the most from me.

" To join the throngs whose efforts prove
   How dear the wealth they earn ;
Or those whose thought the world can move
   To deeds for which they yearn ;
All this were well ; but gold is mined
   In depths that lure below,
And thought more lasting forms can find
   Than lip and line bestow.
When gem and scroll a living soul
   With all its powers may be,
Naught else that might my deeds control
   Can claim the most from me.

" Ah, why through all life's little day
   Should drum and trumpet call,
And cluster'd smoke from many a fray
   Hang o'er earth like a pall ?
How small a space above each fight
   Its rising thunder jars !
The echo sleeps in paths of light
   Where shine unmoved the stars.

To draw toward love like heaven's above
   One's earthly work may be ;
And nothing less than perfect love
   Can claim the most from me."

I spoke, and, ere the beams of day
   Could bar him out, each guest
That I had thought had gone for aye,
   Return'd and term'd me blest.
One call'd me ruler of the land ;
   One chief of hosts enroll'd ;
One brought me wealth ; one bade my hand
   A pen immortal hold ;
And every voice breath'd forth : " Rejoice ;
   O soul, thy wisdom see :—
While love rules all, thy ruling choice
   Must claim the most from me."

————

NOTES FROM THE VICTORY.

AH me, who is ringing those bells ?
   Right merry for funeral knells !
If the winds of hell could ring them as well,
   What woe would the demons lack ?
My light blew out in the gust of the rout :
   My boy will never come back.

And drums !—How lightly they roll !
Coarse drums, can they call the soul ?
Folks, out of breath, do you shout at death ?
Can you rend the tomb ?—Alack,
Vain echoes around, pale under the ground,
My boy will never come back.

Guns too ! O why do they roar ?
Alas, I thought it was o'er.
Though why care I, though a million die,
And all of us wear but black ?
I, too, with the proud have my blood-stain'd
shroud :
My boy will never come back.

Our land !—Who wants it to last !
Its future is doom'd by the past.
And the tears that rise to its mourners' eyes
Will ever dim all they track.
Chill, shivering breast, freeze, freeze into rest :
My boy will never come back.

THE POET'S LESSON.

" O POET vain, put by thy pen,
Put by this dreamy mood,
Move outward through the walks of **men** ;
And do the world some good."

These words I heard, and waived my will,
    And left my rhymes behind,
And past the sill and down the hill
    Went forth my work to find.

And first I spied a romping child.
    " My child," I stopt and said,
" The sun is bright ; the air is mild ;
    Your cheeks with health are red.

" It does you good to leap and run,
    And chase your mates about "—
But ah, my talk had scarce begun
    Before the child cried out :

" O please, man, please keep back, I say !
    O but you spoil my sport !
O but they all will flee away,—
    My prisoners, from my fort ! "

I saw no foe, nor fortress wall,
    My coming had attack'd.
This child, I thought, knows not at all
    A fancy from a fact.

Too young is he ; nor yet has learn'd
    The laws of health, like me ;
Nor cares to know them ; so I turn'd
    And left his fancy free.

A man approach'd with bending frame,
   His eyes by searching task'd ;
A chance, I thought, to help one came ;
   So, " What is lost ? " I ask'd.

" Lost ?—every thing ! " he said, and frown'd ;
   " Ay, every thing I sought.
All day and night, the whole week round,
   My mind had track'd the thought ;

" And just had found it, but for you ! "
   I blush'd at this ; and he,
He craved my pardon, said, he too,
   Had done a wrong to me.

" Nay, I," said I, " should make amend.
   Your search was on the ground ;
And I dreamt not, who saw you bend,
   That thought could there be found."

He answer'd not ; but, passing then,
   With shadows paved the way ;
The while I vow'd that not again
   Would I such help essay.

With this I turn'd my footsteps where
   A man long ill abode,
Assured it would do good to share
   This weary sufferer's load.

"My friend," I said, "your smile is bright ;
　Your pains are lessening then ;
Erelong they all will take their flight,
　Your health be sound again."

"Be sound ?" he ask'd ; "and can it be
　That you misjudge me too ?
Ah, not the thing you deem, set free
　The smile that welcomed you.

"Nay, friend, but wisdom learn from one
　Who long on earth has wrought ;
Our ways would leave us wrecks undone,
　If but of earth we thought.

"A double life we all must live,—
　Of spirit and of flesh ;
And but the former life can give
　A joy forever fresh.

"Look up ; there looms a region nigh,
　And there the Master is ;
And if like Him live you and I,
　Then you and I live His.

"When all day long of Him I muse,
　And all day with Him live,
The glory that the spirit views
　Dims all that earth can give."

I heard his words, and went my way,
  My lesson learn'd betimes ;
No more I felt could I obey
  A voice that rail'd at rhymes.

Oh what were life without the worth
  Of ideality,—
Its home, heaven's halo round the earth ;
  Its language, poetry.

The world of deeds whose armor gleams
  May light the path to right
Far less than rays that rise in dreams,
  And days that dawn at night.

God's brightest light illumes the soul.
  That light this life denies
Till earth's horizons lift and roll
  Like lids from opening eyes.

THE MOURNER ANSWERED.

AMID the twilight's gathering gloom,
  She knelt beside her babe's new tomb.
" My child," she sigh'd, " did heaven not know
How deep and dread would be my woe ?
For this did nature give thee birth,
  For this,—to bury thee ?—O God ! "

She groan'd, then started.   Earth to earth,
    Her lips had kiss'd the common sod.

"Amid life's flowers that fade and fall,
What need to pluck a bud so small?
With ripen'd harvests full supplied,
What need had heaven of thee?" she cried;
Then mark'd the flowers that, while she stoop'd,
    E'en yet made sweet her last-brought wreath:
Those full-blown all had dropt or droop'd;
    The buds alone bloom'd bright beneath.

"Why leave, O God," was then her moan,
"My widow'd soul still more alone?
Why wrest from life the last thing dear?
What harm that love should linger here?"
And lo, the neighboring spire above
    Rang forth its evening call to prayer;
And music fill'd from lips of love
    The House of God whose door was there.

THE VACANT ROOM.

AH, wraith-lit star, that shone afar,
    And lured my eager footseps on!
This door I pass, and find, alas,
    The friend for whom I long'd is gone.

O think how drear mere sands appear
   To travellers worn who pray for springs.
More drear this place without the face
   I sought to cheer my wanderings.

Have diamonds rare no gleams to spare
   The light that their own light would shun?
Do roses droop when many a group
   Of clouds crowd off the autumn sun?
The gem and rose less dull repose
   When all are gone that caused their worth,
Than lip and eye when none are nigh
   With smiles that break in bursts of mirth.

Are lovers wild, when maidens mild
   Their wisest ways of wooing shun?
Do mothers weep, when waked from sleep
   Whose dream restored a long-lost son?
Ah, scarce the man's or mother's plans
   Appear so rudely overthrown,
As his whose thought in vain here sought
   A word to echo back his own.

But time speeds on, and duties wan,
   Like ghosts untombed, forbid my stay;
But though I go, this note shall show
   The loss, my friend, you cause to-day.

It craves a thought for him who sought
　A sight of eyes that light it now ;
For him who waits till kindlier fates
　His hopes a kindlier fate allow.

THANKSGIVING DAY.

I SOUGHT the house Thanksgiving Day,
　And found its inmates all away,
Save her who sat before the fire,
And, by her side, her palsied sire.

At play, betwixt her fingers white,
A needle nimbly glanced the light ;
But oft her eyes it could not stay,
To either side would glance away.

And on her right hand, open spread,
There lay the Book of God she read ;
And on her left I just could trace
An infant namesake's pictured face.

The Book of God, the housekeeper,
The babe that had been named for her,
The book and babe and she between,—
Through doors ajar I mark'd the scene.

And, while she sat before me so,
Content to share another's woe ;
A captive for her sisters gone,
Whom all their joy depended on ;

Cheer'd now to read of heavenly worth
For souls denying self on earth ;
Moved now to do the deed she should,
Lest wrong should lead that child from good ;—

Another soul, my heart felt sure
Could keep, if so surrounded, pure,—
If there God lured his thought above,
And here one shared his name and love.

The scene was homely ; yes, I know,
But homely scenes may haunt one so !—
That still her sweet face with me stays,
My days are all Thanksgiving Days.

A MISAPPREHENSION

NOT UNCOMMON.

IN loneliness I wander'd ;
  When, lo, above me, ringing
    Amid the breeze
    That shook the trees,
  I heard a bird's glad singing.

I looked, and through the leaves could see
The warbler nod and chirp for me.
" One friend is left me yet," thought I,
  And ventur'd near
  The song to hear ;
But when he saw me drawing nigh,
  Alas, in fright
  He took to flight !
Not, not for me had been his care.
He sang to greet the sunny air,
 And serve his own sweet nature.

In loneliness I ponder'd ;
 And lo, sweet laughter woke there
  The gentlest rills,
  That broke in trills
 About the lips that spoke there.
Through smiles and blushes burst the glee,—
And eyes that fill'd and flash'd for me.
" Her soul," I thought, " has heard my sigh " ;
  And, drawing near,
  I bade her hear
My tale of love—but from her eye
  The joy had flown.
  Not I alone,
Alas, not I had been her care.
She fill'd the world with sweetness there,
 To serve her own sweet nature.

AUNTY'S ANSWER.

M Y child, you come, and ask me why,
　　The reason why I stared at you ?—
Ah, darling, one can use her eye !—
　　Nay, did I stare ?—You saw me too ?

I stared, then, at these great round eyes ;
　　And thought of all that each would see,
Of all the cares, and all the cries,
　　Ere you were old, you sprite, like me.

And then I saw these tiny ears,
　　And thought of how they both would grow,
And thrill and tremble, ere the years
　　Had taught them all they had to know.

I saw these dainty limbs here, too,
　　That run and jump and snatch and throw ;
And thought how little mine can do—
　　Ah me, not always was it so !

And what of these things ?—Nothing, dear.
　　You ask'd me only, that is all ;
And old is aunty, old and queer ;
　　So kiss me, child, and catch the ball.

Alas, the darling !—How could I
　　Tell her the thought ?—It touch'd me so
To think how—were she but to die
　　Before she learn'd it all, you know.

HIS LOVE'S FRUITION.

"COME, Love, be mine," the boy implored ;
      And from his fresh young heart there
  pour'd
Full streams of life that flush'd his face
And thrill'd his breast for Love's embrace.
"Nay, nay ; not yet," his Love replied ;
"The worth of boyhood must be tried."
So, like the spring's uncertain sun,
Love lured his hope ; but was not won.

"Come, Love, be mine," the young man pray'd,
As if some angel were the maid ;
And could with bliss have knelt beside
The only power that awed his pride.
"Nay, nay ; not yet," his Love replied ;
"For vintage-time must life provide."
So brightly, like a summer-sun,
Love cheer'd his way ; but was not won.

"Come, Love, be mine," the strong man urged ;
"The mounts above in cloud are merged ;
And, hand in hand with thee, my life
Will better brave the looming strife."
"Nay, nay ; not yet," his Love replied,
"The harvests wait ; the fields are wide."
So, clouded like an autumn-sun,
Love veil'd her light, and was not won.

"Come, Love, be mine," the old man said;
And meekly bow'd his whiten'd head;
Then, while it sank against his breast,
"O Love, has life not won its rest?"
"I come," his Love at last replied;
And clasp'd him; but he only sigh'd.
And, faint and chill, life's wintry sun
In gold had set; his Love was won.

WHAT WOULD I GIVE.

WRITTEN ON A SUNDAY IN GERMANY.

THERE, where the flowers more fragrant lie,
  Crushed by the crowds that have pass'd
    them by,
Stands a chapel; and oft from its door
Hymns of the lowly worshippers pour,
  Crush'd like the flowers, I trow.
O little Church, but what would I give,
What would I give, and how would I live,
  To know as thy sweet souls know!

There, where the trees on the great knoll sway
Swept by the wind that they fail to stay,
Bend great crowds, while organ and bell
Hail God's Host that is deigning to dwell
  Shrined in their church below.

O great Church, but what would I give,
What would I give, and how would I live,
　　To know as thy hush'd throngs know !

There on the cliff that chancels the park,
Nigh to the cloud where is trilling the lark,
Men and maidens dance to the lay
Blown by the blasts of the trumpeters gay,
　　Fluttering to and fro.
O gay Cliff, but what would I give,
What would I give, and how would I live,
　　To know as thy light hearts know !

There, where the sun burns all the view,
What sounds there in the boundless blue ?
Faith—is it more than a meek despair ?
Truth—than one's own note echoed in air ?
　　Hope—than his dawn's bright dew ?
O hush'd Heaven, but what would I give,
How would I love, and how would I live,
　　To know the soul's tale to be true !

DRAMATIC.

IDEALS MADE REAL.

I.

IT seem'd a rare and royal friendship, ours,
  The very sovereignty of sympathy ;
Begun so early too—mere lads we were—
And now I never look back there again
But, swept like shading from a hero's face
In pictures,—those of Rembrandt,—all the school
Appear in hues of dim uncertainty
Surrounding Elbert, shining in relief.

Not strange was it ; too tender was I made ;
Nor oft had felt a touch save that of age,
When moulding all my methods to its own.
Kept back from contact with rough boys at play,
Till sensitive and shrinking as a girl,
A hint of their regard could master me ;
No maiden, dreaming of her wedding day,
Could wake at morning with more trembling hopes
Than I, when looking forward to my school.
But when I reach'd it, not a Bluebeard more
Could have disturb'd a trusting bride's romance.

II.

At first, they lodged me there with such a loon !
" Our clown ! " so said the boys ; and clown he was ;
Would tease all day, and tumble round all night ;
And, every morning, sure as came the sun,
Would start and rout me out, with strap in hand,
Plied like a coach-whip round my dancing shape,
Well put to blush until I dodged away.

A chum had Elbert too ; and, like my own,
A wild boy caged, who seem'd more wild at times
Through beating at his bars, a hapless wretch.
And when our happier love had flower'd in us,
Half pitying each other, half this chum,
Which pity grew, we both stood round, scarce loath
To note his own wild set inflating him
With well-blown whims that swell'd his empty pride
Forsooth, the better bubble he could be,
The better hope we two could have of what
Should blow him from us.   Then the blow came
          on :—
A gust of scolding struck him, and he went,—
Obey'd the call that had been mouthed for him,—
An inn-clerk's, as I think,—and bow'd content
To sink from view like Paul, one gloomy night,
From out the window of his room ; while we,
Much giggling, flung his luggage after him.

III.

My friend, thus widow'd, caused that our school's
    head,
Already nodding o'er his noonday pipe,
Should beck at sever'd dreams with one nod
    more,
And so consent to our dreams.

                    Room-mates made,
We slamm'd his door and woke him ; not our-
    selves.
Our dreamland lasted, that is, when we two
Were by ourselves.   When more surrounded us—
You know boy-friends are shy : is it a trait,
Their shielding of their hearts, that fits them thus
For life-tilts of their manhood ?—How we two
Would rasp each other when the world look'd on !
In truth, each seem'd to wear his nature's coat
The soft side inward, comforting himself,
And turn the rough side only toward the world.
If strangers chafed against it, yet oneself
And friend were saved this.

               When thus Elbert's cloak
Was mine, and mine was his, and both held both,
No proof could have convinced me in those days
His peer had ever liv'd.   What seem'd in him
So mild and beautiful, was more than marks

Mere difference between a porcupine
Provok'd and peaceable.   The kind was new ;
Not human, so angelic.   Ay, that soul,
As pure as loving, and as fine as frank,
I half believe to-day, as I did then,
Stood strange amid his comrades of the play
As dogwood, wedded to the skies of spring,
White in a wilderness of wintry pines.
Ah me, could all find all on earth so dear,
Christ's work were common.   I had died for him.
In fact, to shield the rogue, I just escap'd
That very fate a score of times or more,
Bluft, bruis'd, and battling for him on the green.

IV.

Our love kept warm until our school-day-sun
Had set ; and afterwards the smouldering fires
Were fed by letters, and rekindl'd oft
By friction of a frequent intercourse
Through visits in vacations ; then, for years,
Behind it there was left a lingering light
Pervading moods of memory like the rays
Pour'd through a prism, wherein the commonest
    hues
Will spray to uncommon colors when they break.
In truth, I never see to-day a face
Where flash the kindling feelings of a boy,

But back of it, I seem to feel the warmth
Of Elbert's heart.   No school-boy past me bounds
But his dear presence comes to leap the years,
And rush on recollection, with a force
That brings from depths of joy, still'd long ago,
A spray as fresh as dash'd from them when first
They stream'd in cataracts.   With love like his
To flood its brim, my soul appear'd so full
That, overflowing at each human touch,
Its pleasures could not stagnate.

                But, you know
How fly the clouds above us, and in drought
The old springs fail ; and long we liv'd apart.

V.

Then Elbert, when we met, talk'd much of this :
How, all its chairs made vacant one by one,
Th' applause rose thinner at his bachelor-club ;
How, brief as birds', are human mating-times ;
How men, mere songs forgot, withdraw to nests—
To homes—their worlds, where all the sky is fill'd
With sunny smiles they love, and shadowy locks.
How sweet were life whose light and shade were
    these !

"We, Norman," said he, "were contented once ;
To love each other only ; but men part ;

And I confess that, while this light of love
Plays lambent round so many glowing lips,
I feel as chill, and lost, and out of place,
As one lone dew-drop, prison'd in a shade
Of universal noon."
                              " The sun," said I,
" Will free it, by and by.   Our time will come."

"Must come," replied he, " or I go to it.
Henceforth, let beauty's beams but gleam for me,
I shall not shun them, as has been my wont,
But make my eyes a sun-glass for my heart,
And let them burn it."

                              " May they burn," I cried,
" Until love's fragrant opiate fume so strong
It make your brain beclouded as a Turk's.
But I, alas, though wild o'er many a maid,
Am never mad enough to marry her."

" You poets," laugh'd he, " soar above earth so
That common clouds like these can reach you not.
But why say 'clouds'? for clouds rise o'er a flame
That smoulders.   Love that burns is always clear."

" But mine will not burn clearly, till it show
A woman," said I, "fitted for a mate,
Whose mind, like yours, can really match my own.

Till then must memory, jealous for her past,
Out-do love's hope that cannot promise more."

"But maidens," cried he, "are not loved like men.
Bind beauty to their souls, then weigh the twain.
If one weigh naught, he waives his judgment then.
We must be practical."

        Thus Elbert spoke,
While I, for whom these light and vapory moods
Had gather'd o'er that soul in slightest clouds,
Not tokening the storm that yet should burst,
Smiled only, thinking how, where throbb'd his heart,
Some maid unnamed must surely stand and knock ;
Though this I had forgotten, save for that
Which happen'd later.   You shall hear of it.

VI.

It came in Dresden, something like a year
More late than when my plan for life was changed.
The change seem'd sudden ; but, you know, the
    blow
That swept from me my parents, fortune, all,
Could not but stun me, and I could not think.
No other theme seem'd mine ; I could not write.

So came my change—no myth—I felt it all :—
One time, when, lonely, I to Christ had knelt,

I rose to seem not lonely ; I was His,
He mine.   I vow'd to live then but for **Him**,
To break away from every cord of Earth,
And make my life accordant with his own.
Not only would I think the truth, but yield
Each grain in all my being to the truth,
And sow in wildest wastes, where all should **germ**
In generations growing toward the good.

But still, a novice yet, though, like St. Paul,
To will was present with me ; to perform
I found not how ; but, on performance bent,
Within a chancel chanting with the choir,
I stood before an altar, half the day,
And half before my books, with cravings pale
For church and stole and sermons of my own.

VII.

Then was it Elbert's friendship further'd me.
For finding me, and staring at my face,
And books, and cassock—when the puzzle pass'd,—
He, humbling to my humor, praised the priest
And all the powers of priesthood, till delight
Relax'd the rigor of my rôle ; and then
He wedged the wisdom of his own desire
Within my dreams, and broke apart their spell,
And drew aside the curtains of their couch,
And spoke of dawn, and light for all the world.

"First learn about this world," he urged, "and
    then
Learn how to help it.   Minds like mine," he said,
"Should teach, revise, reform, and start the thought
To counteract ill aim'd philosophy.
Here loom'd an end worth reaching ! which to
    reach
'T were well to cross the sea.—His purse was
    mine.
And go you as a student," Elbert said,
"Nor clad so like a priest, for whom all earth
Will don some Sabbath-day demean ; go free
To find the man, hard by his work, at home."

Thus pleading many days, at last he won ;
And, yielding to his wish, the sea I cross'd.

VIII.

Soon, borne to Dresden for a leisure week,
With whom, one morning, should I chance to meet
But Elbert's elder sister ?—now grown staid
And matronly withal, a second wife,
In charge of half a dozen sturdy boys ;
Though these I saw not then ; but all alone,
Much flush'd and flurried, sweeping up the street,
She stopp'd, and cried abruptly, "Why, my friend,
Are you here, Norman ?—you ?—where from ?—how
    long ?

Not heard of you for years ! That Elbert, drone,
Will never write the news. How glad I am
To see a man on hand when needed once !
Two girls, young friends of mine, just come to
    town,
Have lost their trunks,—and I my husband too,—
And there they stand amid such throngs of men !—
And did you note the statues in Berlin,
In all the streets ?—of warriors, every one !
And these two girls, here travelling, by themselves,
Where might makes right, and woman slighted is,
Not strange it is their feelings toward you men,
In heat of indignation seething up,
Should brew some barm at times of bitterness ! "

IX.

Thus, rattling on, she led me, as confused
As feels a warrior at the morning drum,
Till came a sight supreme, arousing me :—
Two bright eyes only, sparkling in the light,
Where flush'd a face that flared, then hid itself
Behind a travelling hood, befleck'd with dust,
And fring'd with venturous locks of careless hair.

" I have them now ! " it cried ; and straight began
A tale, strain'd sweeter through those lips aglow
Than sunset music. Then, when all was told,

The name I heard was " Edith."

Bowing low,

" Well done ! " essay'd I ; then,—to bandy back
That charge against the men I just had heard
From her who brought me,—" Well done as a man ! "

X.

" That speech," laugh'd she thus bandied, " scarce
    deserves
Our ' Well done as a woman ! '—Edith, hark,
His praise for you is, ' Well done as a man ! ' "

Then Edith, echoing after, naïvely dropt,
" I tell you—nay—I will not say it though."

" Please do ? " I ventur'd.

" Nay ; it may offend,"

Replied she ; while her shoulders gently
    shrugg'd
As if to tempt me like two dainty doors,
Doors all but swung ajar before a heart
That love was dared to enter !

" Nay," I said,

" I vow you such a deal of patience now ! "

" I do not know," she answer'd ; " am not sure.
Your manly patience might break loose to sigh

More hints about my manhood!   Just to think
That half of all mankind are merely girls
And so must borrow all their tact from men ! "

"Not so," I said ; "not so ; but commonly."—

"Ah, commonly ! and what," she sigh'd, " is this
" That men-minds do so well ?—discriminate ?
Yet even I, dull woman, I can see
Brains differ in their grain.   But men, forsooth,
Feel so much matter lodged in their brains—eh ?—
That they weigh mind like matter in the lump,
And judge of character, as if 't were clay :—
This forms a man—has wisdom, firmness, power ;
And that, a maid—is foolish, fickle, frail,
And never can be wholly safe, forsooth,
Except when subject to a man, her lord ! "

"Ah, but," I said, "we men all prize you so !
To hold you ours, our pride seems infinite.
Thus lifted up by you, it is your fault
If we seem lords to you."
                              " Is it ? " she ask'd,
" Or have you seem'd so long our lords, you think
Your lording over us has trained in us
What still needs lording over ?   Fashion yields
A man, at times, exemption from her forms,
But woman never.   Wherefore, pray, is this ?

Do not they both have souls? and both aspire?
Must one class only slave it to her sex?—
I think the soul of woman as of man
May show some mastery over its abode."

"But yet," I said, " You know, her frame divine—
And soul, too—men confuse things—who can tell
Which is the soul?"

         She answer'd absently:
"In truth they do confuse things! only wise,
As owls that blink at light!—so blind—nor see
What day dawns with a wife's enfranchisement;
Ambitious, but forgetting that the meek,
Inherit heaven, or that the oppressor dwarfs
His own surroundings; that if pride stoop not,
Then must the soul; that earthly lords must bend,
And lift their consorts to their own prized seats,
As equals, queens; or else must house with slaves,
And make the slavish habits there their own."

XI.

"Well said!" I thought. "Disown it, though she
    may,
This maiden's mood is manlier than she deems";
And, as with manhood, so my wits went forth
To find a way to test her further still.

Just then the sister of Elbert, gesturing toward
The sister of Edith, Alice, whom she fetch'd,
Cried, half-way introducing us, "My fan!"
I stoop'd, and pick'd it up.   Then, bowing low,
"Your humble slave," I said.   "You know, some
    claim
That genuine friends of either sex are slaves;
And only want of love would snatch a whip,
And snapping it, cry out : ' This way—serve me.' "

"And I, like them," said Edith, slightly flush'd,
"Seem wholly loveless.   You may mourn it less
That yonder carriage waits me.   For to-day,
All thanks for coming ! We may meet once more."

XII.

My face flamed hot as if its veil of flesh
Would burn, and bare the soul, to show I meant
No rudeness.   Elbert's keen-eyed sister laugh'd,
And, walking homeward then, kept bantering me,
To storm my heart with courage womanly,
So sure that love of sex controls us all.
"So fortunate !" she cried ; " Heaven favor'd me.
They had no escort,—I no rival near ;
And I must ply my arts this very eve."

"Ah, but my plans !" I said ;—" I leave to-day
For studies at Berlin."

"Yes, yes ; your plans !—
You serve ideals, like all idiots.
But you are more, much more, than out your teens ;
And—well, you are no hermit, any way."

"Then must I find "—I laugh'd, yet half in earnest—
"The charms to tempt me ! " and my reckoning
Fill'd all my fingers doubly with the traits
Of perfect womanhood.

     "She owns," I heard,
"All these, and more. For once, my poet, dream ;
And full Elysium waits you when you wake.
But mind you, Norman, maids of Edith's kind,
In whose one person love so womanly
With intellect so manly has been join'd,
Need not to marry for a hand or head.
There, hearts alone can win. Bear this in mind ;
And fan your fancy till your words grow warm,
Ay, glow to flash the white heat of the soul ! "
Then, crying from her door, " Farewell till eve,"
True to her sex, unanswer'd yet assured,
The woman left.

XIII.

    And so my will was caught,
The net so deftly drawn, I flounder'd first,
Then, resting, smiled. We fight the hydra, we,

Who war against our nature.   Every head
That reason clove would rise redoubled there.
Forsooth, my rudeness :—that should be explain'd ;
For which a single visit would suffice ;
And this, for scarce a day, need check my work ;
Or, if I linger'd longer, all my life
Lay still before me.   Wherefore haste away ?
Fate might be beckoning !—" Nay, I should not
    leave,"
Sigh'd hope, too warm, at last, by more than half ;
Then roused sweet echoes of faint hints, recall'd
From churchly sources, of one's need to wed,
If he would work the best, for all, with all.
Thus, like two cowards, clinging each to each,
Weak wish nudged wisdom, and weak wisdom
    wish.
Who gets on better ?

XIV.

                    So that night we went.
And, all the way, my gay guide rail'd at me.
" Aha, my bachelor, your roving love,
Aha, has had its day ! Yon sunset hues
But deck the curtains hung before its night."

" Alas," I cried, " if I must through them pass,
Woe me who wish it !   See, in front of them,
The river in the horizon underneath—"

"Your Jordan, ere your promis'd land!" she said;
"You need baptizing for your harden'd heart."

"Ah me!" I sigh'd, yet strangely; for there
        seem'd,
While all the way the twilight thicker sank,
Sweet silence luring dreamward wind and bird
Until the reverent air lay hush'd where came
The hallowing influence of holier stars.
And, all the way, deep folding round my soul,
With every nerve vibrating at its touch,
Fell dim delight, through which, as through a veil,
Some nearer presence breath'd of holier life.
Ah, wandering Heart, and had I had my day?—
With closing gates as golden as yon west?
And whither was I moving in the dark?—
"Who knows?" my spirit ask'd, "who knows or
        cares?
On through the twilight threshold, trustingly!
What hast thou, Night, that weary souls need fear?
Thou home of love entranced, thou haunt of dreams,
Thy halls alone can hoard the truth of heaven!
Thy dome alone can rise to reach the stars!"

XV.

She roused me, crying out, "Look toward the
        porch!"
I look'd, and there beheld our waiting friends,

And, grouped with them, some ruddy German
    maids
Whose deeper hues but finely rimmed with shade
The subtler beauty of our special hosts.
These came from out that western world wherein,
By fresher breezes and by brighter suns,
The Saxon tissue, sweeten'd and refined,
Unfolds, each season, more ethereally.

The two then moving from their sister-maids,
Like petals loos'd from roses when in bloom,
Came forth to welcome us ; and, greetings o'er,
Of Europe, Edith spoke, and Germany,
And books, and music—how the church of Greece
Had carved earth's pivot that earth whirls upon
Within the centre of a flag-stone round
That paves a chapel in Jerusalem.
But she, who track'd that viewless whirl by sound,
And deem'd all harmony to centre here,
A Grecian only in her love of art,
Had found that pivot fix'd in Germany.

XVI.

"True Grecian, she !" the sister of Elbert cried ;
"Each morning brings her fresh from shrines of
    art,
All flush'd, a priestess from an oracle,
To sanctify us grosser mortals here

With vague suggestions ! mutter'd mysteries !
Ah me, to hear her rave once ! "

                          Edith smiled,
"And eyes that see are blest !—and which sees
    most—
My worship, or your wonder ?   Know you, friend,"
She turn'd to me and asked, — "this critic's
    ground?—
The Sistine Babe it was, we spoke of Him.
Because I find art's glass, when rightly held,
Revealing through the real the truth ideal,
I said : 'I seem to see not only Him,
The Babe, but back of Him, His heavenly home.
I seem to enter this—His handmaid there,
And there commune until my soul is blest.'
I said : 'From thence my spirit seems to come,
And feel its arms to be the throne of Christ.
And this,' I said, 'is wrought for me by art.
Some hold that souls transmigrate after death,
But art,' I said, 'makes mine transmigrate here.'
For this you hear of raving.   Do I err ?
The soul of feeling is in thought, not so ?
Then one, to feel refresh'd, must think she bathes
In rills that reach her from the freshest springs."

XVII.

"Ah," said the sister of Elbert, soothingly,
"Our soaring lark here bathes in each bright pool.

So be not frighten'd off ; her plumes but shake
A sprinkling from the bath they had to-day."

"Some please the world," said Edith ; "I, myself,—
My soul, I mean ; nor long to clip that soul
To suit mere wordling's notions. Courting crowds,
A soul lives crampt ; but if one speak the truth,
Crowds leave—good riddance !—place is clear'd
    for friends."

"Clear'd verily !" her sister cried, "Long live
These household pet-gods of our modern homes,
Like sprites to fright the stranger off ! Now own
The fear you felt. It would appease her so !"

XVIII.

To this rose no reply to Edith's lips.
I mark'd, instead, a gentle trembling there,
Like ripples roused upon a tranquil sea
That rise from deep, unseen disturbances.
"They fail to read her rightly," thought I, then—
You know no man can flinch it : woman's grief,
If there be any manhood left in him,
Will rouse his efforts to bespeak her peace—
I found myself her soul's expositor
To clear the channel of its overflow.

"And when the thought is in one, when it springs,
Why, then, not let it spring ? The world is not

So fill'd with thoughts that it can spare our own.
And if we startle folks, jog off the guise
Of their deceit, we spy them as they are.
Between souls thus discover'd, Edith deems
That love must flow ; while friendship caught by
  craft
Is lost by confidence.   I think her right.
Why not ? We all when in our noblest moods
Crave homage for our souls' nobility.
But what our souls are in themselves, who know,
Save as our rôles report us outwardly ?
Did not divine hands form us as we are ?
Who love us as we are, love higher things
Than those who love what earth would make of
  us."

" My champion ! " Edith cried ; and waved her
  thanks,
With white sleeves fluttering from her shapely
  sides—
Ah me, a wing'd one sent to save my soul
Had scarcely stirr'd in me a greater joy.

XIX.

My mien must have reveal'd it.   Like a lake,
Whose fogs unfold, when comes a genial sun,
Her moods unfolded to my sympathy ;

And, brightly imaged in her nature's depths,
I seem'd, at every turn, to face my own.

So new to me such views were, that I felt
As thrill'd as feels the savage maid, when first
She finds her own face in a stranger's glass,
Then spell-bound lingers, learning of herself.
So wrapt, my wonder hung, all wistfully,
About that spirit bright.   What meant it all ?
I could not then believe,—I scout it yet,—
That mortals can afford to slight the souls
Reflecting theirs, who make them mind themselves
And prize the good they own, and dread the ill.

You smile, friend : yes ; and often so would I.
My head would oft, made jealous of my heart,
Deny that reason ruled my impulses.
And oft my heart, to bear such weight of joy,
Would faint from too much feeling.   I would ask
Could I be sane yet find my life so sweet ?—
At least I would be sure ; so like a friend
Who finds a long-lost friend amid a crowd,
And stares, and holds him at arm's length, a time,
Ere clasping him with courage to his breast
That wellnigh bursts the while, I held her off,
This long-sought soul that mine had found a
      friend ;
And did not dare to trust her as I would.

XX.

What struggles then were mine ! Too cautious
    grown,
To dare to risk a fall, though but in love,
How would I brace my powers against her charms
That might unbalance me ! How would my will,
That strove to master my reluctant mien,
Make stiff my every smile ! or, were my heart
Too strong to be suppress'd, how would I thwart
And turn each glance that could reveal one glimpse
Of how I loved her, toward her sister first !
Unconscious Edith,—could she read deceit ?—
'T was all I dared to use. How could I else,
Poor fool, that then I felt myself to be,
Hide my infatuation !

XXI.

                What of her ?—
How could she know me when a mask I wore ?
Was not her sister pleased, when pleasing me ?
Did Edith not please me, when pleasing her ?
And so for Alice only seem'd her care ;
And Alice was a fair and flippant naught,
An empty echo only of my love.
The sweetness of the family all had gone
To fill the elder Edith.
              Then alas,
Too late, I learn'd my error. How I chafed,

Kept back from midnight strolls for sake of Alice!
And jogg'd from tête-à-têtes to give her place !
Then with her left, inspired alone to wish
To be like her a dunce ; and thus to be
Like her, in some way, Edith's all-in-all.

XXII.

Nor could I hint this truth to Edith ; nay.
Unselfish, all ethereal in her thought,
A disembodied soul had held less moods
Touch'd through the senses.   One had sooner
          snared
With tatter'd nets of tow a wind of spring,
Or with his own breath warm'd the wintry air.
Her love's regard in no way could be reach'd.
At times, I would essay philosophy,
Or try to freight her fancy's wings with facts.
Like merest sand, flung off a nervous bird,
My pleas were shaken back.
                              She " There," would cry ;
" Some everlasting everybody's law
Applied again to me !   Nay, nay, this world
Would grind one's very soul to common dust ! "

XXIII.

" And what else are we ? " turn'd I once to ask ;
" Would God we all could free ourselves from laws ;

But half our lives we spend in learning them ;
And half in learning how to love them then.
And but in souls that learn life's laws by heart,
Has wisdom, so it seems, a sway complete."

" 'T is thus with earthly wisdom," she rejoin'd ;
" But earth is ruled by folly,—idiot child
Of freedom fetter'd.   You may live the slave ;
But I choose freedom ! "

            And, as then she left,
" You lawless," thought I, " will you always prove
The water Undine of my wilderness,
All maddening, with strange metamorphoses,
My faint love thirsting to refresh itself ? "—

XXIV.

Oft while I this would moot, she changed, and
    seem'd
A fount of laughter now that sprang within,
O'er-rill'd her lips and rippled round her guise,
The very train's hem shaken by the flow.
" Nay, nay, but I shall trust you yet," I thought ;
" And still believe you good, and hold it true
That maids, like minnows, rarely show themselves
Till, caught and drawn from out the open sea,
They frisk in safety in some household pond ! "

Like this, my moods moved on,—life's usual way,
The mainspring sped by balanced contraries,
And every pulse, whose beating proves we live,
Anon with deathlike voids alternating.
One hour, my faith in her was like the sun,
The next, my doubt was lightless as the night.
All prefaced fitly that which you shall hear.

XXV.

I, once, recurring to my youth, had said
Of Elbert, that he soon, fulfilling plans
Long form'd, would join me here in Germany.

"Why," Alice cried, "to think you know so well
Our Elbert!"
        "Yours?" I ask'd.
                "Ours," Edith said,
"Ay, ay; our families have been friends for years."
But spite her careless tone, her eyes appear'd,
Slipping through lashes long, to shun my own.

And why was this?—And why, too, had she
    flush'd?—
What subtle weapon had been used to cut
Beneath the surface of her mien, and bring
The heart-blood from its core?
                Then I recall'd
How Elbert's moods, of late, had hid themselves

In strange far mists of fancy.—Could it be
That Edith, she was his?—And he, my friend,
Was he the one then that had caged her love,
And placed it where my soul in reaching forth
Could sense but bars of chill indifference?—
I could not ask her nor her sister this;
Nor even Elbert's now, for in the week
When first I met her, she had sail'd for home.
But soon, like worms that would not wait for death,
Fear-fretted jealousies clung round the form
Of dying hope that now prized Edith more,
To feel that Elbert too had prized her so.

XXVI.

A few days later, as we sat and talk'd,
He on us burst, and brought a sudden light
Illuminating her, and paling me,
Blanch'd, ash-like, in the flame of that hot flush
That warm'd her welcome. All my heart and
 breath
Seem'd sunk in silence like the buzzing bees
When autumn steals the sunlight from the flowers,
And frost seals down their sweets. I heard them
 talk
Like one who just has walk'd a glacier path
With boist'rous friends; then, stumbling, slips
 away,

Far suck'd through freezing fathoms down to death,
Yet hears the cruel laughter crackling still.

XXVII.

This hardly tuned my mood for Elbert's glee,
When then we left the sisters. "Ah, good friend,
So glad to see you ! Such a desert, life !
And friendship, such an oasis !—Your health !
Our dusty throats need clearing first, and then
Shall drafts drawn deeper clear our dusty souls."

Thus led he, hurrying on from thought to thought,
Yet not one breath for Edith could he spare.—
Why not ? Could he not trust my friendship yet ?
Half anxious then, half curious to detect,
Though wary still of love so subtly hid,
My lips, bold-braced yet trembling at the deed,
Essay'd a note to touch him,—Edith's praise.

XXVIII.

"She looks well," said he, somewhat absently.
"She looks well !" cried I, half-way nettled now ;
Should Edith be abused, forsooth, to show
What brutes men are who lose their trust ! "She
        looks—
For what then do you take her ? for a frame,
An empty effigy of human shape,

Like what a shopman hangs his gowns upon ?—
Her soul is what I spoke of,—of her soul."

" Her soul ? " he said ; " may be ; but I, may be,
Have never seen it."
     " How ?—this too ! " I thought,
" A slight is it ?—or triumph that he vaunts ? "

He caught my feeling from my fever'd mien,
And words confused and few ; and, warming then,
Made answer : " Norman, if I loved you less,
I more might love, and more might spare myself.
The thing my sister wrote, I deemed her whim ;
Could not conceive it true, yet can it be ?—
I swear, it staggers half one's faith to find
A man, devoted to the aims you claim,
So little circumspect."
     What meant he now ?
Could he believe that I had form'd a plan
To woo his Edith, knowing she was his ?—
And could my sleepless nights, my troubled heart,
My prayerful deeds, my nature that he knew,
Be so misjudged, without some fault in him ?—
" So little circumspect in what ? " I ask'd.

And then with words that could but anger me,
" In what but choice of company ? " he said ;

" No more you think of study, duty, church,
But waste the whole day long with one like this !—
Nay, check me not.   I understand my words.—
This actress, though right artless in her way,
This actress here, would play "—

                       " With me ! " I cried ;
" This ' actress ! ' " and I know not what I said ;
But yet recall what kept him forcing in,
" You err ! "—" You do me wrong ! "—" You know
    her not ! "—
Wild words, the which he ended, saying then :
" Not such am I as you profess to be ;
But had you common-sense, no piety,
You might perceive a farce, if not a fault :
A broad church yours will be then, when your
    mate,
Attracting toward the stage by charms you lack,
Will draw the sinner, while you draw the saint."

XXIX.

Struck blind, I scarcely could have felt more
    stunn'd.
Was this the truth ?   An actress would she be ?
Why had that sister of his not told me this ?—

" Not told you this ? " cried Elbert ; " What ? not
    told ?
Ay, ay, I see.—She hoped that love, perchance—

It is a woman's balm for every ill—
Might woo this Edith from her present life.
She knows her not.— And you—have you told
    her ?—
Does Edith know your plans ? "
                    " She must have known "—
I answer'd back ; and then I check'd myself.
Did not she blush to hear that Elbert came ?—
For fear was it, lest he should tell the truth ?—
To me, her friend ? to me, deceived, her dupe ?
To me, whose love she might have known, yet knew
That all that she had seem'd was not her all ?—
If she had meant deception, could my love
Survive the test ?
            Those watching death-beds, mark
That souls, when dying, ere above they spring,
Breathe deep, then pass away.   And so with minds,
When come the deadliest woes.   Down deep in
    thought,
I scarce had deem'd that aught from hell could roil
Such dregs of bitterness long undisturb'd.

XXX.

The fault, sigh'd conscience, had been all my own :
How safely might one sail the sea of life
If all his reckonings were but true to heaven !
Ah, siren-like, a rivalling earthly love

May lure to realms whose mountain heights are
    clouds,
Clouds warmly hued above a cold gray shoal,
Whose only outlines are the breakers' caps,
Whose only stir, the fury of the storm.

And I, who now had learn'd the truth, what now ?—
Should I turn back to aims I knew were safe ?—
I swore to do it ; yet I thought—and thrill'd—
Could I but hold her soul, but own herself,
Though all things else were lost, this gain were sweet !—
Were sweet, though all were lost ?   Why need this
    be ?
All might be saved.   Did I believe in God ?—
That he could change a life through human means ?
Might not her life be chang'd then ?—What were I
But faithless wholly, did I try this not ?

XXXI.

So, soon, to draw her thoughts out, baiting mine,
Some slur I dropt, suggested by a church :
It touch'd a theatre.   " Extremes," I said,
" Have met."

        " Extremes have met," she said, " before !
I take your meaning.   Elbert has disclosed—
Not what I am, but what I seem to be

To those who will not view me as I am.
You join their lists ?—I hoped for better things."

"But was it right to keep me ignorant ? "

"I hoped it right," she said, "to keep you wise.
What Elbert thought, I knew. With you, had
    hopes,
That she who might not seem so wholly wrong
Might better represent a class unknown,—"

"Without design, might represent amiss,"
I answer'd. "As for you, however class'd,
I fear no class could claim you, all in all.
For all rules have exceptions."

                    " Take but rules
For this time," said she. "Did you ever find
That ever, when the seers look forth through heaven,
They view there pews and pulpits ?—Nay, not so :
Yet oft they note a stage and galleries,
All throng'd with white-robed hosts attendant
    there.
So these, you see, at times may hint of good."

"They may," I said, "but do they, as a rule ? "

"Ah, as a rule," she said, "they hint of life—"

"But mainly life to laugh at or to fear,"
I answer'd.

"When emotion swells and shrinks,
The spirit's wings are moving," she replied.
"And that art moves them most, which mirrors
     most
The life that is, and therefore is the truth.
So often have I heard my father say :
'We read of truth who spell from nature's page ;
And art can best make out the meanings there ;
For 't is the artist's thought that finds each form
A form of thought,—imagination's glass
That views the infinite in the finite fact.
Here moves a man, you say.   What see you ?—
     man ?—
Nay, nay ; that guise material fashions there
The image only of his manliness.
And you can only know his life within,
As from the image you imagine it.
Yon little girl that skips beside the porch,—
I know her, love her, not, save as I pass
Behind that face to reach a region rare
Where dolls are sentient babes, and brothers
     kings.
And yonder maidens, musing in delight,
I know not, love not, till, in sacrifice,
My spirit seems to yield to their desires,
To wait a watchful servant unto them,
To move with motives that inspire their deeds,
To look through their own eyes and see their views,

And thrill with rhythm when their ear-drums throb ;
Then, joining all with all, imagine thus
The movements of their hidden inner moods.
Thus too, through all of life, how know we more ?
All things are fitful images alone,
Reflecting glory from the Absolute ;
And he who can imagine from the part
What marks the whole, walks in the light of heaven.
Find then a life where every child becomes
Earth's animated toy of manliness,
Each man the mass from which to mould a god,
And earth the pit whence all heaven's wealth is
    mined,
You find for thought a life worth living for,
A life the artist gives us : it is he
Discerns a spirit always veil'd in shape,
A soul in man, and reason everywhere.' "

XXXII.

Ah, Edith, so I mused, an artist thou,
Thou art indeed ! but not an actress, no,
Whatever may have train'd thee, save to tread
The stage of truth ! and Elbert's every act
Against my flinty confidence in her
Struck fire and flash'd, each time I met him now ;
The more so, that each time I met him now,
In earnest, or to stir me to distrust,
He flutter'd like her fan at Edith's beck,

Her silence fill'd with subtlest flattery,
Her vacant hours invaded with himself;
Till all my life, at last, appear'd a plot
To steal upon his absence, and then pluck
Love's fruit which once his presence only brought.

XXXIII.

And so, henceforth, I less could welcome him.
How could I do it,—with his views of her,
Yet wooing her?—He wellnigh made me doubt
If I might not mistake her,—doubt I check'd,
Flush'd fiercely soon that Elbert's deeds could hint
Thought so unworthy.   When I spoke to him,
He laugh'd me off.

               " Why, man, I like your friend,
And she likes me ; and with the other sex
The more we like, sometimes, the less we love—
Or think we love.   Do I deceive her, then,
In showing friendliness?—Why think you so?—
Forsooth, if beauty pleases me, I smile ;
If gracefulness beguile me, gaze at it ;
If wisdom awe me, offer my respect.
Good art I laud ; with fancy, am a poet ;
And with emotion, an enthusiast.
What then?—Am I a hypocrite?—How so?—
Must all our sympathy be personal?
Must one appropriate all that he would praise?
Is beauty such a flower, or is a man

So much a beast, that, having taste for it,
He needs must go and gorge it down ?—Go to !—
I watch the fair thing ; of its fragrance quaff ;
Then leave for others.   Edith knows this well ;
For that, trust her."

XXXIV.

But was it, as he claim'd ?
Were both of them so wise ?—Or would he now
By sheer sharp practice cut us two apart ?
This more seem'd like him, and more anger'd me.
Was I a boy that he should foil me thus ?

Yet what to do ?—The more I question'd this,
The more I saw but only one true course.
Our aims—my own and Edith's—differ'd much.
Yet knew I more than this.   Our hearts were one
In all desires that had inspired these aims.
And if our lives and hearts could be but join'd,
Could not my love and hers, together put,
Outweigh such aims as would be hers alone ?
Why not have faith in love, mine join'd with hers ?
What power was mightier in the universe ?
Why not have faith to trust this only soul
That ever I had met, to whom my moods
Could be unroll'd, assured of insight there
To read them rightly ?   Why, 't was all decreed :
Her power to read my soul gave her the right

To know its love, whatever might be hers.
And were I but to speak the truth to her,
So tell her all, why fear the simple truth ?
For I would say I loved her, not her aims.
If then she should prefer her aims to me,
It would be proof that she could love me not.
But if she should prefer me to her aims,
Then surely she could yield her wish to mine.

XXXV.

So, near the sunset of a summer's day,
While walking by the lake within the park,
" I mean," I breathed out cautiously, " to write
A tale of love ; and I have plann'd the tale
To open here.   In after time, perchance,
Those minds to whom it proves of interest
May love to linger here, recalling it.
Look now—this lake.   To gain the full effect
Of palace, park, and yonder heaven unveil'd,
One, gazing downward in the water's depth
Should note them wash'd of gross reality,
And—as in art—reflected.   With this view
This tale of mine shall open.   First of all,
Here, in the sunshine near us—at our feet—
Ay, in the water ; ay, friend, here I mean—
Just underneath us,—mark you, mark you, there,
The hero, and, beside him, his ideal ! "

XXXVI.

And when she saw us two there, "What?" she cried;
And then stood speechless; whereat I sped on,
Detailing all my plans and all my hopes:
How she, with soul so true and aim so high,
Might meet in them the mission meant for her,—
How all the wrongs of earth might be redeem'd
Through sacrificial deeds of such as we.

Still stood she silent.   Then I spoke again:
"But think not, Edith, for my plans alone
I plead with you.   I plead, too, for myself;
And tell my plans that you may know myself;
Not holding that I stand above you, friend.
Nay, nay; I oft feel worthy scarce to touch
Your fingers' tips, or stand erect and taint
The level of the air you breathe in; nay,
I would not judge your life; would only crave,
When we have so much else in sympathy,
That holy state where two souls, else at one,
Would both be God's.—Ah, could you thus be
    mine?"

XXXVII.

Her silence then was broken.   "Well might I
Be proud to be thus yours.   Who could not find
All meet for manhood, in your manliness?
But no, for you forget our different aims.

You never told me of these plans before.
And, Norman, now—no, no; for, through your
    church,
That fann'd some whim of his, left smouldering,
Some spark of doubt to ardent heresy,
My father suffer'd, lost his honor'd name,
His living, all; nor struggled, scrimpt, and starved
To leave his daughter ignorant of the cause.
And I?—no, no; it courses through my blood;
And you would hate my tastes, which cannot be
Like yours religious; no, for I was made
To be the minister of only art."

"But, Edith," urged I, "truth far more includes
Than most men deem who would deem all things
    theirs.—
Your tastes are not religious?—Mine are not,
If by religion you mean piety,—
Religion's brew, froth'd bubbling to be seen.
But how is it beneath the surface, friend?
Down deep within?—is not the substance there?
I never seem'd religious half so much
As when at one with you."
                              She but replied
To tell me how "her father's legacy
Had been her sister, whom she must not leave.
For her sake, seeking means of livelihood,
She first rejected, then accepted what

Her spirit, spurning once, had learn'd to love ;
As had her sister ; and for both of them
Each hope, and joy, and all they thought of now,
Was bounded by the music of the stage.
Nor could my logic change this ; nay," she said,
"Not logic leads the artist on, but light."

XXXVIII.

I heard in vain—I could not give her up.
I urged her still, still hoping her to swerve.
My slight of music, rousing her defence,
But proved my love too weak to rival it.

"My father oft," she said, "would quote your
    Book ;
Say 'music marshall'd all the better life.
What else could sway the soul, yet leave love free
To think and choose and do?'—What different
    moods,"
She added, while before us play'd the band,
"These chords, we hear, arouse in different minds !
That maid may smile amid sweet dreams of love ;
Her dark attendant dream of but her wealth ;
That matron plan some fresh self-sacrifice ;
And that spare fellow, twirling near her side
The soft mustache that downs his pursing lips,
Plan only how to hide their stingy look.

And thus all listen, musing different things ;
And all, with conscious freedom, muse of them ;
And yet one harmony controls them all,
Aroused or calm to match its changing flow.
What else but music frees the mind it rules ?
' Good-will to man,' was first proclaim'd in song."

"Good-will," I said, "but follows will for good."

"And will for good will come," she answer'd back.
"As in the older advent, so to-day,
Would I believe in power behind sweet song
To hold the universe in harmony,
Expelling evil and impelling good
Through all the limits of created life,—
A spirit's power !—What though we mortals here
With eyes material cannot see the hosts
That issue forth in forms that while they move
Awake around us echoes everywhere !
We spring to spy them, but we only hear
Their rustle in the trees by which they pass ;
Or where, with dash of water o'er the rocks,
They leave the sea or linger in the rill.
At times they rest a moment on the earth,
When twilight hides them, sighing gently then,
And lull to dreams, with tones in sympathy,
The lowly insect and the lowing herd.
At times, amid the winds that rise at morn,

They sweep across the land and startle sleep
From nervous birds that twitter in their track ;
And, now and then, in clouds that close the sky,
They bound adown the rift the lightning cleaves
Till sunlight overhead pours through again.
A spirit's power has music ; and must rule
Unrivall'd still as far as ear can heed,
Or reason hark behind it.   All the chords
Of all things true are tuned by hands divine,
And thrill to feel the touch !—

                    But sounds may rise
In souls untuned, like harp-strings when they snap,
Or, though more soft than dreamland breezes are,
May fright like forests when the dark leaves blow
About the solitary murderer—
And sweetest airs to sweetest moods may bring
But foretastes vague of harmonies on high.
The   school-girl   hears   her   comrade's   ringing
    laugh,—
'T is but the key-note trill'd before the tune.
The maiden heeds her lover's mellow plea,—
'T is but the gamut rill'd ere surge the chords.
The dame is moved by tones that cheer her home,—
And they perchance prelude the theme of heaven.
For even blows of toil and battle-guns
May be the drum-rolls of the martial strains
That rise to greet the glory yet to come.
Ay, wait we long enough, we all may hear

In all things music ; far above, at last,
May hear the treble thrilling down from heaven,
And e'en from hell no discord in the jar
That only thunders back a trembling bass."

Thus Edith spake ; while I, left lonely all,
Beheld her, ardent for her art, a cloud,
Aglow by dawn, then drawn away, away.

XXXIX.

I said, I know not what ; but far too proud,
Intoxicated though I was by love,
To let her view the folly of my fall,
I said not all I felt ; but what I felt,
Beneath the first fierce humbling of the storm,
Floods o'er my memory yet with half the woe
That overwhelm'd me then.   Am I, I thought,
So strong in love, and waiting long for it,
And always true to it, to be outweigh'd
By mere brute chaff of manhood, on the stage
Or in the pit ?   I swore 't was ever so
With all her sex.   Worth never weigh'd a straw.
A very satyr could outwoo a sage.—
Weak woman !—yet she must be weak—in brain
Or body.   Better to be weak in brain !
She then, perchance, might serve a husband's
        thought,
And wisdom's voice might rule the family !

But were her moods too strong to serve his thought,
She might serve that in him which could not
    think.—
To wed she-brains, a man should seek to be
Commended as a fool !

XL.

              And then I stopp'd :—
Here raved I, jealous of this fool alone,
This coming clown.—To think of him I blush'd—
But what of her?—of Edith?—She would live,
With faintest smile, to fascinate—ah—crowds !
The rabble would be ravish'd but, forsooth,
To clap with crazy hands the rarer air
Wherein she moved. For them, her voice would
    sound,
With every trill so swaying all who heard
That thronging cheers would thunder in re-
    sponse !—
Her form, so sweet, would plead till foulest lives
Would feel how pure were joys beyond their reach,
And long for things their touch could never taint !
My sweet, sweet love !—
              But, moving at her side,
Should I be aught ?—Alas, I could but seem—
Beside the gilded glory of the stage,
Beside the loud-mouthed suitors of the show,
An unwhipt cur, to wait at some backdoor,

And jar with signalling bark the echo sweet
Of all-the-town's applause.   She mine would be
But as the sun, whose flaming brow has touch'd
The morning sea that flushes far and near,
Is thine, O trembling globulet of spray,
Because, forsooth, his image, glass'd in all
The sea and world, is glass'd, as well, in thee !—
Fool, fool ! yet dear, dear folly !

These my thoughts ;

My words—all I recall now—came at last
When slowly sauntering back we reach'd her home.
"Would God," I sigh'd, "the time might come for
   us,
When, looking toward the future now so lone,
We two should need no more to say good-night."

"Good-bye," she said, and left me in the gloom.

XLI.

Then was it, as I turn'd about, by chance,
I came on Elbert ; and my whole soul rose
To dash at him its briny bitterness.
Is he here, thought I,—he to whom, alas,
The very potion, poisoning all my hopes,
Will prove the sparkling nectar of success,
And bring good cheer, though bringing death to
   me ?—
Then let him share it !—Still, my wiser pride

The purpose check'd, and balancing rash hate
With hateful prudence, closed his opening smile
But with a frown that would not welcome him.

With any truth to self, so argued I,
I could do nothing else ; nor could abide
A town that held him.   So I left the town ;
And so these friends of mine, so prized of old,
And I had parted,—not as friends would part,
With love's high zenith fever'd like the skies
Where eve has rent from them a fervid sun,
Then cool'd and calm'd in starlight sprinkled thick
Until the sun come back.   We crack'd apart,
Like icebergs drifting southward, join'd no more,
And sunn'd alone the while they melt away.

XLII.

No need is there that here I should recall—
I would not if I could—my suffering.
From Elbert, best of friends, my nobler self,
My soul of virtue and my heart of love,
What cause could rightly tear me ?—Asking this,
My heart rose up from reason to rebel ;
Indignant to have found a theory
That dared to hold an innate impulse down ;
While will, caught there, betwixt the heart and
        head,
Each charge would bear, and yet forbear to act.

And Edith, peerless Edith ! how my soul
Would struggle to forget her !   Struggling thus,
How fair her form, conjured by raving thought,
Would rise, a Venus o'er my sea of sighs,
Till I would bend, and seem to plead anon
To be forgiven for forgetting her !
And then, how would I tear her traits apart ;
And pluck the petals from each budding grace
And hope its naked stem some trace would show,
Too void of beauty, to suggest again
The bloom and sweetness of the life I loved.
Alas, but while I wrought for this alone,
How would her virtues but the more unfold !—
Like God's own glory flowering in the skies,
That those detect who would not find it there,
But, when they test the stars, have dealt with light.

XLIII.

I wrought and rested ; it was all in vain.
My highest consolation was the hope
That hard-earn'd sleep might hold me long in
    dreams
Where evermore my soul might with her dwell,
Though every morn I seem'd yet more alone.
Awake, asleep, throned constant o'er my heart,
I served this image all intangible,
This photographic fantasy of truth,
This fairy nothingness of vanish'd fact,

A shape to love, minute yet mighty still,
To senses nothing, but to spirit all.

XLIV.

Thus lived I, triumph'd over ; as are clouds
Whereon the sun sits throned ; all bright are they,
And bright beneath them is the sunset sea.
In splendid serfdom to its love, my soul,
That shone with kindling glory, thence beheld
A kindling glory shine from all about.

No whim of mine was this ; it fills my creed ;
The graft of all true love regenerates.
Those in whom love is born are born anew,
And all their family of fancies then
Bear family traits ; those loving, and those not,
Being wide apart as rainbows and the rain.
I might be superstitious, but to me
The temple of my life's experience
Had been less sacred, had it held no shrine
Whereon to heap sweet tokens of my love.
And all that loom'd around seem'd holier now,
Illumed by holy lights of memory.

Nor long was it ere I had grown to share
In all the love of all with whom I met ;
And oft, too, thus invoking sympathy,
My wishes wrought like witches, and conjured
The thing they wish'd for : sympathy would come.

XLV.

And so my moods, thus moving on, at last
Found special pleasure in a friendship form'd
Upon a day of tramping through the Alps.
Her name was Grace, and gracious was her mien ;
And graces everywhere attended her
Through jars and joys of journeys afterward.
So splendid never as my Edith ; never
So striking, so alluring, or so shunn'd ;
Her brilliance would not dim a rival's eyes,
Nor beauty shade another's face with frowns.
One saw in her a modest, model maid,
A woman loved by women ; and with men
A presence, mellow-lighting like the moon ;
Yet could she shed no light when came my storms,
As now they came full often.   Then it seem'd
Her very mildness made her moods too dull
To penetrate the clouds that cover'd mine.

XLVI.

" It must be lonesome here for one like you,
A stranger-land, indeed, here," would she sigh.
" Why could we not, church people, day by day,
Have converse here, and thus live more at one ? "

When hearts hold secrets, even love that comes,
And comes in crowds, will bring the prying soul

Full drive to spring them open.   How I shrank
To meet with those with whom my soul could find
No source of sympathy beneath the sound
Produced when tongue and teeth and lips combine
To mouth one shibboleth!   A fate like this
Foretoken'd only, made me well nigh faint
As feels a soldier, falling at his post,
With heart shell'd out and emptied of the soul.
I could but find excuses, partly real
And partly feign'd, the fringe of ready whims.

XLVII.

She startled echoes from my inmost soul
By words that named my "life-work."

                             "Yes," I said ;
"We all should sympathize.   All own one lord ;
All wait beside one shore ; all watch one tide.—
So too do snipes and snails ! and so do souls
That yet shall rule in heaven ten towns and one.
Souls differ, Grace ; and John from James, as well
As both from Judas.—Judas lingers too."

"So many," sigh'd she, " sell their Christ, and think
Souls rich, that but receive suggestions rich
From art or——"

                  Had regard for Edith, now,
Made me, at last, a champion of art ?—

"However or wherever plied," I said,
"Real power for good owns good enough to claim
Some courtesy from Christian charity.
If I but fling a stone in yonder pond,
Wherever it may fall, it stirs the whole.
So if I throw out thought for mind or heart,
Through art or through religion, each may move
The whole man thus, and move him for his good."

"Ah, but," she breathed, with slight dogmatic
        stress,
"A simple woman, I would move his heart,
Through love, as Christ too did ; not so ? "
                                    " Do this,"
I said, "you do but what is woman's right ;
And none about you will dispute the right.
But ask me not to limit thus the Christ.
How dare I ?—if our churches teach the truth,
If He incarnated the sum of life
And spirit of all good,—his holiness
His wholeness, and His perfectness, the proof
Of what He was ?   Nor dare I limit those
Who follow Him.—Why may they not live His,
Not aiming here nor there, but everywhere
To make the most of all God meant them for.
And things there are that art can do for man
To make him manlier.   Not the senseless rock
Is all it fashions into forms of sense ;

But senseless manhood, natures hard and harsh,
Great classes crush'd, and races driven to crawl
Till all their souls are stain'd with smut and soil,—
More human seem these when the hands of art
Have grasp'd their better traits and hold them forth.
And men who see these better traits, and see
The tender touch of art that holds them forth,
Behold a beauty never else beheld ;
And all their hearts beat more humanely while
They heed the plea of these humanities.
And so, I think, although the wilderness,
At times, a John in camel's hair may need,
There open too, in ways of life less wild,
More ways, where love may plead in guise more soft.
In short, as long as one may choose his course,
'T is best we do what each can do the best."

XLVIII.

" Oh, you perplexing ! " cried she ; " not for me,
For *your* brain ! Tell, pray, where it rummaged last,
To catch these cobwebs ?—I have seen them, yes ;
These halls are full of them, and libraries,
Old musty things !—But, Norman, soberly,
This German text is bad for eyesight, yes ;
And half I doubt—Come, tell me, tell the truth,
Do *you* see clearly aught that you can do ? "
" Why so ? " I ask'd ; " do you ? "

                              " Why not," she said,

All serious now, " do what shall yield life's day
The most of glory at its evening hour ?—
The sun sets brightest after days of storm."

" What, always ? " ask'd I ; " are you sure of this ?
I know true faith that mainly aims to rid
Our present life from fears of future ill.
To it what need of storms, if sunshine here
May best prepare one for the future calm ?
That future is eternal ; even so
How can we gauge th' eternal save by time ?
How can we judge of joy that will not end,
Save by our own, if ours would only last ?
What is it to be blessèd, if not this,—
To find our process of becoming blest
Made permanent, our young weak wings of faith
Full fledged and flying by habit ?—and if so,
Heaven's habits are form'd here.   Suppose a youth,
That, by and by, he may enjoy much wealth,
Act miserly,—what gains he by and by ?—
Much wealth, perhaps ; but, holding with it, too,
The miser's moods, establish'd now as traits,
Incorporated modes of all his life,
He with them holds what most unfits the soul
To use wealth, or enjoy it.   So on earth
When avarice, aim'd for heaven, makes man a monk,
What can he gain thereby, save monkish moods,
Become establish'd in him now as traits.

Incorporated modes of all his life?
But, holding these, the soul must with them hold
What most unfits it to enjoy—not here,
In any sphere at all,—a life of love."

XLIX.

"You surely would not mean," she ask'd and
        paused,
"That you could throw aside your hopes? your
        vows?
Your life-work?—seek enjoyment?"

                                "Ah," said I,
"Enjoyment is the man's most heartfelt praise
To Him that fram'd his being.   What should I,
A child of God, do here but live God's life?—
Which is not now, nor then, but evermore.
My soul must thrive the best, as best I make
My now, eternal; my eternal, now.
So when a storm comes, let me bar it out;
And, braced against the present ill, grow strong;
And when the sunshine, let me open wide
To that which makes all nature grow more sweet.
Thus, realizing in my earthly state
The aim of heaven, why do I praise Him less
Whose life is that of heaven, than those who wear
The guises of that slattern of the soul,
Asceticism, shuffling toward far good,
Slipshod and snivelling?"—

                       " Now, that goes too far ! "
Cried Grace.   " Do I do this ?—Ah, but I know
A man so moody !—Own it.   Were I you,
I just would set to work.   To work off whims,
The best way, say they, is to work them out ;
One hand at work is worth ten heads that shirk."

" You find me moody!" sigh'd I ; " and complain ;
Deem moods not meet.   Oh, no ; they prove we
    feel !—
Nor pious they : they prove we think ! "

L.

                                And yet,
I could but blame myself ; so fain to draw
This gentler soul from her still streams of life
Toward waves thus fiercely dash'd about my own !
You know, though, how it is : our thought, like
    light,
Opposed, will vaunt itself ; and brightest play,
Glanced off from things it does not penetrate.
So, more to shock her than for sympathy,
My thought play'd round the surface of her life :
It had been shaped so—to so smooth a thing—
I burn'd to warp it of complacency.
Oft, though unconscious of the least mistruth,
I feign'd a fall in fancied depths of ill,
And mock'd that I might hear her call me thence ;

And learn'd therein to envy some the rake.
For what a charm it were to hear—not so ?
That is, if one were vicious, through and through—
Such pleas for love from lips that aye were pure ?
The very depth of one's unworthiness
Would whet such relish for a thing so strange !

LI.

But weeks and months went by, in which she fill'd
A certain void in life ; and, every eve,
We parted for the night made better friends.
Once, ending thus, the pleasures of the day,
We chanced upon a path where, sauntering too,
Lo, Elbert enter'd and encounter'd us.

At first scarce friendly, after divers tests,
And in the new light of my life with her,
His older love return'd with oldest warmth :
" To think so thin a fancy," he exclaim'd,
" As last I found you folded in, should screen
Our genuine hearts, a moment, each from each ! "

LII.

The fancy thin !—I let him keep his word ;
I would not argue.—Still, with care not loath
To guard some credit yet for having sense,
I hinted at the truth,—how I had changed,
And how had changed my thoughts about myself,

About my life-work.   "For that fancy, friend,
That fancy thin my own true self reveal'd.
If spray it were, it left a constant sea
That heaves and heaves.   With moods that move
    like mine,
So madden'd by traditions, calm'd by dreams,
Content scarce ever, till at hazard dash'd
Through ways that lead to sheer uncertainty,
Where fancy more may seek than matter shows
In things that are but matter,—what am I
For life-work such as priesthood, sure in creeds
And sureties for the soul, whereon may lean
All weaker faith, with warrant not to bend?"

LIII.

Then Elbert laugh'd.   "Ah, were you but a bow,
Your bending most would shoot most.—Not a
    priest?
A man alone?—You yet a brother are
To many a soul that sails the sea of life,
Where oft the horizon trembles with the change
Of wind and wave ; and hope, too hale, oft mourns
Fair promises, like skies that fade in fog.
A man alone?—And yet the moods of man
May make men love us for our manliness,
Who draw them, Christ-like through our sympathy,
Toward self,—God's image here, and thus toward
    Him."

"But draw them how?" I cried.   "Woe me, I stand,
A poet born, who deem'd his Muse had fled ;
That time and trouble had a stone roll'd up,
Her sweet form sealing in their sepulchre.
And yet one breath of love could rouse the dead.
All day the subtle spirit haunts me now,
Thrill'd through and through to sound her sweet-
      ness forth."

"Then let it sound !" he said.   "Rare rest it were,
Were all one's recreation freshen'd thus ;
And slumber serenaded by the Muse."

"One's recreation ! slumber !" I exclaim'd ;
"Is mind a deep that wells with most of thought
When void the most?   I tell you none can draw
A truthful inspiration save from truth.
The poet's ken may people heaven like clouds,
All phantom shaped, and splendid as their sun ;
But all his fairest forms were vapors first
That heaven drew, mist-like, from the earth beneath.
Thought decks itself in holiday attire,—
Turns fantasy,—to expend the inertia large
Of large reserves of philosophic force,
Forced into play, the night's dream opening where
The day's work closes."

                    "Close work thus," he said ;
"And all the measures of your verse may show

How sweet can be the echoes waked anon
By labor's ringing anvil."
                              "Nay," I sigh'd.
"Such work would bring too much of sleep,—no
    dreams.
When born with souls like harps the Muse would
    play,
What better can men do than toil to keep
Their thoughts and feelings close in tune with
    truth?
For this will tax them wholly. They, who try,
With those few strings that fate has given to them,
To play all parts of all the orchestra
Will help the play of no part. We are men;
And straight and narrow must our pathways be.
If, Adam-like, we would be gods, we fall.
Not given to mortal is the life supreme,
In naught unbalanced, laden light in naught,
Existence evermore at equipoise,
Complete with that which on itself depends.
Oft, who his worth would double, nothing does
Except to break the back of worth that was,
While doubled burdens fall to doubled waste.
We men should humbler be, and pray to heaven
To have horizons hanging nearer us.
Our views too broad unfit us for the earth,
Yet fit us not for loneliness divine,—
The wide chill chaos, back behind the stars."

LIV.

Thus would I talk, and trouble Elbert much,
For he would rouse me in his rattling way :
" Why, Norman, you are hedging all our hopes.
Do not you pity moods that dote on you ?
If, man, your metaphysics be not yet
Beyond all physics, pray you, cure yourself ;
Be more material ; or material powers
Will alienated grow, and so forget
And count you out in all their reckonings ;
And you who are of earth, will earth own not ;
And you who would be heaven's, will heaven own
        not.
To own yourself and only own yourself,
Is worse than serfdom that has earn'd a smile,
Though but from wrinkling cheeks of sham good-
        will."

LV.

Then, through my gloom exploring for its cause,
His thought would light on Edith.   He was right ;
Perhaps less right, grew garrulous of Grace.
For deeming love's return my only hope,
And, seeking this, resolved, as well, to find it,
My slightest flush could furnish him a glow
As bright to light his pathway as the day.

Of course I could deny it ; say I held
No key to spring the latch of love like hers.

Our lips, but parting e'en to speak of love,
Infringe on Cupid ; and, before they shut,
Some tingling arrow of that jealous god
Will make them drop all soberness.

He laugh'd :

" Now say you never saw the sea, for waves ;
Or stars, for twinkling ; or the trees, for leaves ;
But tell me not, you never saw the heart
That bosom heaves ; nor ever saw the play
Of faith and freak within that twinkling eye ;
Nor ever saw the spirit when the smile
That breaks in laughter shakes the form aside.
Come, friend, I know you better.   Say you err ;
Or, by my soul, I never read you yet."

" And more," said I ; " she is not my ideal."

He laugh'd again : " Most men who court ideals
Have first their idol ; and, the false god fell'd,
Hoard then the fringe that dangled on its train,
And spend their lives in hunting other trains
To match but forms and colors of the first.
It strikes me, friend, that all things truthful grow.
E'en love outgrows the fashion of its youth :—
The world whirls on apace ; and different hues
Turn toward the noonday-sun.   No dawn returns.
What form or color robes the infinite ?—
Yet aught to worship matches that alone.

So look you less for worship, than for worth.
You need a mate, friend ; not a mystery."

"A mate," I said, "but she for whims could waive
The truth whereto was anchor'd all my soul."

LVI.

Still Elbert parried me : "To hear you prate
Of truth—with women !—Why, you tried that once,
With Edith, not so ?—and she liked it, eh ?
Herself had love for that same truth ? — What
　　then ?—
How very strange, when yesterday she pass'd,
She craved no more of it."

　　　　　　　　　　　　" She pass'd ? " I cried.

"Ay, ay," said he ; "while you, so wrapp'd in
　　Grace,
Walk'd near,　and noted nothing.　How she
　　turn'd !—
Then spoke of 'haste, such haste, she could not
　　stay' ;
And bade me 'not to tell' you.—Thus, you see,
I keep my word ; I promised nothing though.'

At this, I blush'd ; it but encouraged him.

"This flame of sympathy you deem'd so bright
Extinguish'd was—you may have thought by me.

If so, I tell you, friend, 't was lightly done.
I but outblew you ; and the moral is :—
True flames, these women flicker with the wind.
But use you breath enough, their natures yield.
Yet blow for their sakes, not for your ideals.
One seldom finds a sweetheart sweet enough
To love her suitor's pinings for mere whims.
Nay, they alone our all-in-all would be ;
And so are jealous of our male ideals.
Then, too, they are creative less than we,
And cling more to the creature, love and serve
Embodied life that may be seen and felt.
You doubt me ?—Test it.—Read that rhyme you
     wrote,
Inspired by fancy.—Say so ;—still they hint.
' Ah, this was she, or she, whom once he loved.'
It may be, Grace does waive your love of truth.
If so, 't is better ; more you seem her own."

"More likely," cried I, " I and all my truth
Seem like champagne,—a thing that pops and
     shocks,
But yet enlivens when the hour is dull."

"She likes the shocking," said he.   "Know you not
Most maids love mastery ? and the closest cling
To those who show the strength to hold them fast ?
Full many a suitor, when he wins his love,

Will treat her merely like some petted puss,
Caress, then cuff her, till she yield at last,
Won solely through his wondrous wilfulness.
If one defer to her, she pities him;
And names him friend, because she feels him frail.
Her favorite cavalier seems less a friend,
At first, than foe who stays the brunt in time
To seem to save her when she seems to fall."

"And should make him fall," cried I.   " 'T is not strange
Such onsets numb her senses!   Heaven preserve
The world from women rear'd to feel but weak,
Whose whole experience, nurtur'd not to think,
Unfolds in passions pert of wishes dwarf'd,
Afraid of truth and dodging to deceit!
Let loose from home, their thing that ought to think
Is dry and hollow as a sounding-board
Behind a tongue that, like a weather vane,
Creaks with the windy scandal of the town
Till endless malice make one's ear-drum ache,
At one spot hammer'd sore, and o'er and o'er,
With humdrum gossip of surrounding naught.
Small gain are they, to crown our courtships grand,
Prinked out with flowers and flattery!   Wise man;
Flowers draw the bee, and flattery the fool.
One stings; the other—Laugh not, Elbert, nay,
You know it well, what friendship craves; and these

Light, simpering women, testing manhood's woof
By worthless nap that tickles their vanity,—
O I shall wait some coming woman, I,
Who needs no suing since in soul we suit ;
Nor ruling either.—Love shall rule us both."

" You true Pygmalion," cried he, " make a maid !—
But all maids grow to us, when wedded once ;
For practical, they are, far more than men,
And bow to powers that be.   Though caught, like
       fish,
Through bait they crave not ere men tender it,
They cleave to love once offer'd them ; nor turn,
Like male-friends, clinging—true as iron, forsooth—
To each new stronger magnet !   Were they thus,
Our homes might hardly hold our rivals there.
Accept the facts, friend ; in this world of reals,
Ideals must give way.   So look to Grace,—
Despite your protest, your true mate ; and love
In maids like her is limitless when won.
You like her, too ; now, now "—

LVII.

And so we talk'd.
I never thought it meant much ; for we talk'd
Of all things, almost ; and, in play, at times,
Would I indulge in hopes that he was right.
Once too, far up in clouds, my fancy feign'd

To question if her friends, or she, would wish
My calling to be hers.   I scarce had dream'd
Of Elbert's giving weight to whims like this.
Yet after that I mark'd him much with Grace ;
But naught surmised until, one time, he said :

" All right, my Norman ; I have talk'd with her ;
All but to tell her why I talk'd with her ;
And with her parents talk'd, and now they all
Agree in praising plans of life like yours ;
These latter actually sighing oft,
' Would we but had a son for work like that ! '
So, friend, your way is clear."

LVIII.

But was it clear ?—
So sure was it, that I could pluck this fruit ?
If sure, so sure the Eden open'd not
To tempt, as well as bless me ?—Could it be
That love could yet be mine ?—The hope seem'd
    sweet ;
Yet strange ! — Why strange ? — The change ? —
    Seem'd all change so ? —
Yet marriage ?—Why did mortals marry then ?—
For love, they said, for love.   And what was love ?
What more than liking well ?—Whom liked I so ;
And all in all, and always ?—Edith ?—What ?—
And liked her calling ?—If I liked not that,

I liked not her, not wholly.   If not her,
Then liked I no one wholly ; and my will
In love, as in all other earthly states,
A choice must make,—take one of different boons,
And all imperfect.   Why should not my love
Serve thus my judgment ?   Grace could stand this
    test,
And life with one like her so sweet could be !

LIX.

I thought ; but all my thinking stirr'd but thought
Until, one time, I mused of other days ;
How once, and at the merest hint of love,
My younger blood, like some just conquering
    host
That trembling hope bears on, would bound through
    veins
That thrill'd and thrill'd while shook each trodden
    pulse ;
How, hot as deserts parch'd by swift simoons,
And wild as forests fell'd by sudden blasts,
My frame would glow and bend at every breath
That tidings bore me of the soul I loved.
Love Grace did I ?—How then had love been
    tamed !
Mere self-control was it, that now, grown strong,
Had broken in, at last, that bounding blood,
And held the rein to joy ?—Ah, self-control,

The rest rheumatic of a zest grown old,
It came with time ; but mine had come from care.
Cold self-control, the curse of northern climes,
The artful despot of the Arctic heart,—
Before my summer scarce had warm'd me yet,
Was it to freeze me with its wintry clutch
Of colorless indifference ? chill and check
The springs of love till still'd in ice-like death ?

Woe me ! I sigh'd ; but then, with nobler cause,
More nobly moved, I mourn'd that older love.
It aye had come from regions far and pure,
From sacred heights of dream-land and desire,
And trailing light like Moses from the mount,
With one hand clasping mine, one pointing up
To something earthly, yet more near the sky.
It aye had thrill'd the throbbing veins it near'd
And made my brow flush proudly as the boor's
When king's hands knight him, and he bears away
Ennobled blood forever.—My mood though —
This lax-limb'd, loitering, sisterly regard,
So cold, so calm, so cautious,—what was this ?—
To call it love my spirit could have swoon'd,
Shrunk like some parent's when he first has found
His fair babe's brain to be a gibbering blank.—
And then, down underneath my deep despair,
Where heaved a sigh that loosen'd all my soul,
Like some sweet kiss of sudden death that draws

To sudden bliss, when men to heaven are snatch'd
From all the roar and rage of war, there came
One hope for Edith ;—and my shaken powers
Lost hold of Grace forever !

LX.

                    Still would doubt
Survive, and question if, when off my guard,
In fancy rampant, I had Grace deceived
As I had Elbert ?   Could it be, indeed,
That I, who wish'd it not, had won her love ?
And if so, what ?—The problem wore me thin.
My very wits, indeed, seem'd whittled off
To point and probe it.
                    Strangely was it solved.
I dropp'd a vague surmise,—how two " should act,
In case one loved, and love were not return'd."

She arch'd her answer with so rare a blush,
That all my doubts dissolved ; and, catching truth
From hers contagious, like a boy confused,
All fused in frankness bubbling o'er the brim,
I blurted out about my older love ;
To root it out would root out love itself,
And not to do so, leave none else a place.

" I love not you ! " she cried, with look so changed,
My weight of shame had sunk me through the floor.

But, driven to words, like one some startle shocks,
I stammer'd "Elbert!"—and stood shock'd in
    truth ;
For had I wrench'd it from her bodily,
Scarce redder had her flushing brow repell'd
My wresting rudely such a secret thence.
At one bound then my honor had return'd.
A bandit had I been, to force the spring
That lock'd her secret—but had spied her soul !—
And back to right it brought me. "Pardon,
    Grace,"
I breathed, then hush'd : With strange and holy
    power,
New-welling love seem'd fountain'd in my heart,
And shower'd and stream'd through all my thrill-
    ing veins ;
And then I check'd it. She was not for me,
Alas, unworthy ! She was Elbert's—all !

"Grace," breathed I, "you are doubly now my
    friend,
And doubly dear, since Elbert's dearest friend ;
Thank Heaven that you have loved so true a man.
I go to him."
                    "Nay not to him," she urged.

But I, though yielding to her, as it seem'd,
Made loose the letter for the sake of spirit ;
Nor promised aught, unless he loved her not.

LXI.

But Elbert, found, the whole sweet truth confess'd,
With all his love for her so satisfied,
And all the sacrifice for me so clear,
I honor'd God the more from this, the hour
I found His honor so encased in man.
" Nay, thank me not," he said.   " You brought me
    her.
Nor did I dream I loved her, ere I sought
Your cause to plead ; and, aim'd for what it wills,
My will is wilful.   There, you know the whole."
And soon, as if he fear'd our former strife
Were not yet still'd, "And you, perhaps, were right
With Edith, too," he said ; " at least, were safe.
Hold still to truth.   It yet may save us both."

LXII.

And then I learn'd—as many a friend has learn'd—
Who with them strove my joy for them to share,
How much more joy was theirs, when theirs alone.
But this could scarcely turn my thought aside
From self, left lonelier now than e'er before.
I strove to drown my grief in work.   The work
Was but a worm's that eats from day to day
The morrow's bed, at morning dragging on
A soulless trunk, through troubles void of hope.

My soul to startled sighs was roused alone

When Edith cross'd my vision.   Then my mood,
As gloom would gather round again, would grieve
To think, in sorting souls, fate bungled so,
And let our traits be judged of by our trades,—
The dusty imprint of the things we touch.
" As well," cried I, " to judge of winds of heaven,
By bogs they brush, or fogs they bear away !
We two that so could trust each other's hearts,
Why should we not join hearts, and leave to them
The hands ?   If wiser than the world we were,
Why should we act, forsooth, in worldly ways ?
What need that all should don the uniform
That fits men for the social march of fools ?
What need ?—Ah me," I thought, "all need,
      indeed,
If one wish influence in the world or church.—
Or church !—Must it then crucify the soul
To save appearances ? the body ? form ?
The Christ gave up all these to save the soul.
'T is treason when His churches join the world,
And courting smiles from bigotry appeased,
And grinning hell that holds the whole its own,
Preach up the crucifixion of the soul
To save the body, save the outward form.
A church is His no more, whose rites or creeds
Keep souls untrue to truth within that shows
God's tempering there, the touch that makes man
      man."

LXIII.

I swore it should not be, it could not be ;
No life could so be cleansed,—by wringing thence
The blood that warms the heart ; no face made pure
By turning pale the blush of beauty cast
By shadows where sweet love goes in and out.
Love, love should never be a slave, but free.—
" Come, Edith ! "—Then I question'd, Would she
    come ?—
Nay, not to my life.   Mine must go to hers.
But this, mine could not,—could do nothing
    there ;—
And would not !—Whence then sprang my call to
    her ?—
If not from reason, from my wish, forsooth.—
My wish for what ?—for her ?—as now she was ?—
Not so ; but rather might be.—Whence then sprang
This ' might be ' ?—whence, alas, but from myself,
As I kept moulding it within my soul ?
Why rail'd I, then, against the church and world ?—
Not these alone, but I would have her changed.
These all but echoed back my own soul's voice ;
And yet, augmented by the voice of all,
In heeding them, I heeded not myself,
But something greater, grander than myself.
For if a single man may image God,
Then many men who join their partial gifts
And parted wisdom,—till the whole become

Not merely human but humanity's,—
May watch our ways and keep them circumspect
With eyes that often wellnigh stand for His
Who still more fully in mankind than man
Rules over truth in each through truth in all.
Why term me slave, then, when I serve my kind?—
Through serving it, I best may serve, as well,
My godlier self !—Let general thought take shape ;
What better can incarnate sovereignty ?
What stir to nobler dreams or grander deeds ?
The soul in reverence may kneel to it,
Yield all to it.—So may my neighbors reign,
And I may be their slave, yet own myself ;
And deify, while I defy my pride !

LXIV.

A new conversion, say you ?—call it so.
The truth converts one oft, if he be true.
The true man loves his own, and fights for it ;
And, since his own is little and God's is large,
He often fights to fall.   Yet ranks on high
Now throng with heroes, whose too slender blades
Were wielded but for slender causes once ;
Nor sheathed, ere flying shatter'd from their grasp,
Till truth they fought had proven too strong for
    them.
Then, when they knew themselves, and knew the
    truth,

And knew its mercy too, they loved the truth,
And came to be its champions, evermore.
So now with me : rebellious though I was,
Rebellion wrought my rescue.   Truth trium-
        phant
Enlisted duty for a loyalty
That made all life seem lordlike.   Work began.
Thank God, we all have heads above our hearts ;
And, if we let them reason with us well,
They rule us for our best.

LXV.

                        What Elbert wish'd,
When   first   I   cross'd   the   sea,   was   more   than
        wrought.
I brought back not alone what books could give,
But in myself a sense of others' wants,—
For in my heart a wondrous wealth of love ;
Ay, wealth it was ; though, like the ore in mines,
It only proved that that which lived had died.
What though my life, complete with her alone,
Seem'd always rent ? a weight of broken quartz
That only gleam'd where it had fractur'd been ?
That weight was wealth that sparkled back to greet
Each glance of sunshine.
                        Thus I found that love
At times may prove a treasure even dead,
If dead enough in spirits yet alive.

Mine, thwarted so, had made me more the man
That Elbert wish'd,—a man for all mankind :—
No special pleader for a special class
Whose grasping greed crowds out the general
    good ;—
But one who pleads for all fair rights for all .
Nor would I bide content with utter'd words.
Too often, these, when widest welcomed, wake
But echoes brief as breath from which they spring.
I craved the mission less of roaring waves
Than of the rare wrought shells that, evermore,
When storms are gone, suggest their living presence.

LXVI.

Anon it happen'd that through others' hands
My tales, pour'd forth to voice my loneliness
In echoing talk and song, were framed in plays,
And then were phrased in music ; and, in time,
Arose like sighings of a human wind
Above a human sea, while, all about,
There swept, like surgings of a rhythmic surf,
The shifting scenes and singers of the stage.
And, chief of all the singers in those throngs,
Who best of all could body forth the truth
That most of all had seem'd to be inspired
By Edith's influence, while in all I thought
Her love had ever lured expression on,
Was her own self.

LXVII.

But love outstrips my tale.
Erelong, from shores where surged that surf of song,
Like gems the ocean casts upon its coast,
About me lay a growing store of wealth.
And then, with broaden'd means, led on to push
Toward broaden'd purposes, I spoke and wrote;
And found, anon, while aiding here and there
Where aid was rare, wide opening to my view,
A worthiest mission in this new reform
That seeks to make the server and the served
Walk hand in hand, while wage gives way to share,
And, furthering all men to their furthest due,
Thus lifts the low and lost.

LXVIII.

At last, one day,
There came a letter from our bureau's head,
With it, another, sent him, so he wrote,
"By some enthusiast, a character—
A woman, and a woman too of mind;
And yet, withal, who had been strangely led,
Through doubtful ways, he thought, toward doubt-
ful ends,
Till doubts had wrought reaction,—as when clouds
That course on clouds, at last, bring lightnings
forth
That clear them off. And now her vision, clear'd,

Had found within her soul a wish to work,—
In new ways truly for a cause like ours,—
For us and with us.   But I held her note,
She dwelt near by me : could I visit her?
And give my judgment then ? "

LXIX.

           This note, so sent,
Was—would you guess it?—Edith's.   What she
    wrote,
Weighs love against all liking to this hour.
All thrill'd with hope, yet trembling for my fate,
I spell'd out all her tale :—" Her sire—his aims—
And her fulfilment of them—her success—
Earth seem'd a kingdom prostrate at her feet,
And she, a queen ; alas, but, like a queen,
Was doom'd to hold a throne where rivals came,
To spy her weakness out, and wrest away
A power that could be kept by power alone.—
How sad for woman when her hopes were based
On practice that must all her heart conceal,
That must be conquering ever or be crush'd !
At first her love for art had kept her up,—
And for success, and for a sister dear,
Who shared her earnings, who, while cheer'd the
    crowds,
At last, had died, and left her all alone.
And, after that, her soul had loathed applause,

Had found her nature so belied, misjudged,
Her life the embodiment of hollow sound,
And all surroundings echoing back but sound,
Chill admiration in the place of love,
Her friends but flatterers, and herself unknown.

" With this, her world had grown so hard, so parch'd,
Without one source affording sympathy—
She took no credit to herself for aught ;
The weakest sigh that could have heaved a breast,
A dying breast, had crack'd so dry a crust—
She rose, one morn, and swore to free her soul,
Let pent-up love in softening currents flow
Till something human, ay, and heavenly, too,
Were nurtured by the wish from which it sprang.

"She could not work now for herself alone ;
For she had learn'd that all life's purposes
Are held like lenses that a soul may use
To gather in heaven's light and flash it round
Upon its world illumin'd ; or, not so,—
If turn'd on self,—to but inflame and dim
Its own self-centered vision.   So she now
One only purpose knew,—to pledge her gifts
To those who most might need them ; and she
        came,
With all she was or hoped she yet might be,
Her gifts of nature and her skill in art,

To work for us, whose aims were plann'd so well,
To further all men to their furthest goals,
And lift the low and lost."

LXX.

           And then I rode,
As fast as trains could take me ; and I wrote,
Like one intoxicated, from the inn :
"The bureau's agent here abides your wish " ;
And, signing not my name, awaited thus
The welcome sure to seem more sweet than life.
It came.   I went.

       " You ? " Edith cried, " and whence ? "
" From whence ? " I said.   " Each slightest spark
    of good
Flies upward, and the heaven returns it where
It fires the most ?—and where were tinder found
Like my heart ? "

       " Why is this ? " I heard ; " My note—
Did it miscarry ?—Would you thwart me now—
Or, though my gifts could aid them, do they wish
No help from me ?—My heart was fix'd on it."

" On my cause," breathed I.   " Did you never think
That work with them would make you work with
   me ? "

"Why think of that ? " she ask'd.—" Enough to know
I sought my own work here."

                                    " Why, Edith, friend,"
I answer'd—"Why could not your work be mine ?
What parts us now ?   What though, like mine, your
        soul
Had come to look down life's long dreary vista,
And watch yourself alone.   Why bide alone ?
I, I, at least, through all these years have seen—
Not you yourself, for that too dear had been !—
But I have seen a vision, seeming you
Within the far horizon of my hopes,
The sweet mirage before me.   Now, at last,
I know those misty outlines veil'd the truth ;
It must have meant that you would yet be found—
That we should meet.   Heaven surely meant it so."

LXXI.

Her mien had chang'd ; and yet she ask'd again,
" But how with Grace ? I thought "—
                                    " Alas," I said,
" With your dear spirit thron'd above my love,
What were I but a traitor, wedding Grace ?
This heart was yours, your dwelling-place alone
Nay, now I do not come to give it you :
It only opens to an owner old.
How sacredly I guarded it for you !—
A holy place, though there, above the shrine,
The niche was empty.   Ah, has earth seem'd rude ?
Some reason was there ; surely some there was.

We war with Providence, who war with life.
We seek to mould our own existence out ;
But life, best made, is mainly for us made.
Each passing circumstance, a tool of heaven,
Grates by to smooth some edge of character,
And model manhood into better shape.
Has nought been wrought with you ?   Ah, idol
    mine,
You living image of all hope, would God,
Love's niche were fill'd, love's altar stood com-
    plete ! "

LXXII.

Then Edith lean'd her face against her hand,
And slowly came the words that seem'd so dear :
" It may be, Norman, may—I know—I feel—
It must be earth, so roughly handling one,
Should round experience for some wise design.
Yet this—it cannot be—how can it ?—nay—
For me you come—and you ? your voice I hear ?
No echo void, oft, oft so sweet in dreams ?—
Nor now to wake me ?—Nay I trust.   You may—
'T will stray no more—take back your wanderer."

" My wanderer ! " I answer'd, when I could ;
" Ah Edith, you but wander'd as the lamb ;
My spotless, worldling-mediator, you !—
It wander'd ?—yes ; it cross'd a threshold chill ;

A proud cathedral enter'd ; there found one
Too pleased with what he had, to gaze outside.
To him those arches low seem'd high as heaven ;
And all the sweet and sunny air without,
When strain'd through stain'd and smoke-wreathed
           window-panes,
Gleam'd lurid as were hell.   This man spied you :
He saw you shun him—leave him.   He pursued—
Out, past the doorway—and he found God's world
So much more broad than walls named after Him ! "

LXXIII.

"And Norman," said she, " think you, evermore,
Recalling you, the worldling could forget
How walls exclusive could exclude not love ?
Or, love rejecting, gain from all the world,
Though brimm'd with but applause, one draft so
           sweet ?—
But then earth held such promise yet, so lured ;
How could I know that merely sighs there were
Could thrill me more than all its thunders could ?
Ah, did I love you then, so loves he heaven
Who has not courage yet to leave the world.
I might have left it never ; but, you know,
That sister mine—At last, life meant but this,—
To envy that cold tomb, all night, all day,
That held her only.—Norman, pardon me :

Such woe, such loneliness,—ah, strange was it
That oft then I recall'd your form, your words?
And when I render'd forth upon the stage
Scenes you had visioned, phrases you had fram'd,
That then I came to do as you would do,
And think as you would think?—or that my tongue
Should linger o'er your language, as o'er sweets
Re-tasted still again?—or that, anon,
Those accents ardent with your own dear aims,
Should fire mine own to ardor?—or that then
My soul should flash forth light that flamed within,
And tracing far the rays that sped from it,
Should find here "—

        " One to help you, friend? " I asked—
" Then let us both thank heaven that made us
     weak.
So may a mortal pair bide, each to each,
Both priest and partner; like the church, their
     home;
For what are churches here but chosen courts
Of One pure Spirit, moving all to love?
And, think you, writ or vestment, art or arch,
Can image Him, or His domain unbound?
Nay, trust my word, we worship Him the best,
When two or three together, loving truth
And one another, thus repeat, once more,
An incarnation, imitating Christ."

LXXIV.

" I catch it, Norman," cried she, " the ideal !
Henceforth our aim be this,—the art of life.
I saw it not before : the stage of spirit
So much more broad is than the stage of sense !
Comes on the soul now, actor, all divine,
At play no longer ; nay, but shadowing forth
A love complete that personates a God !
And what love is complete that walks alone ? "

" None," answer'd I. " In true love, hand in hand,
Each leads his like. For this the whole world
    waits.
It waits for love,—why say not love like ours ?
When souls touch souls, they touch the springs of
    life ;
For them the veils of sense are drawn aside,
Are burn'd away in radiance divine,
The while their spirit's contact starts afresh
The electric flash that scores new glory here,
And lights the lines of being back to God.
Then, with their whole existences renew'd,
Far up these lines, the souls that thus commune,
Discern anon that sacred home on high,
Where boundless rest is blest by boundless love
And dreams the dreams of bounty absolute.—
They find that home, whence issue floods of light,
Which, flowing forth from white mysterious heights,

Flame down and flash and burst anon in sparks
That star the dark through all life's firmament ;—
They find that home, whence whirl the cycles
　　wide
Where all the wastes of nature fuse and form,
And all the things that thought can touch take
　　shape,
Until the restless wheels of matter, roll'd
Through roadways worn to waste by speeding years,
At last in fatal friction fire themselves,
And light returns to light from whence it sprang.
Through all, where souls commune with central
　　love,
They stay secure, awaiting birth or death ;
The Spring that starts the blossom blown to fall,
Or Fall that drops the seed that springs afresh.
They watch nor fear whatever change evolve,—
The splendor grand of epochs borne to waste,
The ruin wild of times that end in law,
The monarch mail'd whose lustre dims his folk,
The people's guns whose echoes hush their king.
What though dark clouds loom up and storms de-
　　scend?
True faith would not bemoan the forms they
　　wreck ;
For forms if true are formulas of love
That still is ardent to consume them all.
Though lightnings thunder till they crack the sky,

What unroofs rage leaves heaven to dome our peace.
The more convulsion shakes and fire consumes,
The more of love and light may both set free ;
The earlier may they end these earthly days
That fret our lives with flickerings vague below
Of steadfast light in endless day above ;
The earlier may the power of hate give way,
And good awake, and every path be bright,
While hope of glory gilds the gloom on high.
We too—come, Edith.   Christ will go with us ;
And by and by the glory so shall flame
Heaven cannot hold the halo !—Edith, come ;
We join the plans above."

LXXV.

                           But hold—I rave—
I know, I know—no matter, so would you.—
But find your soul's ideal, and you would find,
If common-sense be reason, you would rave,
Till you forgot that common-sense could be—
Though I forget it not.   My tale is told.
Why talk I more ?   I know one household now
All radiant through its mistress !   Where she
     dwells
A sweet content pervades the very air,
And genial sympathy smiles on to make
Each whole long year one summer of delight.

PATRIOTIC.

AMERICA, OUR HOME.[1]

THIS land of ours, we love it.
   'T is Freedom's own, where reign
No tyrants throned above it
   O'er serfs that wear their chain;
Where birth and wealth to worth give way,
And none in camp or court have sway,
   Except as all ordain.

CHORUS:

O Land that leaves the true man free
For all the soul would do or be,
Thank Heaven for life that gave us thee,
     America, our home!

Kind homes are ours that wake us
   To life whose morn is bright.
Free schools are ours that make us
   Believe in truth and right.
Our churches all are churches taught
That conscience guides the wisest thought,
   And love wins more than might.
    CHORUS: O Land that leaves, etc.

[1] Sung, to music composed by the author, at the anniversary of the battle of Concord, at Concord, Mass., 1898.

We love the rule that trains us
    To duty, self-control'd,
And honor'd toil that gains us
    What order helps us hold ;
Where never, save for threaten'd right,
Our starry flags, like stars at night,
    O'er war's dark storms unfold.
           CHORUS : O Land that leaves, etc.

We love the life that bears us
    Toward all that seers can see,
And, led by hope, prepares us
    The whole world's hope to be,
When, in the day that war shall cease,
Our GOLDEN RULE shall keep the peace,
    And all mankind be free.
           CHORUS : O Land that leaves,etc.

HAIL THE FLAG.[1]

HAIL, all hail, the flag above us.   Oh, how oft,
    to right
Wrong that war alone could end, that flag has led
    the fight,
Streaming on with fire and shot till, through the
    smoke, the light
    Burst on the victory of freedom !

[1] Sung, to the music of " Marching through Georgia," at the anniversary of the National Society of the Children of the American Revolution, held in Columbia Theatre, Washington, D. C., Feb. 22, 1899.

CHORUS :

Hurrah ! Hurrah ! beneath the flag to be !
Hurrah ! Hurrah ! its loyal wards are we !
Where the STARS AND STRIPES are flying over
    land or sea,
        Under the flag there is freedom.

Hail, all hail, the flag above us.   Peace is in each
    hue ;
Storms are signal'd not by stars, or skies red, white,
    or blue ;
Peace is in it e'en in war, for, when the war is
    through,
        That which has won then is freedom.
            CHORUS : Hurrah ! Hurrah ! etc.

Hail, all hail, the flag above us.   In its blue more
    bright
Shine the stars to guide our way than in the dome
    of night ;
Higher aims the hope that sees them, for their
    spotless white
        Symbols the pure light of freedom.
            CHORUS : Hurrah ! Hurrah ! etc.

Hail, all hail, the flag above us.   Nature never
    knew,

In the dawn's red ladder-bars where daylight climbs
　　to view,
Stripes that brought as fair a day as these anon
　　shall do,
　　　　When all the world turns to freedom.
　　　　　　　CHORUS : Hurrah ! Hurrah ! etc.

————

EXPANSION.

NOT mountain chains, nor streams that cleave
　　the plains,
Nor the wide ocean that around them rolls
Can bound the realm of Freedom's loyal souls
Who serve the Spirit that above it reigns.
Not the mean few who snatch for selfish gains
Through pathways opening toward the noblest
　　goals
Can shake Heaven's children's faith that Heaven
　　controls
That life the most which Earth the least enchains.
O ye who see but lust for wealth or rule
Where love would end one more wrong'd people's
　　thrall,
As your sires ended yours, how blind are ye !
Who says there is no God is no more fool
Than he who hears not God's voice in each call
To loose man's bonds and let the oppress'd go free.

A PRAYER FOR PEACE AND GOOD WILL.

CREATIVE Spirit, Source of Life,
　　And Father whom we trust,
Keep us and keep our state from strife
　　Through deeds to all men just.
Teach us that each, though poor or base,
　　Is yet a child of Thine,
And born, whate'er his rank or race,
Or wheresoe'er his dwelling-place,
　　To destiny divine.

Let not one nation's pride of might
　　On other nations prey
With brute-like hosts that boast a right
　　To plunder and to slay.
If one land's war-lord claim his own
　　To be Thy Spirit's call,
Teach men that no God so made known,
No God of but one land alone,
　　Was ever God of all.

Grant all, oh Lord, through lives of love,
　　A glory to attain
As far as heaven's could be above
　　What earthly battles gain.
Grant all, wherever patriots view

Their country's flag unfurled,
The right to think that service due
God's country calls for patriots too
Whose country is the world.

END

THE AZTEC GOD, AND OTHER DRAMAS

By GEORGE L. RAYMOND

16MO, CLOTH EXTRA, $1.25

"It is not with the usual feeling of disappointment that one lays down this little book. One reads 'The Aztec God' with pleasure. . . . 'Cecil the Seer' is a drama of the occult. In it the author attempts to describe the conditions in the spiritual world exactly as they exist according to coinciding testimony of Swedenborg, of the modern Spiritualist, and of all supposed to have explored them in trance states. Indirectly, perhaps, the whole is a much needed satire upon the social, political, and religious conditions of our present materialistic life. . . . In 'Columbus' one finds a work which it is difficult to avoid injuring with fulsome praise. The character of the great discoverer is portrayed grandly and greatly. . . . It is difficult to conceive how anyone who cares for that which is best in literature . . . could fail to be strengthened and uplifted by this heroic treatment of one of the great stories of the world."—*N. Y. Press.*

"One must unreservedly commend the clear, vigorous statement, the rhythmic facility, the copious vocabulary, and the unvarying elevated tone of the three dramas. . . . The poetic quality reveals itself in breadth of vision and picturesque imagery. One is, indeed, not seldom in peril of forgetting plot and character-action in these dramas, because of the glowing imagination."—*Home Journal.*

"The time and place make the play an historic study of interest, aside from its undoubted high poetic quality and elevation of thought. . . . The metre of the dramas is Shakespearian, and that master's influence is constantly apparent. It is needless to say to those who know the author's remarkable abilities that the plays are substantial and reflect perfectly the author's mind."—*Portland Transcript.*

Modern Fishres of Men. 12mo, cloth, gilt top . $1.00

"This delightful novel is written with charming insight. The rare gift of character delineation the author can claim in full. . . . Shrewd comments upon life and character add spice to the pages."—*Nashville Tennessean.*

"Deals with love and religion in a small country town, and under the facile pen and keen humor of the author, the various situations . . . are made the most of . . . true to the life."—*Boston Globe.*

"Such a spicy, racy, more-truth-than-fiction work has not been placed in our hands for a long time."—*Chicago Evening Journal.*

"Essentially humorous, with an undercurrent of satire . . . also subtle character delineation, which will appeal strongly to those who have the perceptive faculties highly developed."—*San Francisco Bulletin.*

A LIFE IN SONG

By GEORGE L. RAYMOND

16MO, CLOTH EXTRA, $1.25

" An age-worn poet, dying amid strangers in a humble village home, leaves the record of his life in a pile of manuscript poems. These are claimed by a friend and comrade of the poet, but, at the request of the cottagers, he reads them over before taking them away. The poet's life is divided into seven books or ' notes,' because seven notes seem to make up the gamut of life. . . . This is the simple but unique plan, . . . which . . . forms but the mere outline of a remarkably fine study of the hopes, aspirations, and disappointments of life, . . . an American modern life. . . . The author sees poetry, and living poetry, where the most of men see prose. . . . The objection, so often brought against our young poets, that form outweighs the thought, cannot be urged in this instance, for the poems of Prof. Raymond are full of keen and searching comments upon life. Neither can the objection be urged of the lack of the human element. ' A Life in Song ' is not only dramatic in tendency, but is singularly realistic and acute. . . . The volume will appeal to a large class of readers by reason of its clear, musical, flexible verse, its fine thought, and its intense human interest."—*Boston Transcript*.

" Professor Raymond is no dabbler in the problem of the human spirit, and no tyro in the art of word painting, as those who know his prose works can testify. These pages contain a mine of rich and disciplined reflection, and abound in beautiful passages."—*Hartford Theological Seminary Record*.

" Here are lines which, if printed in letters of gold upon the front of every pulpit, and practised by every one behind one, would transform the face of the theological world. . . . In short, if you are in search of ideas that are unconventional and up-to-date, get ' A Life in Song,' and read it."—*Unity*.

" Some day Dr. Raymond will be universally recognized as one of the leaders in the new thought-movement. . . . He is a poet in the truest sense. His ideals are ever of the highest, and his interpretation is of the clearest and sweetest. He has richness of genius, intensity of human feeling, and the refinement of culture. His lines are alive with action, luminous with thought and passion, and melodious with music."—*Cleveland World*.

" The main impulse and incident of the life are furnished by the enlistment of the hero in the anti-slavery cause. The story of his love is also a leading factor, and is beautifully told. The poem displays a mastery of poetic rhythm and construction, and, as a whole, is pervaded by the imaginative quality which lifts ' a life ' into the region of poetry,—the peculiar quality which marks Wordsworth."—*Christian Intelligencer*.

" It is a great work, and shows that America has a great poet. . . . A century from now this poem will be known and quoted wherever fine thought is appreciated, or brave deeds sung."—*Western Rural*.

BALLADS AND OTHER POEMS

By GEORGE L. RAYMOND

16MO, CLOTH EXTRA, $1.25

" In the construction of the ballad, he has given some notable examples of what may be wrought of native material by one who has a tasteful ear and practised hand. If he does not come up to the standard of the ancient ballad, which is the model, he has done as well as any of the younger American authors who have attempted this kind of work, and there is true enjoyment in all that he has written. Of his other poems, the dramatic poem, ' Haydn,' is finished in form, and has literary value, as well as literary power."—*Boston Globe.*

" The author has achieved a very unusual success, a success to which genuine poetic power has not more contributed than wide reading and extensive preparation. The ballads overflow, not only with the general, but the very particular, truths of history."—*Cincinnati Times.*

" It may well find readers in abundance . . . for the sake of the many fine passages which it contains. . . . ' Ideals made Real ' has one point of very high excellence . . . we have in the conception of the character of Edith the work of a genuinely dramatic poet. . . . In Edith we have a thoroughly masculine intellect in a thoroughly feminine soul, not merely by the author's assertion, but by actual exhibition. Every word that Edith speaks, every act that she does, is in accord with this conception. . . . It is sufficient, without doubt, to give life to a less worthy performance, and it proves beyond doubt that Mr. Raymond is the possessor of a poetic faculty which is worthy of the most careful and conscientious cultivation."—*N. Y. Evening Post.*

" A very thoughtful study of character . . . great knowledge of . . . aims and motives. . . . Such as read this poem will derive from it a benefit more lasting than the mere pleasure of the moment."— *London Spectator.*

" Mr. Raymond is a poet emphatically, and not a scribbler in rhyme.' *London Literary Churchman.*

" His is no mere utterance of dreams and fancies. His poetry takes hold on life; it enters the arena where its grandest and purest motives are discussed, and by the vigor and beauty of the language it holds itself on a level with the highest themes. . . . Every thoughtful reader . . . will wish that the poems had been longer or that there had been more of them. It would be possible to quote passage after passage of rare beauty."—*Utica Herald.*

" . . . Rhythmical in its flow and deliciously choice in language . . . indicating a deep acquaintance with human nature, while there is throughout a tone that speaks plainly of a high realization of the divine purpose in life . . . Not the least charming characteristic is its richness in pen-and-ink pictures marked by rare beauty and presenting irresistibly that which the poet saw in his mind's eye. . . . We confidently promise that any one taking it up will enjoy the reading throughout, that is, if there is any poetry in him."—*Boston Evening Journal.*

Books by Professor Raymond

Dante and Collected Verse. 16mo, cloth, gilt top . **$1.25**

"Epigram, philosophy, history—these are the predominant elements . . . which masterly construction, pure diction, and lofty sentiment unite in making a glowing piece of blank verse."—*Chicago Herald.*

"The poems will be read with keenest enjoyment by all who appreciate literary genius, refined sentiment, and genuine culture. The publication is a gem throughout."—*New Haven Leader.*

"The poet and the reformer contend in Professor Raymond. When the latter has the mastery, we respond to the justice, the high ideals, the truth of all he says—and says with point and vigor—but when the poet conquers, the imagination soars. . . . The mountain poems are the work of one with equally high ideals of life and of song."—*Glasgow* (Scotland) *Herald.*

"Brother Jonathan can not claim many great poets, but we think he has 'struck oil,' in Professor Raymond."—*Western* (England) *Morning News.*

"This brilliant composition . . . gathers up and concentrates for the reader more of the reality of the great Italian than is readily gleaned from the author of the *Inferno* himself."—*Oakland Enquirer.*

Pictures in Verse. With 20 illustrations by Maud Stumm. Square 8vo, in ornamental cloth covers . . **$ .75**

"Little love poems of a light and airy character, describing pretty rustic scenes, or domestic interiors. . . . As charming for its illustrations as for its reading matter."—*Detroit Free Press.*

"Simple songs of human every-day experience . . . with a twinkle of homely humor and a wholesome reflection of domestic cheer. We like his optimistic sentiments, and unspoiled spirit of boyishness when he strikes the chord of love. It is all very true and good."—*The Independent.*

The Mountains about Williamstown. With an introduction by M. M. Miller, and 35 full-page illustrations from original photographs ; oblong shape, cloth, gilt edges. Net, postpaid **$2.00**

"The beauty of these photographs from so many points of vantage would of itself suffice to show the fidelity and affection with which Professor Raymond pursued the theme of his admirably constructed poems. The introduction by his pupil, friend, and associate is an exhaustive study. No better or more thorough review could be written of the book, or more clearly point out the directness and power of Professor Raymond's work. . . . Among his many books none justifies more brilliantly the correctness and charm of his rhetorical instruction, or his facility in exemplifying what he commends."—*Hartford* (Conn.) *Courant.*

Rhythm and Harmony in Poetry and Music. 8° . **$1.75**

"The reader must be, indeed, a person either of supernatural stupidity or of marvellous erudition, who does not discover much information in Prof. Raymond's exhaustive and instructive treatise. From page to page it is full of suggestion."—*The Academy* (London).

Professor Raymond's Art-Books

Art in Theory. 8vo, cloth extra. . . . $1.75

"A well grounded, thoroughly supported, and entirely artistic conception of art as a whole, that will lead observers to apply its principles . . . and to distrust the charlatanism that imposes an idle and superficial mannerism upon the public in place of true beauty and honest workmanship."—*The New York Times.*

"His style is good, and his logic sound, and . . . of the greatest possible service to the student of artistic theories."—*Art Journal* (London).

The Representative Significance of Form.

8vo, cloth extra. $2.00

"Evidently the ripe fruit of years of patient and exhaustive study on the part of a man singularly fitted for his task. It is profound in insight, searching in analysis, broad in spirit, and thoroughly modern in method and sympathy."—*The Universalist Leader.*

"An original thinker and writer, the charm of his style and clearness of expression make Mr. Raymond's book possible to the general reader, though worthy of the study of the student and scholar."—*Hartford Courant.*

Painting, Sculpture, and Architecture, as Representative Arts. With 225 illustrations, 8vo. . $2.50

"Expression by means of extension or size . . . shape . . . regularity in outlines . . . the human body . . . posture, gesture, and movement . . . are all considered. . . . A specially interesting chapter is the one on color."—*Current Literature.*

"The whole book is the work of a man of exceptional thoughtfulness, who says what he has to say in a remarkably lucid and direct manner."—*The Philadelphia Press.*

The Genesis of Art-Form. Fully illustrated. 8vo. $2.25

"In a spirit at once scientific and that of the true artist, he pierces through the manifestations of art to their sources, and shows the relations, intimate and essential, between painting, sculpture, poetry, music, and architecture. A book that possesses not only singular value, but singular charm."—*N. Y. Times.*

"A help and a delight. Every aspirant for culture in any of the liberal arts, including music and poetry, will find something in this book to aid him."—*Boston Times.*

Proportion and Harmony of Line and Color in Painting, Sculpture, and Architecture.

Fully illustrated. 8vo. $2.50

"No critical person can afford to ignore so valuable a contribution to the art-thought of the day."—*The Art-Interchange* (N. Y.).

"One does not need to be a scholar to follow this scholar as he teaches while seeming to entertain ; for he does both."—*Burlington Hawk-Eye.*

"The artist who wishes to penetrate the mysteries of color, the sculptor who desires to cultivate his sense of proportion, or the architect whose ambition is to reach to a high standard will find the work helpful and inspiring."—*Boston Transcript.*

Books by Professor Raymond

Poetry as a Representative Art. 8° . . . $1.75

This book is an attempt, in accordance with modern methods, aided by the results of modern investigation, to determine scientifically the laws of poetic composition and criticism, by deriving and distinguishing the methods and meanings of the various factors of poetic form and thought from those of the elocution and rhetoric of ordinary speech, of which poetry is an artistic development. The principles unfolded are illustrated by quotations from the first English poets.

"I have read it with pleasure, and a sense of instruction on many points."—*Francis Turner Palgrave, Professor of Poetry, Oxford University.*

"Dieses ganz vortreffiche Werk."—*Englische Studien, Universität Breslau.*

"An acute, interesting, and brilliant piece of work. . . . As a whole the essay deserves unqualified praise."—*N. Y. Independent.*

The Essentials of Æsthetics. Fully illustrated. 8° $2.50

A compendium of all the art-volumes, designed as a Text-Book.

"So lucid in expression and rich in illustraton that every page contains matter of deep interest even to the general reader."—*Boston Herald.*

"It can hardly fail to make talent more rational, genius more conscious of the principles of art, and the critic and connoisseur better equipped for impression, judgment, and appraisement."—*New York Times.*

The Orator's Manual. 12mo . . . $1.50

A Practical and Philosophic Treatise on Vocal Culture, Emphasis, and Gesture, together with Hints for the Composition of Orations and Selections for Declamation and Reading, designed as a Text-book for Schools and Colleges, and for Public Speakers and Readers who are obliged to Study without an Instructor, fully revised with important Additions after the Fifteenth Edition.

"It is undoubtedly the most complete and thorough treatise on oratory for the practical student ever published."—*The Educational Weekly,* Chicago.

"I consider it the best American book upon technical elocution. It has also leanings toward a philosophy of expression that no other book written by an American has presented."—*Moses True Brown,* Head of the Boston School of Oratory.

The Writer (with Post Wheeler, Litt.D.) 12mo $1.00

A Concise, Complete, and Practical Text-book of Rhetoric, designed to aid in the Appreciation, as well as Production of All Forms of Literature, Explaining, for the first time, the Principles of Written Discourse by correlating them to those of Oral Discourse.

"A book of unusual merit . . . prepared by practical teachers, and the end in view is evidently to teach rather than to give information."—*The Pacific Educational Journal.*

"The pupil will forget he is studying rhetoric, and will come to express himself for the pure pleasure he has in this most beautiful art."—*Indiana School Journal.*

BOOKS BY PROFESSOR RAYMOND

Ethics and Natural Law. 8vo . Net, $2.25.

A Reconstructive Review of Moral Philosophy, Applied to the Rational Art of Living,—a Book that is in effect a Continuation and Completion of the Author's well-known Æsthetic Works, showing the Relationship of the Principles underlying Art to the Culture of Character.

"The student of ethics will considerably fortify his knowledge of the history of ethical thought by reading the book, especially the first twelve chapters. In these Mr. Raymond embodies, with copious references, his extensive knowledge of what has been written and thought by moral philosophers. On pp. 63–67, for instance, will be found in footnotes a kind of classified anthology of all the definitions given of conscience by modern writers. The various ethical theories holding the field do not, he thinks, recognize as indispensable the coöperation, in every slightest detail of thought and feeling, of the two necessary factors of every desire; and he claims that his own doctrine keeps to the purpose he avows in his opening chapter,—to draw no inference, and to advance no theory, not warranted by known facts as ascertainable in connection with the operations of natural law. . . . Chapters XIII to XXIII deal acutely and comprehensively with the various sides of American life."—*London* (England) *Times.*

In an article entitled *A Desirable Acquaintance, Prof. A. S. Hobart, D.D. of Crozer Theological Seminary,* after mentioning his twenty years' experience in teaching Ethics, says, "I find this book the only one that has come within the range of my reading which has, for the basis of its system, what I have found to be satisfactory. The writer assumes that there is in the nature of things a law of ethical conduct as continuous and self-evincing as is the law of physical health. . . . The study of psychology has opened the mind to inspection as we open the back of a watch-case and see the wheels go round; and this study lays its crown of victorious explorations at the feet of ethics. . . . His view is that conscience is the sense of conflict between bodily and mental desires. . . . therefore not a guide; it is only a sense of lostness in the woods, that wants a guide. Good sense and good religion are the guides to be consulted. By many illustrations and very clear reasoning he verifies his view. Then, . . . he takes up the task unusual in such books—of showing how the leading moral qualities can and ought to be cultivated. In view of my own careful reading of the book I venture to call attention to it as a most fertile source of instruction and suggestion for ethical teaching.—*The Baptist.*

"The book is clear and comprehensive. His theory in regard to conflict is reasonable, and the principles deduced from it have philosophic foundation."—*Boston Transcript.*

"Professor Raymond extracts a fundamental principle that largely reconciles existing ethical theories . . . makes distinctions that have vitality, and will repay the necessary study and application."—*Scientific American.*

BOOKS BY PROFESSOR RAYMOND

A Poet's Cabinet and An Art Philosopher's Cabinet.

Two books containing quotations, the one from the poems, and the other from the æsthetic works of George Lansing Raymond, selected by Marion Mills Miller, Litt.D., editor of *The Classics, Greek, and Latin.* Each book 8vo. cloth-bound, gilt top. $2.00

"Dr. Raymond is one of the most just and pregnant critics, as well as one of the most genuine poets, that America has produced. . . . His verse generally, and his prose frequently, is a solid pack of epigrams; and hundreds of the epigrams are vigorous, fresh, telling, worth collecting and cataloguing. . . . Probably from no other American but Emerson could a collection at all comparable be made. Many of the phrases are profound paradox. . . . Others are as hard-headed as La Rochefoucauld. . . . Some are plain common sense, set in an audacious figure, or a vigorous turn of phrase. . . . But few or none of them are trivial. . . . As an æsthetic critic, Professor Raymond is, by training and temperament, remarkably versatile and catholic. He is almost or quite equally interested in architecture, painting, sculpture, music, poetry. . . . Each is as definitely placed in his system as the several instruments in a great orchestra. . . . If Dr. Raymond had been born in France, England, or Germany, he would, no doubt, have enjoyed a wider vogue. But it is just as well that he was none of these; for the, as yet, æsthetically immature New World has sore need of him."—*Revue Internationale,* Paris.

"We risk little in foretelling a day when all considerable libraries, private as well as public, will be deemed quite incomplete if lacking these twin volumes. Years after the thinker has paid the debt to nature due, his thoughts will rouse action and emotion in the hearts and minds of generations now unborn."—*Worcester* (Mass.) *Gazette.*

"This Poet's Cabinet is the best thing of its class—that confined to the works of one author—upon which our eyes have fallen, either by chance or purpose. We can't help wishing that we had a whole book-shelf of such volumes in our own private library."—*Columbus,* (O.) *Journal.*

"The number and variety of the subjects are almost overwhelming, and the searcher for advanced or new thought as expressed by this particular philosopher has no difficulty in coming almost immediately upon something that may strike his fancy or aid him in his perplexities. To the student of poetry and the higher forms of literature . . . the volume will be of distinct aid."—*Utica* (N. Y.) *Observer.*

"Dr. Miller's task in selecting representative extracts from Professor Raymond's works has not been a light one, for there has been no chaff among the wheat, and there was an ever present temptation to add bulk to the book through freedom in compilation. He thought best, however, to eliminate all but the features which revealed the rare rich soul and personality of the poet, and each quotation is a gem."—*Albany* (N. Y.) *Times-Union.*

"To study the works of any one man so that we are completely familiar with his ideas upon all important subjects—if the man have within him any element of greatness—is a task which is likely to repay the student's work. . . . This fact makes the unique quality of the present volume . . . quotations which deal with practically every subject to be found in more general anthologies." *Boston* (Mass.) *Advertiser.*

BOOKS BY PROFESSOR RAYMOND

The Psychology of Inspiration. 8vo, cloth. (New Revised Edition). Net, $2.00; by mail, $2.14

The book founds its conclusions on a study of the action of the human mind when obtaining and expressing truth, as this action has been revealed through the most recent investigations of physiological, psychological, and psychic research; and the freshness and originality of the presentation is acknowledged and commended by such authorities as Dr. J. Mark Baldwin, Professor of Psychology in Johns Hopkins University, who says that its psychological position is "new and valuable"; Dr. W. T. Harris, late United States Commissioner of Education and the foremost metaphysician in the country, who says it is sure "to prove helpful to many who find themselves on the border line between the Christian and the non-Christian beliefs"; and Dr. Edward Everett Hale, who says that "no one has approached the subject from this point of view."

The first and, perhaps, the most important achievement of the book is to show that the *fact* of *inspiration* can be *demonstrated scientifically*; in other words, that the inner subconscious mind *can* be influenced irrespective of influences exerted through the eyes and the ears, *i. e.*, by what one sees or hears. In connection with this fact it is also shown that, when the mind is thus inwardly or inspirationally influenced, as, for example, in hypnotism, the influence is *suggestive* and *not dictatorial*. Not only so, but such faith as it is natural and right that a rational being should exercise can be stimulated and developed in only the degree in which the text of a sacred book is characterized by the very vagueness and variety of meaning and statement which the higher criticism of the Bible has brought to light. The book traces these to the operation and requirements of the human mind through which inspiration is received and to which it is imparted. Whatever inspires must appear to be, in some way, beyond the grasp of him who communicates it, and can make him who hears it *think* and *train him to think*, in the degree only in which it is not comprehensive or complete; but merely, like everything else in nature, illustrative of that portion of truth which the mind needs to be made to find out for itself.

The sane, fair, kindly attitude taken gives of itself a profitable lesson. The author proves conclusively that his mind—and if his, why not another's?—can be at one and the same time sound, sanitary, scientific, and essentially religious."—*The Examiner*, Chicago.

"The author writes with logic and a 'sweet reasonableness' that will doubtless convince many halting minds. It is an inspiring book."—*Philadelphia Inquirer*.

"It is, we think, difficult to overestimate the value of this volume at the present critical pass in the history of Christianity."—*The Arena*, Boston.

"The author has taken up a task calling for heroic effort, and has given us a volume worthy of careful study. . . . The conclusion is certainly very reasonable."—*Christian Intelligencer*, New York.

"Interesting, suggestive, helpful."—*Boston Congregationalist*.

Books by Professor Raymond

Fundamentals in Education, Art, and Civics: Essays and Addresses. 8vo, cloth. Net, $1.40; by mail, $1.53

"Of fascinating interest to cultured readers, to the student, the teacher, the poet, the artist, the musician, in a word to all lovers of sweetness and light. The author has a lucid and vigorous style, and is often strikingly original. What impresses one is the personality of a profound thinker and a consummate teacher behind every paragraph."—*Dundee Courier*, Scotland.

"The articles cover a wide field and manifest a uniformly high culture in every field covered. It is striking how this great educator seems to have anticipated the educational tendencies of our times some decades before they imprest the rest of us. He has been a pathfinder for many younger men, and still points the way to higher heights. The book is thoroughly up-to-date."—*Service*, Philadelphia.

"Clear, informing, and delightfully readable. Whether the subject is art and morals, technique in expression, or character in a republic, each page will be found interesting and the treatment scholarly, but simple, sane, and satisfactory . . . the story of the Chicago fire is impressingly vivid."—*Chicago Standard*.

"He is a philosopher, whose encouraging idealism is well grounded in scientific study, and who illuminates points of psychology and ethics as well as of art when they come up in the course of the discussion."—*The Scotsman*, Edinburgh, Scotland.

"Agreeably popularizes much that is fundamental in theories of life and thought, The American people owe much of their progress, their optimism, and we may say their happiness to the absorption of just such ideals as Professor Raymond stands for."—*Minneapolis Book Review Digest*.

Suggestions for the Spiritual Life—College Chapel Talks. 8vo, cloth . . Net, $1.50; by mail, $1.63

"Sermons of more than usual worth, full of thought of the right kind, fresh, strong, direct, manly. . . . Not one seems to strain to get a young man's attention by mere popular allusions to a student environment. They are spiritual, scriptural, of straight ethical import, meeting difficulties, confirming cravings, amplifying tangled processes of reasoning, and not forgetting the emotions."—*Hartford Theological Seminary Record* (Congregationalist).

"The clergyman who desires to reach young men especially, and the teacher of men's Bible Classes may use this collection of addresses to great advantage. . . . The subjects are those of every man's experience in character building . . . such a widespread handling of God's word would have splendid results in the production of men." —*The Living Church* (Episcopalian).

"Great themes, adequately considered. . . . Surely the young men who listened to these sermons must have been stirred and helped by them as we have been stirred and helped as we read them." —*Northfield* (Mass.) *Record of Christian Work* (Evangelical).

"They cover a wide range. They are thoughtful, original, literary, concise, condensed, pithy. They deal with subjects in which the young will be interested."—*Western Christian Advocate* (Methodist).